COMPUTE!'s
Beginner's Guide to the
AMIGA

Dan McNeill

COMPUTE! Publications,Inc.**abc**
Part of ABC Consumer Magazines, Inc.
One of the ABC Publishing Companies
Greensboro, North Carolina

Printed in the United States of America

10 9 8 7 6 5 4 3

ISBN 0-87455-025-4

The author and publisher have made every effort in the preparation of this book to insure the accuracy of the programs and information. However, the information and programs in this book are sold without warranty, either expressed or implied. Neither the author nor COMPUTE! Publications, Inc. will be liable for any damages caused or alleged to be caused directly, indirectly, incidentally, or consequentially by the programs or information in this book.

The opinions expressed in this book are solely those of the author and are not necessarily those of COMPUTE! Publications, Inc.

COMPUTE! Publications, Inc., Post Office Box 5406, Greensboro, NC 27403, (919) 275-9809, is part of ABC Consumer Magazines, Inc., one of the ABC Publishing Companies, and is not associated with any manufacturer of personal computers. Amiga, AmigaDOS, Kickstart, and Workbench, are trademarks of Commodore-Amiga, Inc. IBM is a registered trademark of International Business Machines, Inc.

Contents

Foreword

Whether the Amiga is your first computer or you've moved up to it from another machine, *COMPUTE!'s Beginner's Guide to the Amiga* will be a reliable companion to ease you on your way. First of all you'll learn how to set up the Amiga. Then you'll progress in easy, logical steps to an understanding of the machine's hardware. You'll see how to operate the system by using the keyboard, numeric keypad, mouse, and menus. Discussions of optional peripherals such as light pens, touch pads, and speech recognition devices will give you suggestions about expanding your basic system. And you'll learn about creating output for various types of monitors and printers.

After this comprehensive grounding in the basics, *COMPUTE!'s Beginner's Guide to the Amiga* examines all the software available for the Amiga—word processors, spreadsheets, databases, graphics and music programs, and games. When you're ready to buy software, you'll find tips on evaluating your individual requirements that will help you avoid making mistakes.

The Amiga's music and graphics really shine. Here, again, software is available that can turn you into an artist and change your Amiga into a music synthesizer. You'll take a look at some of the programs available for both the amateur and professional.

Finally, with your Amiga you can branch out into the fascinating world of telecommunications, accessing vast databases that contain information ranging from up-to-the-minute stock market information to complete encyclopedias. You'll be able to communicate by electronic mail and can even shop and bank electronically. When you and your Amiga have finished working for the day, you can tune into one of the bulletin boards and talk to new friends—electronically.

Dan McNeill's conversational style and thorough descriptions provide the reliable information that COMPUTE! books are known for. As you learn about this remarkable new machine, you'll gain the confidence to explore everything it can offer.

Preface

The Amiga is one of the most fascinating computers ever built, and this book is a guided tour of it. You'll see how it works, what it can do for you, and what you can do for it. You'll also receive tips on hardware and software, so you can talk to computer dealers without feeling they are leading the high-tech revolution.

I've arranged the book in a rough chronological order. It begins with events that occurred before the Amiga appeared, and moves on to the items you'll encounter in approximately the sequence you'll encounter them. The story breaks down into five parts:

1. The background of Commodore, the essential contours of the Amiga, and the experience of setting up.
2. The hardware, including not only the computer, but accessories like the printer and video display.
3. Software, the major types and the Amiga's potential for extending their powers.
4. Video and audio, two special realms in which the Amiga excels.
5. Telecommunications, or how to make the Amiga's screen a pipeline to the world.

A few words before setting out:

First, if you don't understand something, don't worry. You will.

Second, I've tried to shield you as much as possible from jargon—that is, terms that are arid, pretentious, and even unpronounceable. The task is ultimately impossible. You can't talk about a machine like the Amiga without using a word like "interface," any more than you can talk about baseball without mentioning RBIs or ERAs. In a way, learning the terminology is learning the topic.

Yet any sort of verbal underbrush is unfortunate, and particularly so in the field of computers. For the topic is fascinating, and, despite its reputation for chrome-like impersonality, very human. The people behind computers—the hardware engineers, programmers, entrepreneurs—have pronounced personal qualities, and their creations may have wit, charm, and grace. The Amiga is ultimately a machine, but you may find yourself speaking of it, or to it, in rather human terms.

Welcome to this book.

Acknowledgments

The author would like to thank: Paul Freiberger, for unstinting aid and encouragement along the way; Phillip Robinson, for expert advice graciously given; Gene Beisman, for generous technical comments, and for the emergency loan of a monitor; David Leon, Jeanne Polevoi, and Soames, for contributing a subtext invisible to the reader; and Stephen Levy, my editor at COMPUTE!, for guiding this book into print with special care and frictionless efficiency.

Dedication

To Rosalind Gold

PART ONE

Getting Started

For some, this was the train to Sullivan Square or Milk Street or, at the very most, Orient Heights; for me, it was the train to Patagonia.

Paul Theroux
The Old Patagonian Express

Commodore

Two years ago, the idea that Commodore might launch a state-of-the-art computer upon the world would have seemed pretty farfetched. The company made serviceable, inexpensive machines and sold them in bulk, in department stores. Its unofficial motto—"We make computers for the masses, not the classes"—almost ridiculed the high-end market.

Now it has the Amiga, a machine with features so advanced that you'd have to buy several expensive computers to match it. You might approach its basic business capacity with the upscale IBM PC AT, but to equal its graphics you'd need at least a $10,000 computer, and to exceed its sound you'd need a good Moog synthesizer.

The emergence of this computer signals a dramatic change in the nature of Commodore, and behind it lies a fascinating tale about the American Dream. But there are reasons beyond dramatic interest to know about this company. A food processor or a vacuum cleaner can stem from spontaneous generation, at least as far as you're concerned. But a computer has both a background and a future. It comes from a particular maker, which offers ongoing support for it. Commodore already sells hardware and software compatible with the Amiga, and should offer periodic upgrades. So you do not leave Commodore behind in the computer store the day you bring the Amiga home. It's always there, hovering invisibly, occasionally emerging into light, and it's thus worth knowing about.

The Legacy: Jack Tramiel

The story begins with World War II.

In 1939, the Polish city of Lodz had 200,000 Jews. One of them was Jack Tramiel, then twelve years old. After the Nazi blitzkrieg, he labored on road gangs—it was one way to get food—and he claims he helped build the Autobahn. In 1944, the invaders shipped him to concentration camps, first Auschwitz, then Bergen-Belsen. At the war's end, he was one of 970 Jews from Lodz still alive.

CHAPTER ONE

Tramiel arrived in the United States in 1947 with only five years of formal education. He drove a cab in New York City, served a stint in the army, and in 1954 started a business in the Bronx, fixing typewriters. He called it Commodore Portable Typewriter. Two years later, he moved the firm to Toronto and was soon making adding machines under the illustrious name of Commodore Business Machines. He obtained capital from the Canadian investor Irving Gould, who received a controlling interest in the firm, but let Tramiel run it. Tramiel liked running things. He had become a tough, shrewd cost-cutter who believed a hardtack regimen was vital to survival in the business world.

In 1968, he began making electronic calculators, and the company became prominent in this field. It was a new, exciting technology with much promise for a canny entrepreneur. However, Commodore had been buying calculator chips from Texas Instruments, and in 1972 the latter decided to make and sell its own calculators. Texas Instruments leaped into the market, slashed prices, and stirred up a dogfight from which only a few companies would emerge. Since it manufactured its own chips, Texas Instruments had an edge over clients like Commodore which had to buy them. In two years, the price of the average calculator fell from around $150 to around $25, a breathtaking plummet. Commodore lost millions of dollars, and Tramiel saw the lesson. He decided to make his own chips and purchased MOS Technology. This act led him into the personal computer business.

The first commercial personal computer was the Altair, announced in January 1975. The Altair was a build-it-yourself kit with no screen, no disk drive, and often defective memory. Its only input device was switches, and its only output was flashing lights. Yet it was a tremendous breakthrough, and it surprised almost everyone by tapping a vast and eager market. Its manufacturer, a small company called MITS, worked out of a former sandwich shop in an Albuquerque shopping center. It was completely unprepared for the spate of checks in the mail. It shipped the kits as fast as it could, yet the backlog ballooned, becoming immense. The delightful scent of bonanza wafted into the breeze. Soon rival computers appeared from other companies: IMSAI, Processor Technology, Radio Shack, Apple.

Thus, when Chuck Peddle, a talented engineer at MOS Technology and the designer of several important chips, offered Tramiel a plan for a personal computer, he found the boss receptive. The machine first appeared at the Consumer Electronics Show in early 1977. It was called the PET. Publicly, Peddle said that this name stood for "Personal Electronic Transactor." In fact, it honored Pet Rocks™.

Tramiel formulated his marketing strategy for the PET very carefully. Many companies now offered personal computers, and he wished to outflank them. He decided, first, not to compete in the same price range as Apple or Radio Shack, but to make cheaper machines and sell them in bulk. Second, he focused on Europe, virgin territory he hoped to cordon off before his American competitors could reach it. And finally, he brought his own spartan theories of organizational efficiency to bear.

"I'm not in business to be loved. I'm here to make money," Tramiel once declared. Indeed, he viewed unnecessary costs the way surgeons view rats in the operating room. He employed a minimum of staff, insisting that vice presidents shoulder the tasks normally done by middle management. This tactic gave top managers detailed knowledge of firm projects, yet it sometimes slowed operations and certainly burdened executives with heavy workloads. Tramiel never hesitated to eject anyone who wasn't producing. Turnover was perpetual, and gave the company a fluid aspect, like water drifting past a rock.

But the approach worked. In less than two years, Commodore gained over 80 percent of the market in Germany and Britain. Tramiel followed the PET with the VIC-20 and then, in 1982, the Commodore 64, which had the cash registers singing a merry tune indeed. The Commodore 64 grew into the bestselling computer in the world. In 1982, the company sold over one million computers. In 1983, a price-cutting war commenced, and the cost of the Commodore 64 fell to around $200. The firm sold over a million computers in the last quarter of 1983 alone, and its share of the home computer market was estimated at 45 percent. Finally, it drove Texas Instruments limping from the field, a sight which must have caused a merry dance somewhere in the heart of Jack Tramiel.

On January 13, 1984, Tramiel abruptly resigned from Commodore, walking out of a meeting of its board of directors

CHAPTER ONE

and directly onto a plane for California. Employees were stunned and bewildered. It seemed that Tramiel and Irving Gould had reached some dark impasse, perhaps over Tramiel's desire to move his three sons into management, perhaps over Gould's choice for a new president.

Six months later, the former chairman pulled a real doubloon from his ear. He purchased Atari, Commodore's major rival, from Warner Communications. Within a month, Tramiel had cut Atari's staff from 5000 to 1500. By 1985, he had come out with the Atari 520 ST, the "Jackintosh." He now faces his old company from across the net, and the game is not for Coke and donuts.

Tramiel's legacy to Commodore is complex. Much of it is positive. He left it with a commitment to vertical integration. Since the company owns MOS Technology, it, unlike, say, Apple, can make its own chips and pass the savings on to you. He also rode Commodore to a position of power in the industry and gained for it the financial basis necessary for a serious venture like the Amiga. Yet he alienated many computer retailers and software developers. He was not in business to be loved and didn't earn much corporate good will. He also bequeathed the company a reputation for bargain-basement computers, and hence you'll not see the Commodore name on the Amiga. Commodore owes much to Tramiel, and is trying to live down much else.

Marshall Smith and the Amiga

Tramiel's replacement, Marshall Smith, was a tall, snowy-haired executive with decades of experience in the steel industry. Smith quickly won repute as a low-key, pleasant individual with a keen appetite for new ideas. He promoted a few people from the lower echelons of Commodore, but also recruited many important executives from companies like IBM, AT&T, Apple, and Pepsi-Cola. Since many of Tramiel's followers also left during transition, his philosophy burned off somewhat, and management took on a more familiar cast.

Coincidentally, at the very time Tramiel departed, a remarkable new computer had appeared. During telecast of the 1984 Super Bowl, Apple presented its famous Big Brother ad: An attractive young woman races into an auditorium where a Leader harangues a crowd of gaping skinheads from a screen the size of Wyoming. She flings a hammer through the screen, liberating everyone. A few days later, Apple announced the Macintosh.

Marshall Smith

The Macintosh made computer use much simpler and more pleasurable. It shunned the standard approach, which compelled the memorization of many commands and made selecting position on the screen a chore. Instead, using extensive graphics, it displayed available commands on the screen and let you choose among them. It also let you move around the screen instantly with a small handheld device called a mouse. The Macintosh had many other innovations and was quickly acclaimed a major advance in the field.

In August, 1984, seven months after the door slammed on Tramiel, Commodore purchased Amiga Corporation, a Silicon Valley firm which had been working on the Amiga since 1982. This computer had humble origins. It began as the brainchild of a group of Midwest investors who wished to cash in on the vogue for videogames. They formed a firm called Hi-Toro, and set out to build an inexpensive home computer with resplendent graphics and sound.

The company first hired Jay Miner, who had helped design a number of special graphics chips for Atari computers. Miner says Hi-Toro originally intended to sell the product for between $300 and $400, and to call it the Amica, Latin for "friend." But this name was legally preempted, so they changed one letter and arrived at Amiga, Spanish for "friend." The company also brought on David Morse as chief executive officer, and it was Morse who eventually negotiated the sale of the company to Commodore for $25 million in 1984.

It was a good deal for both sides. The Amiga needed money and Commodore not only supplied it, but retained the management and generally encouraged the project. In return, Commodore earned the rights to a gem. For, with time and under the influence of the Macintosh, the Amiga had matured from a game machine into an all-purpose, Mac-like marvel.

The Amiga was announced on July 23, 1985 at Lincoln Center in New York to an enthusiastic reception. Hard-boiled computer reviewers routinely described its attributes as "amazing" and "incredible." One can see why. Though costing about the same as a Macintosh, the Amiga surpassed it in almost every way: It had color; it worked much faster; it had more graphics tricks; it had much better sound; it performed several tasks at once; and it was expandable. The Macintosh is a fine computer, and if the Amiga leaves it behind, it makes other machines look like artifacts from the Troad.

Yet as the Amiga debuted and Marshall Smith toured the country promoting it to retailers, Commodore faced mounting troubles. The company had begun racking up huge quarterly losses. The Commodore 64 was no longer selling well, and other machines were unable to take up the slack. And the

CHAPTER
ONE

Amiga, though announced on July 23, was harder to find than a penguin in the Kalahari. August passed, then September, and no Amigas reached the stores. The machines began trickling in in mid-October, and it remained unclear whether the December sales would bring smiles and backslapping to the Commodore Christmas party.

Chairman Irving Gould has stated that the Amiga is Commodore's future. Commodore has also suggested that the Amiga is the first in a line of similar computers, and the most elementary at that. This kind of commitment matters, for once a company abandons a computer, the makers of software and peripherals drift away from it, too. It's hard to imagine the Amiga will be abandoned. It's not just a commodity. It's a new technology.

A Tour of the Amiga

The Amiga is the computer Merlin might have owned. It creates vibrant images and breathes life into them with sound. Indeed, it is perhaps the first computer to approach the mesmerizing audiovisual power of television. You can sit before it entranced by something as simple as a bouncing ball.

There is, of course, more to the Amiga than great mimetic prowess. It is the compleat computer, superb at almost any task imaginable, yet its splendid presence has tended to conceal its deeper potential for business applications like spreadsheets. In fact, it is a seemingly endless bag of tricks, so full of features that software authors will be exploring it for years to come. It's not just in a different league from other computers. It's playing a different game.

Look at its attributes:

• *Speed.* The Amiga is probably the swiftest personal computer available. Its speed alone lifts it into another realm, and makes it what some have called a "supermicro." It extirpates a host of petty delays from your day, and makes almost all other effects possible.

• *Dazzling graphics.* The Amiga's screen is a wonderland. It offers not just minute resolution and endless colors, but a full graphics environment with an array of features like sprites, playfields, and multiple windows. These endowments will lead to extraordinary games, charts, animation, and other video feats.

• *Superb audio.* The Amiga imitates musical instruments, synthesizes speech, transforms sound in myriad ways, and even plays along with you as an accompanist.

• *Multitasking.* The Amiga runs several programs at once, so you can compare two documents, write from notes, or keep different projects percolating at the same time. It also allows simultaneous use of the computer, printer, and modem. You can print out or mail a document over the wires while you

are writing or calculating. The Amiga performs multitasking
with breathtaking ease, and it may be the single greatest feature of the machine.
• *IBM compatibility.* The Amiga runs the cornucopia of software
for the IBM PC. These programs are particularly common in
business, where the PC holds general sway, and compatibility thus greatly extends the Amiga's powers.
• *Expandability.* The Amiga, like most computers but unlike the
Macintosh, is fully expandable. You can enrich it with a
plethora of extra devices, and some of these devices may be
exotic indeed.

These are qualities which become more and more impressive the closer you look at them. Yet the Amiga does not
flaunt them with a slick exterior. In fact, it may be the most
deceptive-looking personal computer on the market.

The Facade

At rest, the Amiga looks completely conventional. It consists
of a flat, off-white console about the size of a stereo, which
houses the inner workings of the machine. The front of this
console, the part that faces you, is a strip somewhat narrower
than a bumper sticker. In its upper-left corner stands a chro-
matic check, the Amiga's hallmark, and next to it, the legend
"AMIGA" itself. A pair of vertical lines trisect the panel, and a
long horizontal indentation parallels the bottom. Two tiny red
lights lie at either end of the horizontal line. The left one
lights up whenever the computer is on, and the right one,
whenever the disk drive is working.

The right third of the panel is the scene of much ado. It is
dominated by the great slot called the disk drive. Here you insert disks containing the software that will bring the Amiga to
life. The drive has a squarish recessed area to ease disk handling. Just below it to the right is the knob that triggers ejec-
tion of the disk.

The console is just the core of the Amiga, and requires
auxiliary devices around it—peripherals. Beneath the console
there is room for the keyboard to slide in and out, a thought-
ful touch that yields instant desk space if, say, you want to jot
down a handwritten note or sign a letter. You also need a
video display, and you'll probably place it atop the console,
which can hold 40 pounds. This arrangement will leave slen-

der shoulders on either side, on which you can stack other peripherals, thus reducing the system's "footprint."

The outside of the Amiga very much resembles the IBM PC: solid and unprepossessing, not ugly, but no swan either. It scarcely matters. Once you turn the Amiga on, the exterior has about the same importance as the design on a teacup.

The Amiga

Entering the Amiga

You progress into the Amiga in a series of steps, all very simple. First, you turn on the monitor, then the computer. The fan begins to hum and pale blue light floods the screen. Soon you hear the little startup song and see the picture of a large hand feeding the Kickstart disk into the disk drive.

Kickstart contains part of the Amiga's operating system, the software it needs to perform its most elementary chores, so you require it to spur the Amiga into action. While the Amiga absorbs the information on this disk, the red warning light stays on. Do not touch the disk-eject button at this time or you could destroy the Kickstart disk, a loss which will lock you out of the Amiga until you can get a new one. Wait till the light goes off and you see the hand inserting the Workbench disk. Then press the disk-eject button and pull Kickstart out of the drive.

The next step depends on your software. If you have a program that doesn't need the Workbench, you ignore the onscreen cue and simply slip it in. Otherwise, you insert the Workbench disk, and set the Amiga up for further tasks.

The Interface: Portal of the Amiga

The Workbench is really your gateway to the Amiga. It is an elaborate portal, full of important entry information as well as little aids which you can exploit or not at your pleasure. Here, we'll look mainly at its interface, that is, the zone where you and the computer conduct basic interaction. The Workbench also lets you carry out important disk operations like initializing and copying, and we'll deal with them more fully in Chapter 10.

A computer's interface is in many ways its style, its personality. Some interfaces place the burden of communication on you, forcing you memorize endless commands to get through to them. They are like quiet, passive individuals who may be very willing to please, yet wait for unambiguous cues before responding. The Amiga's interface is more like a genial host. It takes over the burden of communications, constantly offering you its resources so you can select them at your pleasure.

Let's look at its fundamental elements. You'll pick them up very quickly from a few moments of playing with the machine. But they're worth skimming over, for they are the foundation of the Amiga experience.

The crux of the interface is the pointer, which is rather like a magic wand. You move it freely about the screen with the mouse. When it's over an item, you can click a mouse button, and it will respond as if a magic wand had touched it. There is instant action. Touched items open up, fold down, or cause myriad changes, and you thereby gain mastery over the machine.

There are three kinds of items that react to the pointer's touch: icons, windows, and menus.

Icons. Icons are small pictures. They can represent disks, drawers, tools, or projects. The first two are containers for the second two, and the second two are the reason you bought the Amiga.

CHAPTER
TWO

Disk icons are easily recognizable, as they resemble the disks you slide into the disk drive.

Drawers are repositories for tools and projects, and they usually look like desk drawers.

Tools is Amiga-ese for programs, like *Graphicraft* or the Clock. Tools let you create pictures or documents, and their icons can look like anything a programmer can imagine.

Projects are the files you create with programs. The painting you do in *Graphicraft*, for instance, is a project.

Icons are like doorways leading into various parts of the system. Disk and drawer icons open up upon further icons, while tool and project icons show you actual work areas.

When the Workbench interface comes up, you see the disk icon in the upper-right corner, labeled "Workbench." This icon is the first entranceway. Place the pointer over it, double-click the left button of the mouse, and a window appears with new icons inside it. You've moved into a foyer.

The Workbench window reveals a number of possible options. On the left, you see four drawers. Opening a drawer—again, you double-click it—creates a new window with other icons in it. It essentially moves you from the foyer to a smaller anteroom. If you click the Utilities drawer, for instance, a window with the Notepad icon appears.

The Notepad is a tool, one of the ultimate destinations in the system. Double-click the Notepad icon, and the Notepad window opens up. Here, you can jot down random thoughts and memos to yourself. You have reached the equivalent of a room, and you have no more doors to enter.

The Workbench has three other icons besides drawers. One is the Clock. If you click it, a ticking clock appears onscreen, giving you the time. Another is the Trashcan. To erase a project you have no further use for, drag it over to the Trashcan. The Trashcan is a kind of drawer, and also a kind of limbo. It holds onto the file in case you want to recall it, for deleting a file is an act of consequence. Once you select Empty Trash from the Disk menu, however, there is no return.

The third icon is Preferences, which depicts a question mark over the front panel of the Amiga. Double-click it, and you enter the central command post of the Amiga. Here, you can dictate clock time, date, text size, mouse speed, double-click speed, Workbench colors, and numerous other matters. Preferences is actually a series of three screens layered over

one another. Normally, you see only the first, the one most
often used. But click Change Printer, and the second screen
appears. It allows you to set printer variables—an important
function you cannot ignore. The second screen is also your
entryway into the third. Click Graphic Select, and you leaf
down to the final screen, which lets you alter graphics on their
way to the printer.

Icons do not exist solely to be opened. You can move
them around too. Click an icon once with the left mouse button, and it darkens. You have selected it. Hold the button
down and move the mouse around. The icon follows. When
you get it where you want it, you release the button and it
stays. Selecting also lets you act on icons from menus. To de-
select the icon, click the pointer again somewhere outside the
icon.

What's the point of moving icons? Well, it can change
their status, as it does when you drag them to the Trashcan.
You can also shift them in and out of drawers, by dragging
them from one window to another.

Windows. Windows are simply opened icons. They per-
vade the interface. When you click the Workbench icon, for instance, its contents appear in a window, and when you click
the drawers, more windows fly open. Indeed, windows are a
highlight of the Amiga, and the computer can have as many
as 50 of them onscreen at once. It's chaotic, but the power is
there if you want it.

The pointer can control windows easily by clicking little
symbols on them which trigger big changes. These symbols
come in two types. The tiny, boxlike ones are gadgets, and the
long, slender ones are bars.

Windows can have up to four different gadgets, as the
Workbench window does. They are the close gadget, the back
and front gadgets, and the sizing gadgets:

The close gadget is the square with the dot inside in the
upper-left corner of the window. Click it, and the window
vanishes back into its icon. This operation is the reverse of
double-clicking the icon.

The back and front gadgets. In the upper-right corner are
two gadgets which look very similar: the back and front gadgets. They help you shuttle windows behind or before each
other on the screen, and you'll need them because sometimes
the screen looks like a wild stack of pages. These two symbols

are easy to understand. Both have one white box and one dark one. The back gadget shows a white box in the rear; the front gadget, in front. The white box is your current window, and the gadget indicates its destination.

The sizing gadget sits in the lower-right corner of the window, and shows a specklike box attached to a larger, vertical rectangle. It's meant as a before-and-after shot, since the sizing gadget lets you turn a small window into larger one, or into any size window you want. You place the pointer on the gadget, hold down the left button of the mouse, and pull the mouse. The window expands or contracts till its new size pleases you, and you release.

Windows can also have two different bars. One lets you shift the entire window about the screen like a hockey puck, while the other lets you move contents within the window.

The drag bar is the set of parallel lines at the top of the window. If you point to it, hold down the left mouse button, and pull the mouse around, the window will follow.

The scroll bars. The contents of a window are not limited to its onscreen size. They can be much larger. In such cases, the window acts like a viewfinder looking down on a roll of microfilm. And the scroll bars on the right and bottom let you move the contents below so you can see them. Click on an arrow at either end of a scroll bar, and you'll shift half a window. You'll still have part of the old contents, to give you bearings, but you'll enter new territory as well.

Often, with several windows onscreen, you'll have to choose which of them is to be active. You do so by simply clicking the left mouse button once on the window you want. It's just like selecting icons, and means the same thing: the file is ready to be acted on. You'll recognize inactive windows by their ghostly contours.

Menus. There is one final element to the Workbench triad, and it's crucial. It is the menu. All along, the screen has displayed a title bar across the top, notifying you that you are in Workbench version whatever and have so many thousand units of free memory left. If you click the right button of the mouse, the title bar changes at once into a menu bar with a string of menu titles on it. Workbench, for instance, has the menus Workbench, Disk, and Special.

What are menus for? Well, icons and windows let you open, close, move, and delete files, yet many more specialized tasks remain. Menus let you perform them. They are simply lists of words, and can thus be very flexible.

Normally, menus are hidden from view to give you more screen space. To see them, you place the pointer over the menu title and hold the right button down. The menu rolls out below, unveiling a series of menu items. You drag the pointer down to the item of choice, and release. The Amiga then executes the task upon whatever you have selected.

Menu items are either commands or options. They differ mainly in their finality. A command has a clear termination point. It executes, then ends. For instance, the Print instruction generates printout until there's no more text, then stops. An option, on the other hand, has no clear termination point. It sets a condition that persists until you select a different one. For instance, if you open the Notepad and select Diamond from the Font menu, the Notepad stays in Diamond till you select another font. You may recognize an option by the check mark you leave beside it.

Some menus have submenus appended to them. They flash out on the right as you pull the pointer down the menu. To select a command or option with a submenu, you shift the pointer over to the submenu and release at the chosen subitem.

One menu item worth knowing about is Info, under Workbench. Info provides current data regarding the disk, drawer, tool, or project you have selected, including estimates of size. You don't want to write excess software to disks, and these estimates help avoid the problem.

The Workbench menu has some commands that merely replicate simpler mouse operations. The Open item, for instance, does the same thing as double-clicking an icon. Since to use Open you must first single-click that icon anyway, to select it, it's not exceptionally helpful. But you will use other menu items all the time, particularly in applications like word processors and spreadsheets, where specialization is the point.

Most Workbench operations involve disk management. If you move an icon to the Trashcan and select Empty Trash, for instance, the disk drive whirs and the Amiga deletes part of the disk. The Workbench is thus an interface to the Amiga's disk operating system, called AmigaDOS, the software that controls disk operations. The Workbench isn't AmigaDOS per se; only one pipeline to it. In fact, AmigaDOS also has a sec-

CHAPTER
TWO

ond interface, called the Command Line Interface or CLI. The CLI resembles more conventional computers in that it requires explicit, typed commands, yet it gets you deeper into AmigaDOS itself, and offers raw power. We will examine the CLI in Chapter 10, on the operating system.

The Workbench disk has both AmigaDOS and the Workbench interface on it. All programs require AmigaDOS. However, if a program already has it, it may not need the Workbench, and you can insert it right after Kickstart.

We've seen how to negotiate the Amiga interface to reach a program or document. The variety of such software is vast, and the Amiga will inspire new programs of a scope yet unimaginable. But though we cannot anticipate this software, we can at least outline the Amiga's special powers. The best programs will exploit them, and they give the Amiga its crestline.

Video: The Iridescent Plane

The screen is your first sight when you turn the Amiga on, and it is impressive. Indeed, the names of some of its items— sprites and playfields—suggest an elfin paradise, where imps dance and cavort. It is in fact a visual delight, and the absence of real fairy spirits doesn't mean that it can't cast a spell.

First, the Amiga renders color. That's not unusual, since among the major personal computers today, only the Macintosh does not. However, the Amiga offers 4,096 different colors, a near-infinite palette, far more than any other personal computer now on the market. Imagine an ordinary spectrum divided into 4,096 slices and you get an idea of the Amiga's finesse.

The computer also gives you excellent screen resolution. At its highest level, it yields a picture 640 dots wide by 400 high, remarkably clean and fine. Resolution really matters. A screen with abundant, sparkling detail is like a bayscape after a day of rain.

Moreover, like the Macintosh, the Amiga has its whole screen mapped out in memory. It has a bitmapped screen. This technique confers great precision and flexibility. It means that you can print out exactly what you see on the screen, as well as render text in endless fonts, styles, and sizes. Computers without bitmapping use a rough shorthand to control the screen, and it handicaps them.

Audio: The Universal Instrument

We don't normally think of a computer as an audio device, but that's because few personal computers have ever shown much aptitude in the field. The Amiga could turn this situation completely around.

The Amiga has four independently programmable sound channels, which can mimic instruments like vibes or banjo with stunning fidelity. These channels can also act as four music synthesizers. You can not only dictate the melody, but also give distinctive curves to the volume of each note, and even create timbre—that elusive quality of tone that sets an oboe apart from, say, a trombone. In effect, you can invent new musical sounds.

You can also attach a microphone to the computer and gain an accompanist. With the right software, you can play "Summertime" on a kazoo, and the Amiga will harmonize, speeding up and slowing down as you do yourself.

In addition, you can hook other synthesizers up to the Amiga through a special interface called the MIDI, and control them all at once. The computer thus lets you conduct a veritable orchestra of powerful instruments.

Finally, the Amiga is specially adapted for voice synthesis. It allows both male and female voices, with an eight to nine octave range. This feature should make for remarkable new software. For instance, a program could teach you how to run it vocally, or characters in computer games might speak to you directly, giving them unprecedented immediacy.

Multitasking: The Amiga As Juggler

Because the Amiga is so fast, it can run several different programs at the same time, a capacity called *multitasking*. Each program gets its own window on the screen and acts as if it is the chief and sole glory of the computer. Future uses of this feature depend on the cleverness of programmers and are almost impossible to spell out, but people will likely make fortunes thinking them up.

One aspect of multitasking is clear right now. It lets you print out or transmit projects over the modem while you're also using the computer to do something else. It doesn't sound like much. But printout and modem transmission can take up large chunks of time, during which the computer is paralyzed.

19

CHAPTER TWO

And since the computer is the hub of operations at your desk—your typewriter, calculator, file cabinet, and more—you can be truly inconvenienced. This element of multitasking alone has a great many current users eyeing the Amiga with dewy fondness.

Emulation: The Amiga As Chameleon

The Amiga's great speed lets it emulate other computers, and hence run software written for them. Its $99 *Transformer* program already emulates the IBM PC quite well, and the Amiga can thus tap into its base of excellent business software. IBM emulation should help ease the Amiga into offices, where companies could run their IBM software on the Amiga.

Significantly, the Amiga emulates with software rather than hardware. Most previous "emulation" has required a company to take the brains of one computer—its CPU—and add it to another, creating two computers in one. That's not emulation—it's the real thing. It's also expensive and clumsy. Software is not only cheaper and more elegant, but it's removable. You can change it. Today you use *The Transformer* and emulate IBM. Tomorrow you may be able to use another program and emulate the Apple II.

Hence, the Amiga could be the first computer that runs programs written for any machine. It is hard to convey the importance of such an achievement to the computer community. For years, this El Dorado has shimmered just beyond the horizon, and many have believed in it, some sacrificed for it, and others scoffed at it as mirage. If the Amiga can reach it, or even come close, it will make history.

Expandability: The Amicable Amiga

The Amiga console itself has no speakers or video display. To use these devices, it must be physically linked to them. Without screen and keyboard, the console is just a costly paperweight, and thus all personal computers attach to such devices.

But some limit the scope of connectability. The Macintosh, for instance, can handle only two disk drives and requires a technician to add extra internal memory. You can attach a few peripherals, but otherwise you can't link up to the fundamental architecture. The system is considered nonexpandable.

The Amiga is not so constrained. First, it has a memory expansion port, located behind the middle third of the front panel. You can buy a simple memory upgrade, plug it in here, and double the Amiga's internal memory at once. More important, it also has an expansion bus, beneath a panel on the right side of the computer. The expansion bus hooks into the basic circuitry of the machine. It allows you not only to connect many existing hardware devices to the Amiga, but to invent entirely new ones.

This capacity is particularly significant with the Amiga. Because of its remarkable graphics and audio, it will become the tool of specialists who will devise novel hardware for it. Such ingenuity has a trickle-down effect. Devices are invented for the space race and wind up on your kitchen drainboard. Hence, the Amiga's expandability may well lead to new and fascinating retail products. Finally, one of the Amiga's most impressive feats is almost as much political as it is technological. Most computers lean toward either ease of use or power. Machines which open the door for you and let you bounce into the front seat do not always take you very far. And super-charged computers, which let you conquer hill and dale, often bristle with complexity. Each type has advocates, and the debate between them has sometimes grown warm.

The Amiga resolves it. It is almost as easy to learn as the Macintosh, which takes about three minutes and has transformed the instruction manual from a thick text to a chatty guide. At the same time, it offers a trove of features for those willing to explore them, and these can require and repay a little study. For instance, users who prize comfort can stay with the Workbench, while those who like to open the hood can delve into the Command Line Interface. Fans of the mouse and keyboard, often at odds, will find the Amiga caters to them both. Some users can scull along with graphics programs, while others venture onto the high seas of the genlock interface and the videotape. The Amiga speaks to everyone.

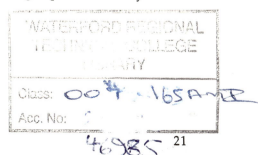

Setting Up

There can be a real thrill in opening the Amiga packages, laying out the contents, and getting them to work. Part of the excitement lies in the half-magical nature of the device itself, and part in the drama of hooking it up. If you have always relegated mechanical tasks to some realm beyond the sea, where individuals with arcane knowledge exist to help you out, you may experience special pleasure in meeting the challenge of Amiga setup, since the odds are heavily in your favor. Commodore has provided a manual that is simple and straightforward, and it steers you through the process without delay. However, the booklet is brief, and as the topic is important, this chapter fleshes it out a little.

When you get the Amiga boxes home, you may find they contain a bit more than you expected. The basic console is there, of course, clasped between two styrofoam flats. But in addition you'll have:

The Amiga user guides. A thick loose-leaf binder comes with *Introduction to Amiga* and an explanation of the BASIC language, and these documents will lead you through the specifics of Amiga use. The binder, like the computer, is expandable and will easily hold upgrades and other booklets.

Disks. The User Guides binder also contains disks for the Amiga. These disks include the *Amiga Tutor*, which welcomes you to your new possession, as well as *Kickstart*, the *Workbench*, the graphics demo *Kaleidoscope*, and a version of BASIC.

The power cord. The power cord is the dark gray wire with the three-pronged plug. This cable connects the Amiga to the nation's electrical supply.

Warranty card. The warranty card has two parts. The top explains Commodore's 90-day guarantee and offers a subscription to *AmigaWorld*, the first magazine devoted entirely to the Amiga. It also has room for you to write down your serial number. The serial number is on the underside of the computer, and if you don't record it now, you'll have to move mountains to do so later. The lower part is a detachable business reply card. You should fill it out and send it in at once, for it is your warranty registration.

The entire package is meant to get you on the Amiga as fast as possible, and it does this job well. Yet setting up demands a little prudence. The Amiga is not a china doll; it can stand a certain amount of everyday handling. On the other hand, it is no Raggedy Ann, and should be treated with as much care as possible. And there are some things you simply should never do to it.

A Place Out of the Sun

We generally think of plug-in appliances as the gleaming symbol of modern convenience. You plug a toaster into an outlet and instantly the device works. But a toaster is a simple implement. A computer like the Amiga is one of the most complex machines you are ever likely to buy, and it asks somewhat more of you. You should accommodate it.

First, you should find a good place to use it. The task is not quite as simple as it appears. You need to consider at least three factors: space, temperature, and outlets.

Space. The Amiga requires a fair amount of room. By itself, it takes up no more space than a breadboard. The monitor goes on top of it, and so adds nothing to the footprint. But the keyboard and mouse both need territory, and a printer does, too. In addition, you will likely keep your disks nearby, as well as papers and other handy items. If you simply cannot find the space for the Amiga and its appurtenances, you might want to consider specially designed computer furniture, though you should check out its cost very carefully. Some manufacturers apparently think computer owners like to stand by the railing and fling their money into the mall.

Temperature. A second vital factor is temperature. The Amiga can be stored at between −40- and 60-degrees Centigrade or −40- and 140-degrees Fahrenheit, a wide range indeed. However, it can operate only between 5 and 45°C or 41 and 113°F, and you should thus avoid using it in extreme heat or cold. And even though 113°F is rather high, don't place the Amiga near a heating register or a crackling fireplace. There's no need to play brinksmanship with the machine.

The Amiga, of course, is not the only thing you'll have on your desk. You'll have the monitor and probably a printer,

CHAPTER
THREE

and these devices have their own temperature limits. Moreover, you'll probably also have disks. Disks are vulnerable to direct sunlight—and the Amiga isn't wild about it either—so you should look for a place beyond the rays of the sun.

Finally, you can use the Amiga at up to 113°F only if you use it properly. Otherwise, it will wilt very fast. You may have noticed the grills the Amiga has in back and on the bottom. The computer also stands on an I-shaped ridge, leaving plenty of empty space beneath the machine. These are not casual accidents of design. Both grills and ridge act to cool the computer, and it's a crucial function.

Computers, like the human body, give off heat which absolutely must be dissipated. As every jogger knows, people have a number of biological mechanisms for getting rid of excess heat, such as sweating and vasodilation at the skin surface. If these means somehow fail, we suffer heatstroke and possibly death. Likewise, the Amiga needs a means of wafting its heat away, or it, too, will collapse.

Thus the grills and the ridge. The grills are ventilation slots, allowing air to enter and leave the machine. The ridge lifts the Amiga above the desk, for the same reason that Polynesian houses often stand on stilts a few feet off the ground. It fosters convection. As the Amiga warms up, a fan blows heat out the back vent. You can hear its slight whir and, if you place your hand nearby, feel the rush. At the same time, cooler air flows in through the bottom vents. A current is set up, like a slow breeze, and it keeps the Amiga comfortable.

Hence you must never leave papers, books or anything else next to the vents while you are working on the machine. Avoid using the Amiga on a thick rug or storing anything in the narrow crawlspace as you work, no matter how crowded your desk is. If you block the Amiga's vents, you will be forcing it to do the equivalent of calisthenics in a sauna.

Outlets. Outlets are a third consideration in situating your Amiga. If possible, you should have two or even more outlets nearby. The Amiga needs only one electrical source, but the monitor, printer, and modem each require one as well. If you have just one outlet, you may eventually want to purchase a power strip, an extension cord which can multiply a single outlet into three or six.

It is worth selecting your outlet with care. The Amiga should not have to share it with a food processor, refrigerator,

24

large fan, or other appliance with a motor. These machines generate electrical noise which can hiss back up the wires into the Amiga, much as a running blender interferes with a TV picture. In the Amiga, this noise may destroy your data. The problem is less severe than previously, since most computers now come with a device to help preserve them from fluctuations in electrical power. Nonetheless, losing information generally makes people quite animated, and it is a good idea to minimize its likelihood. You should also seek an outlet not prone to short circuits. The Amiga uses much less electricity than you would expect and will rarely overload a circuit by itself. But a short or any failure of power will erase your screen, and if fuses in a certain room tend to blow every time someone turns on the hair dryer, you should put the Amiga elsewhere.

You also need an outlet with a ground connection. Look at the power cord. Its larger end has three prongs: two flat like the head of a screwdriver, and a third like a rounded icepick. The flat prongs work just like those in the average plug. One leads electricity into the device, while the other carries it away and completes the circuit. The third is the ground connection. It channels errant electricity away from the Amiga, so it doesn't harm the computer or you yourself. In the absence of grounding, stray electrical charges can collect in the computer and ruin it, or even give you a shock. A ground connection is thus imperative. It is like a seat belt that buckles automatically.

If your home or office already has three-hole sockets, you have no problems. Even if you have two-hole sockets, you can still buy an inexpensive adapter at most hardware stores. You insert the power cord into one end of the adapter, plug the adapter into the two-hole socket, and attach a wire or clip leading out from the device to the screw in the center of the plastic outlet plate. However, in some buildings even this arrangement will not work, and if you have any doubts at all about this matter, you should talk to an electrician.

Plugging In

The climax of this careful preparation is the act of plugging in. First, be certain that the on/off switch on the left side of the Amiga is off. Then find the smaller end of the power cord. It goes into a plug on the right hand side of the rear panel, in a recess immediately below the TV and video ports. You may

CHAPTER
THREE

have to hunt a bit to find it, as it is tucked in rather deeply. Fit
the plug onto the three flat prongs, then stick the other end
into the outlet.

Now that you've got the Amiga plugged in, what can you
do with it? In fact, almost nothing. You could slip a disk in the
disk drive, and the computer would read it in and act on it.
But you'd have no command of the Amiga, and no idea what
it was doing. You need to attach some peripherals.

The Amiga with a 1080 Amiga Monitor

The Ports

As we've seen, the Amiga has a long line of plugs for peripherals. The plugs are called *ports,* and the nautical association is fitting, since the various cables lodge here like ships docked at a city.

The Amiga has two ports on the right side and nine on the back. Each has a drawing or icon above it. The icons represent an attempt to internationalize the machine, to create a pictorial vocabulary the whole globe will eventually understand. Unfortunately, some of the peripherals are harder to depict than others, and the meaning of the icons does not always leap out at you. It doesn't matter. If an icon has you stumped, just look beneath the port where its name is spelled out in English.

Even a cursory glance will show that about half of the ports are very long and flat. These are called D-type connectors—they look a little like squashed D's—and support a large number of pins. D-type connectors usually conduct the most complicated signals, with each pin relaying information about one aspect of the whole. They also have screws to insure that the connection does not break at some critical juncture and turn your work into linguini.

The other common kind of port is called an RCA female jack. The rear panel has three of them. RCA female jacks have a small, ivory circle which accepts a rounded tine much larger than the pins for other ports. The plug has four metal projections which clasp the jack and tighten the connection. These ports are used for the speakers and the composite and monochrome monitors.

Let's review the ports, first on the right side—the honorary rear panel—then the rear panel itself. Don't worry if you don't yet understand what the items at each port do. You will. For now, the important thing is to lay out the map.

The right side has the two hand controller ports for various input devices you move around by hand. You will use these ports most often to plug in the mouse, the little device that moves a pointer on the screen. But they will also accept paddles, joysticks, light pens, digitizer pads, and optical scanners.

The rear panel has nine ports, from left to right:

Keyboard port. This connector resembles a phone jack and takes the cable from the keyboard. The cable clicks in briskly and easily.

CHAPTER
THREE

Parallel port. The parallel port generally links you up with the printer or other color plotter, a specialty device for drawing high-quality graphics. It is called a parallel port because it uses parallel transmission to communicate with other devices. Parallel transmission involves sending eight or more signals down the cord at the same time. It requires that you give it a cable with numerous wires, and repays the courtesy with greatly enhanced speed.

External disk drive port. Disk drives read information from magnetic disks into the Amiga's memory. The Amiga comes equipped with one disk drive, but if you add another, you will have to plug it into this port. The icon here shows a floppy disk.

Serial port. Some printers and most modems use serial transmission, and this port handles them. Serial transmission is the opposite of parallel. It involves sending signals one at a time through a single wire. The industry has standardized serial signals, and a common protocol is the Recommended Standard 232, or RS-232, which you will see fairly often. The serial port is female and the parallel port male, so you should not accidentally mistake the two.

Speaker ports. These two jacks attach to the speaker in the Amiga monitor or to your hi-fi speakers and let you bask in the computer's sound capacities.

RGB monitor port. This port links the Amiga to the color display called the RGB (red-green-blue) monitor. The icon shows a TV tube with three dots in it, emblematic of the three colors.

TV port. The TV port sends signals to your TV set. You won't confuse it with either the pancake-shaped RGB port on its left or the nozzle-like video jack on the right, for it is the only port in the form of a circle. It takes several pins around its edges and one at the middle.

Video port. While the RGB and TV ports have clear, unequivocal names, the "video port" is vaguer. It connects you to the leftover miscellany: the color composite monitor, a type of screen somewhat inferior to the RGB, and the monochrome, or one-color, monitor.

The rear panel is where the Amiga forms its bonds with other machines. It may look technical and forbidding, the haunt of gnarled and invisible gremlins ready to spook your work. But it's really rather staid. Its main challenge involved your prudence.

CHAPTER THREE

Connecting the Peripherals

Connecting the peripherals demands a bit of caution, but people do it every day, and if you follow two basic rules, you will have no difficulty.

First, *be absolutely certain that the Amiga and the peripheral are both off.* If you try to connect the Amiga to the peripheral while one of them is on, you may damage the computer. This stricture pertains to any device you ever want to plug in. *Always make sure that the Amiga and whatever you are attaching to it are off before linking them up.*

Second, never try to force a connection. Many of the ports have numerous slender pins, and rough treatment can break them. If a plug feels tight, rock it gently—very gently—back and forth to ease it in. It should fit snugly, but if you meet resistance, look the situation over before trying again. The pins are delicate, and this is definitely not a case where might makes right.

You should have no trouble hooking up most peripherals to their ports. The documentation explains the procedure very clearly. The mouse, for instance, simply plugs into the first hand controller port. The RGB monitor goes into the RGB and the speaker ports. But there are a few more interesting cases.

The keyboard. The Amiga has a detachable keyboard, so you must plug it into the computer. Its cable is a long, helical, springlike wire, like a telephone's, and the keyboard port also looks like a phone jack. (Do *not* for this reason try to attach a telephone to this port.)

Connecting the keyboard is an unusual operation. Commodore wanted the keyboard to fit under the computer when not in use, an excellent idea. But this goal raised a problem with the cord. It seemed that either the cord would have to snake out of the recess and around to its port—a clumsy arrangement—or the user would have to repeatedly detach it—not much better. Commodore solved the problem by, in effect, digging a tunnel. It cut a small notch in the I-shaped ridge on the machine's underside, and placed the keyboard port on the far left of the rear panel. You plug the cable into the port, then lift the computer, string the cable through the notch, and carefully lower the computer again. If the cable hasn't fit into the notch, the Amiga lies atilt and you try again. Then you just snap the other end of the cable into the keyboard.

CHAPTER
THREE

Television. You don't need a monitor with your Amiga. You can use a TV set for display. If you do, however, you'll have to link the Amiga to your TV set. This operation is the trickiest part of setting up because it requires: a few new parts, a chain of connections, and a screwdriver.

The parts include an RF modulator (also called a TV modulator), a cable, and a switch box. They don't come standard with the Amiga, and you'll have to purchase them from your Amiga dealer or local hardware store. They aren't space age technology and should cost around $30.

The chain of connections is easy to figure out. To hook up a device like the printer to the Amiga, you simply link the two machines with a cable. Anyone can do that. A television set needs a cable, too. But it also requires a pair of small boxes, one at either end: the RF modulator at the Amiga side and the switch box at the TV. Thus, instead of a three-part sequence like Amiga-cable-printer, you have: Amiga-RF modulator-cable-switch box-TV.

Making a chain of these items is not much harder than making one of paper clips. The first step is to locate the RF modulator. Plug it into the TV port, the second one from the right, with the legend TV MOD beneath it. Note the switch on the RF modulator. This mechanism selects the television channel you will be using. You have a choice between 3 and 4, and to avoid interference you should pick whichever one isn't used in your area. If both are used, choose the one with the weaker signal.

Once you plug the video cable into the RF modulator, you've got a cord leading from the TV port over toward the TV itself. If you have a newer TV designed for VCRs or videodisc players, you'll have no trouble here. You don't even need the switch box. Just insert the video cable into the VCR outlet, and you've got a screen for your computer. Whenever you want to watch TV again, unplug the cable.

However, if your TV lacks this genial capacity, you must make the connection with a screwdriver, and since you don't want to have to fiddle with wires every time you go from *Graphicraft* to the evening news, you need the switch box.

The switch box is just what its name implies: a switch. You insert it in the path of the broadcast signals that the antenna carries down from the air into the TV. You then either leave things as they are, in which case the set continues to show TV, or you cut the connection to the antenna and shift it to your video cable, in which case the set displays signals from the Amiga.

Attaching the switch box is normally the highlight of the day. Generally, you will do it like this. Somewhere in the rear of your television will be two screws labeled VHF. You want to break the line to the antenna at this point. First, you loosen the screws, freeing a pair of wires that come straight from the antenna. You attach them to similar screws on the switch box. Now you've got a line running from the antenna to the switch box, which dangles in midair. To reconstitute the path, you take the two forked metal prongs called spade lugs, make each one straddle a VHF screw on the TV set, and tighten the screws.

Once you've plugged the cable into the switch box, all you need to do is open Preferences and select the 60 gadget opposite the word Text. This figure refers to the number of characters per inch that the device can display clearly. If you have an RGB monitor, you should make sure that "Text" is set to 80.

You are now ready to turn the Amiga on.

Turning On

On the left side of the computer, near the front, is the rocker switch which turns the Amiga on and off. The side closer to you is on, the side farther away, off. Plugging into the wall sets up the potential for electricity to flow through the Amiga, but this switch actually closes the circuit and starts the current moving. It works just like the switch on a lamp.

It's a good idea to turn on the peripherals first, before the Amiga. When any machine is switched on, it sends electrical current back through the wires. This kick won't destroy the Amiga, but it's wise to preserve the computer from as much stress as possible.

Final Precautions

There are a few more things you should be aware of once you get the Amiga on the road. The manual mentions them, but they are worth emphasizing.

First, avoid drinking or eating near the computer. If you spill root beer onto the Amiga, for instance, you can really

CHAPTER
THREE

damage it. Such accidents can happen to anyone. They're accidents—that is, unintentional. Moreover, if you somehow get
food on the ports or plugs, you can interrupt the connection
and cause further hazard to your work.

Don't put more than 40 pounds on top of the computer
console. The Amiga is not a weigh station and simply can't
hold it. Most monitors or small portable TV's will not exceed
this amount. But some TV's are beefy indeed and will crush it.

And don't open the case. Opening the case voids your
warranty, and there is simply no reason for you to do it, as its
secrets reveal themselves to visual inspection about as fast as
those of Linear B. If you're curious about how it works—and
curiosity is an admirable trait—look at subsequent chapters of
this book.

PART TWO

The Hardware

*Machines have less problems. I'd like to
be a machine.*

Andy Warhol

The Universal Machine

In 1936, a brilliant English mathematician named Alan Turing published a paper in which he described a "universal machine," one whose function the user could alter at will. Most machines like, say, automobiles have their purpose frozen into a fixed structure. They are created in factories where molten steel, plastic, glass, and other materials take on shapes dictated by blueprints. The process is irreversible. Once the blueprints are carried out, they give rise to a rigid object with a narrow, unchanging role. However, the universal machine would perform an almost infinite number of tasks because you could blueprint it yourself, and reblueprint it, and reblueprint it again. It would resemble the factory where cars are made rather than the cars themselves. Rearrange the insides of a factory, and it will turn out chandeliers or swimsuits or grapefruit knives.

The universal machine would deal with information. Feed one set of instructions into it, and it would follow them and manipulate data in one way. When you replaced them with new rules, the device would follow those and act on data in another way. The instructions would describe and create special-purpose submachines, without the bother of mining metals and refining petroleum, and hence without the limits of corporeality. Such machines could be called to life and destroyed in seconds. Thus, for instance, instead of having both a typewriter and an adding machine on your desk, you could have a universal machine, which would act like either at your behest.

The key to this pleasing vision is the idea of information acting on other information. The scheme, therefore, requires two tiers of input. The first creates the submachine. It resembles a formula, like, say, $5a + 27 = x$. It defines actions the computer will take automatically and leaves blanks for items you can choose: a and x. We call it the program.

CHAPTER
FOUR

The second-level information plugs into these blanks and causes the computer to react. It's the raw data. Raw data is familiar to us, since most machines require it. In a car, for instance, we enter it by pressing down on the accelerator or moving the left-turn indicator. We give the vehicle information, and it responds. In the formula above, we enter raw data by providing specific numbers. For instance, if we decree that a equals 2, the computer instantly replies with $10 + 27 = 37$.

Of course, computer programs are hardly limited to math formulas. They can reproduce typewriters, filing systems, drawing boards, and much else besides. Hence, in a computer, raw data goes far beyond mere numbers. It is whatever information the program lets us feed in—letters, lines drawn across the screen, commands to fire destructive little dots, anything the program will respond to.

Of course, Turing didn't have the video arcade in mind in 1936. He wasn't even sure exactly how his machine would work. Physically, he envisioned simply a box with printed paper tape running through it with symbols for instructions and data. The machine could read them and perform logical operations. Little steps of logic would be the great secret of the universal machine. A few such operations might not be impressive, he said, but combine enough of them and an Emerald City would rise.

Turing was an unusual individual. He had a high-pitched stammer and a weird, crowing laugh that irritated even his friends. He was tall and often slovenly, and when hay fever struck him, he did not hesitate to wander around in a gas mask. But his concept of the universal machine led directly to the development of ENIAC, the first large-scale vacuum tube computer, in 1945.

The Amiga is also a universal machine. It works in two phases: programming and execution. Slip a program in the disk drive and you create the submachine. Enter raw data and the submachine acts. You can program it in myriad ways, and, like every computer, it has two main components: *software* and *hardware*.

Software is the program itself, a set of instructions. Hardware is the physical apparatus that carries them out. Software is always intangible, hardware always tangible. Kaleidoscope, for instance, is software. The disk it comes on is hardware.

It's like the difference between a book with blank pages and one filled with words. An empty book is hardware. We could buy one, but then we'd have to supply it with words of our own creation, a vexing task. A novel, on the other hand, comes complete with verbiage. The words take time to devise and may well take talent. They're ideas—intangible—but we value the labor and skill that went into them, and pay more for a novel accordingly. A program on a disk is similar. It is a pattern of tiny magnetic instructions, and it too takes time and talent to create. It also far exceeds the value of the medium. A disk without software costs only a few dollars, but with software, it may cost hundreds.

The nature of software is elusive partly because it entwines so closely around hardware. Without overstating the matter, we can say it's a bit like the relation between intelligence and training. Hardware, like intelligence, creates the potential for performing tasks. Software, like training, constitutes the method. The better the hardware, the more it can do, but it must have software or it does nothing. At the same time, the more good software it does have, the greater abilities we tend to attribute to the hardware.

The Elements of Hardware

The individual most responsible for the configuration of computer hardware is John von Neumann, one of the most important mathematicians of the twentieth century, who laid out the basic pattern at the end of World War II. Let's approach his scheme pragmatically, as he did, by considering those powers any item requires to act as a universal machine. For an analogy, we can start with ourselves.

The brain is a universal "machine" too, in a way, though an extremely complex and subtle one. (Actually, a spitfire controversy now rages over whether the brain really is a supercomputer, and the combatants are tearing each other to pieces.)

An example of human problem solving will help. Imagine you are back in elementary school. You have previously learned the formula for long division, and now the teacher asks you to divide 369 by 3. To carry out this task, you need at least four essential hardware capacities:

Sensory power. You must have eyes, ears, or tactile sensitivity to register the formula and data, and you must have nerves to carry them to the brain.

CHAPTER
FOUR

Processing faculty. You must have a center of awareness in the brain from which to structure the problem. This center must understand it, access your memory, perform the calculation, and prepare to express the answer.

Memory. You must have a store of memory, containing not only the formula and data, but also much information you take for granted, such as the rules of language and the neuromuscular memory needed to talk and coordinate vision.

Expressive power. You must be able to communicate the answer to the teacher, by speech, writing, or some other method. Otherwise, you have the falling-tree-in-the-wilderness syndrome. Is there a sound? Is there an answer? No one but you can know. And to others, your own knowledge is not enough. The task remains unfulfilled.

Figure 4-1. Elements of Human Problem Solving

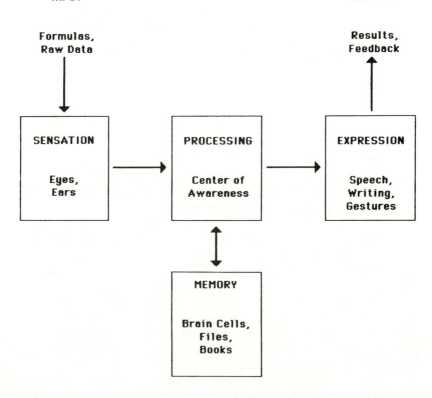

INPUT

OUTPUT

Formulas,
Raw Data

Results,
Feedback

SENSATION

Eyes,
Ears

PROCESSING

Center of
Awareness

EXPRESSION

Speech,
Writing,
Gestures

MEMORY

Brain Cells,
Files,
Books

Of course, the problem need not have been one of calculation. We could just as well have been asked, "Is Socrates mortal?" The elements would be identical. We would first have to sense the words, then process them. We would call up another formula from memory, however—another kind of program. This time it would be a logical one: All men are mortal. We would plug Socrates into the formula and reach the woeful conclusion. We would then express it, fulfilling the request. Our "hardware" would be working in the same basic way, but performing a different function.

Computers also go through this cycle of sensation-processing-recall-expression, and, like us, they have a variety of instruments for the stages:

Input devices. Input devices conduct programs and data from you into the computer. Generally, programs enter the computer through the disk drive. The disk drive is a slot which accepts floppy disks, magnetically coded platters which the disk drive reads like a record player. Your first act after turning the computer on is normally to insert a disk into the drive, to create the submachine of the moment. Raw data comes in through a variety of devices. The most common is the keyboard, which takes information directly from your fingertips. Another is the mouse, a small, handheld item which you roll on your desk to move a pointer about on the screen. The joystick is a peg you shift up or down, left or right, to control the action in arcade games. Other, newer input devices include touch screens, light pens, touch pads, image processors, optical scanners, and speech recognition devices. On the far, downswell side of the technological wave, input devices used with the early behemoth computers, such as punched card readers and paper tape readers, are virtually deceased.

CPU. The CPU (Central Processing Unit) is the machine's processing faculty, its "center of awareness," a microchip of silicon with thousands of transistorized switches and connections. The Amiga has numerous chips, but the CPU, or microprocessor, is the special one. The CPU carries out all the little steps of logic, so fast they hardly seem to exist. It also controls the rest of the computer. It is like a very busy man with a hundred arms sitting in the middle of congested floor, continually receiving instructions and information, depositing them in the proper box, retrieving them in order, executing them,

CHAPTER
FOUR

and relaying their results to the correct place. The CPU is the headquarters of the Amiga or any computer, and its capacity and nature in many ways determine the computer itself.

Memory. Any instruction or piece of data not being acted on by the CPU at any given moment must be stored in memory. It can be kept anywhere, as long as the CPU can reach it when it needs to. There are hence several kinds of memory devices, which vary in size and accessibility. Information which must be available immediately or continually goes into memory chips, silicon slivers like the CPU. For instance, memory chips hold part of the Amiga's operating system, the software which corresponds to human neuromuscular memory, and constantly performs little chores in the machine. However, other types of information, such as game programs or written documents, we use less frequently. To save space inside the computer, we store this data on floppy disks. More expensive kinds of memory include hard disks and hard disk drives, hermetically-sealed disks and readers capable of storing large quantities of information. And laserdiscs, which can hold the equivalent of 180 rolls of microfilm—far more than the Encyclopaedia Britannica—offer fantastic memory potential. At the tag-end of the technology, cassette tape remains in use, though it is inefficient and survives mostly on small, cheap machines.

Output devices. Output devices communicate back to you, the user. They give you not only your ultimate result, but a great deal of feedback en route. They are clearly essential, for a computer that solves problems without telling you the answers belongs somewhere like the Marianas Trench. The most important output device is the video display screen, or the CRT (cathode ray tube). The CRT is the picture tube in TV sets, but the term also includes video screens made especially for computers, called monitors. The CRT normally lets you know exactly what you have keyed in, so you can check for typos and generally contemplate your work. It allows programs to ask you questions, and sometimes shows error messages. Another important output device is the printer, which gives you hard copies. You don't need a printer for playing games, finding solutions to mathematical problems, or keeping track of large collections of information. But it is vital for word processing, graphics, and much business software. The Amiga has a third output device: the speaker. It can mimic musical instruments, generate special effects for games, create near-human voices, and in general fill the room with splendor.

Figure 4-2. Elements of Computer Problem Solving

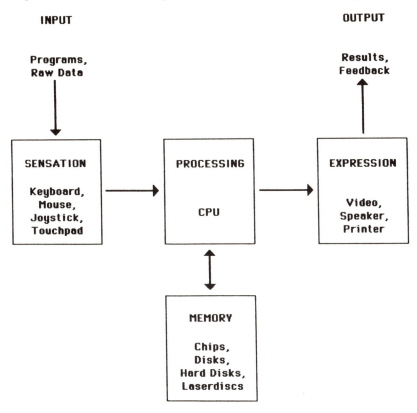

These four elements—input devices, CPU, memory, and output devices—make up the computer hardware universe. The manufacture of each has bred enormous and lucrative industries. The following four chapters will discuss them in turn.

Input and output instruments are often collapsed into the same category as I/O devices because they share the aspect of communication between machine and outside world. But this is an engineer's perspective, not a user's. From the viewpoint of the CPU, they are indeed similar. From your viewpoint, they aren't.

These four elements—input devices, CPU, memory, and output devices—make up the computer hardware universe. The manufacture of each has bred enormous and lucrative industries. The following four chapters will discuss them in turn.

Input: From Thought to Chip

Input devices get your ideas into the Amiga's circuitry. They're your scepters, giving you sway over the waiting Amiga. The more powerful they are, the more control they grant you over the computer, and the easier they make your work. And today, some bestow a dominion that is breathtaking.

These devices are rapidly proliferating. They already come in a wide variety, and new ones seem to be appearing every day. At the moment, we can fit them into three categories:

- *Basic input mechanisms.* The disk drive, keyboard, and mouse are foremost among these, but the trackball is attracting fans, and the joystick has long been popular for games.
- *Graphics input.* Touch screens, light pens, and digitizer pads promote precision artwork, while image processors let you use the Amiga like an instant camera, and optical scanners read printed text.
- *Audio input.* Piano keyboards let you play the Amiga like a Steinway. Microphones let it record and respond to immediate sounds. And if speech recognition devices can ever get out of the laboratory, they'll turn your utterances into words on the screen and revolutionize the office.

All of these instruments require software tailored for them, and the extent of that software determines their usefulness. You can't just buy a light pen and expect it to work with *Graphicraft.* Moreover, many of these devices are not yet available for the Amiga. But events move swiftly in the computer industry, and the Amiga's special talents invite attention. Before you know it, you may have your choice of the field.

The Disk Drive

Most of the time, you'll program the Amiga by slipping a 3-1/2-inch disk into the disk drive, the slot on the right of the computer console. This disk contains all the instructions needed to create a submachine, and thus you won't have to worry about this stage of the process. Even when you want to program the Amiga yourself, you'll normally slip a program translator into the disk drive first, then use the keyboard to create the program. The disk itself is a memory device—it holds data—but it and the disk drive are so closely related that we will discuss them together in the "Memory" chapter.

The Keyboard

The keyboard is the input device you work with most often, and it affects your entire experience with the Amiga. If you have written on a typewriter up till now, you might naturally think that the keyboard is a simple item, and that real computer savvy lies elsewhere, say, in understanding the mysterious chips. But a computer's keyboard resembles a typewriter's only superficially. The Amiga keyboard is not just a place to enter letters, but a full control panel, and the more you know about it, the better you will feel at the helm.

The differences between a typewriter and computer keyboard reach down to fundamentals. In a mechanical typewriter, pressure on a key translates directly into force behind the letter, driving it to strike paper. A computer keyboard, however, is electronic. When you press an Amiga key, you send an electrical impulse to the computer. Special software inside—part of its operating system—assesses the row and column that the impulse comes from and translates the information into an ASCII (pronounced "AS-key," for American Standard Code for Information Interchange) number. The 128 ASCII numbers have been standardized for all microcomputers. Pressing *A* thus generates the number 65 within the Amiga. Whenever this character goes out to the screen or to print, the computer's software translates the 65 back into *A*.

The Amiga's keyboard is about as comprehensive as any you'll find. It has 89 keys, all of which repeat automatically if you hold them down past the brief waiting period. In addition, Commodore has given them tactile response. When you press an Amiga key, it moves inward smoothly for a bit, then seems to shudder slightly, signifying receipt of the signal. This feedback tells you how much pressure to apply, and thus hastens typing speed. It also gives a certain psychological assurance, as if the Amiga were saying, "Okay, I've got it!" after each entry.

CHAPTER
FIVE

The keyboard is divided into two parts: the alphanumeric keyboard and the numeric keypad. The numeric keypad is the array of number keys on the far right, separated from the alphanumeric keyboard by a narrow empty corridor. In fact, both of these sections have number keys. This kind of duplication is typical of the Amiga keyboard, and indicates not sloppy design, but rather a concern for easing your life. Let's look at the alphanumeric keyboard first, for it will engage most of your attention.

Even a casual glance at the alphanumeric keyboard shows that it has two types of key. In the center, like the white in a loaf of bread, are the character keys. They feed letters, numbers, and punctuation marks into the computer. Around the edge are the command keys, which give the Amiga instructions.

Character keys. The Amiga has the familiar Sholes or QWERTY layout of keys. The first six letters left to right on the top letter row spell out QWERTY. Why QWERTY? Why this whole layout, which looks like someone turned a Scrabble pouch upside down? The reason is historical. QWERTY is a fossil from the early days of typewriters, when it had this fine feature. It was the slowest layout anyone could think of.

Christopher Latham Sholes (1819–1890)—in succession, a printer, newspaper editor, postmaster, and state senator—is generally credited with inventing the typewriter, though he really only enhanced the 50-odd versions completed before him. He also gave it its name, *type-writer*, in 1867, after trying "writing machine" and "printing machine." But before he could market his device, he had to solve a vexing problem. Most earlier machines laid out the keyboard in alphabetical order, and their keys jammed even at low speeds. Human fingers were faster than the mechanism, and he needed to slow them down. He asked his brother-in-law, a schoolmaster and mathematician, to help rearrange the keys so they would tend to come up from opposite directions. After much experimentation, he settled on QWERTY, selling it to the public with the explanation that it was scientific and added to speed and efficiency.

The Sholes machine was a commercial success. In 1905, a large international meeting was called to establish a standard keyboard. Delegates offered more efficient layouts, yet QWERTY prevailed, and among its main exponents were teachers of typing, who did not want to have to re-learn their fundamental skills.

But challenges to QWERTY kept arising. For instance, in 1932, Agustin Dvorak, a professor of education at the University of Washington in Seattle, created his Dvorak layout, based on time and motion studies of champion typists. He claimed it would increase typing speed by 35 percent, and its supporters say it can bring a beginner up to 40 words per minute in 18 hours. But it was largely ignored, and the embittered inventor later said that proposing a new keyboard was like trying to "reverse the Ten Commandments and the Golden Rule, discard every moral principle, and ridicule motherhood."

However, technology can sometimes succeed where reason fails. Since the meaning of computer keys is controlled by software, you may find a utilities program that converts your QWERTY layout into the Dvorak. You could thus alternate at your pleasure between the comfortable old and the initially demanding new, till you found out which you liked best. If you're a fast typist and wish to control all operations from the keyboard, the Dvorak layout would make you even faster.

This possibility shows that pressing a character key doesn't always give you that character. In some game software, certain characters move you around or fire rockets. In music programs, characters may act like piano ivories, and deliver audio input. Like many of the command keys, the character keys are pliable.

The character keys have one final refinement: tiny bumps on the F and J keys. Touch typists commence by placing their index fingers on these keys, and the little knobs make it easier for them to determine their starting point.

Command keys. Around the margin of the keyboard are keys with cryptic names implying exotic technical operations. These command keys may look intimidating, but in fact there's no reason at all to fear them for you'll either be familiar with them from the typewriter, or you'll need them only in special situations where their use will be spelled out as plainly as a face at Mt. Rushmore.

The command keys fall into three rather hazy categories:

1. Cursor-movers, like TAB or the arrow keys, shift the cursor, the blinking line or box which shows where your next character will appear on the screen. They are positional keys.

CHAPTER FIVE

2. Function keys, like the F keys along the top, spark events on their own. They are autonomous actors.
3. Modifiers, like CTRL or SHIFT, work in tandem with other keys and change their meaning. SHIFT, for instance, turns a lowercase letter into a capital. Modifiers are like adjectives, helpless alone but powerful in combination.

The boundaries between these groups are permeable, so a single key can pop up in more than one category—a fact that undermines the taxonomy. But it does give a fair overview of the types of operation that the command keys carry out.

Let's examine these keys in order, going around the ring in a counter-clockwise circle. We'll start with the stormcloud gray keys across the top.

The ten **F** or function keys carry out acts independently, without assistance from other keys. In PolyScope, for instance, they let you launch the color swirl of your choice. The software always tells you what these keys do, if anything.

The **ESC** or escape key can be either a function key or a modifier. As a function key, it commonly allows you to jump from one branch of computer logic to another. In PolyScope, for instance, it gets you out of a mesmerizing color pattern and back to the main menu. You may also find it used as a modifier, performing diverse and sundry tasks. Like many other keys, the effect of ESC varies according to the program you are in.

The **TAB** key resembles its cousin on typewriters. That is, it shoots the cursor a certain number of spaces to the right. It's used mainly in word processors, where you set the TAB key to provide paragraph indentations, column markers, and other quick layout enhancements.

CTRL, the control key, is a modifier that can perform a variety of feats. Some CTRL functions mimic those of other keys on the board. For instance, CTRL-m acts like the RETURN key. CTRL-i does a TAB, and CTRL-h replicates the left arrow. Like other modifiers, the CTRL key works by altering ASCII number values. If you press a, you get ASCII number 97, but if you press CTRL-a, you get ASCII number 97 minus ASCII number 96, or 1. The computer reads CTRL as a message to subtract 96 from ASCII 97.

CTRL has one major function you should not overlook. If you press it together with both of the Amiga keys, you will reset the computer. That is, you will take it back to the point just after you have loaded Kickstart. Reset is valuable in two ways. First, it lets you restart the Amiga at once, rather than turning it off, waiting 10 or 15 seconds, turning it on again, waiting 10 more seconds, inserting Kickstart, and waiting for it to load. Instead, you go right back to the point you were when you loaded the Workbench. Second, it helps preserve the computer. Physically, turning the machine on and off puts a little strain on it, and reset circumvents that. Pressing the three keys at once is a clumsy maneuver, but it insures that you won't reset accidentally and thereby erase work in progress.

The **SHIFT** key is a third modifier. On a mechanical typewriter, it alters the position of either the striking key or the platen. In the computer, it simply subtracts 32 from the ASCII value for letter keys. Thus, SHIFT-a results into 97 minus 32, or 65, the ASCII equivalent of an uppercase A. Note that it only subtracts 32 from letters. It makes individual adjustments for the number and punctuation keys, since the ASCII values yield differences other than 32 between the paired characters on nonletter keys.

CAPS LOCK is similar to the Shift Lock key on mechanical typewriters, but with one important distinction: it shifts only the letter keys. It gives you no new punctuation marks like the dollar sign or question mark, just capitals—hence the name. If CAPS LOCK is down and you want to type an asterisk, for instance, you have to push SHIFT down too or you'll get an 8. This arrangement can be disorienting at first. But it is clearly sensible, and the only reason it doesn't appear on mechanical typewriters is that it can't. It gives the keyboard two new characters in place of the uppercase period and comma. It lets you type numbers while locked in uppercase. And pressing SHIFT to type a character unavailable in CAPS LOCK is much easier than releasing the Shift Lock, typing a character, and setting the lock again.

The Amiga CAPS LOCK has another ingratiating feature: a red light which turns on while the key is engaged. This light eliminates the need for that sometimes unsuccessful squint to determine the status of this low-profile key.

The two **ALT**, or alternate, keys lie at either end of the bottom row, and state their nature as modifiers in their name. They act like a second SHIFT key, opening up a whole new realm of characters. Press ALT and other keys and you can generate Greek letters, the angstrom sign (Å), the pound ster-

ling symbol (£), and many more. If you press both ALT and
SHIFT along with the character keys, you get a fourth set of
symbols.

ALT has a second important use, with the left and right
Amiga keys, as we'll see below.

The **Left** and **Right Amiga** keys—depicted by filled and
hollow *A*'s, respectively—flank the space bar like bookends.
They are modifiers like CTRL, and among the most potent
keys on the board.

The Amiga keys are mouse surrogates. They carry out the
three basic mouse functions:

1. Positioning. The mouse normally moves the pointer. But
   press an Amiga key and one of the arrow keys, and the
   pointer scuttles away in the direction of whichever arrow
   key you pressed. To move it faster, press an Amiga key, the
   SHIFT key, and the arrow.
2. Menu operations. The mouse normally controls the menus.
   But press the right Amiga and right ALT, and the keyboard
   can control them too. Right Amiga-ALT duplicates the effect
   of pressing the right-hand menu button. You hold both keys
   down and press the arrow keys till the pointer reaches the
   menu item you want. When you release, the item springs to
   life.
3. Nonmenu operations. The mouse takes care of a number of
   other tasks, and the keyboard can do most of these, too.
   Press the left Amiga and left ALT together, and you duplicate the effect of pushing the left-hand selection button of
   the mouse.

The Amiga keys are awkward and lumbering at many of
these tasks—no competition for the agile mouse. But there's
one way they can beat the mouse cleanly. They can be shortcuts. They let you issue certain mouse commands to the computer at once, without touching the mouse at all. For instance,
to select a menu item without pulling the menu down, you
press the right Amiga plus the predefined key, say, Q. A menu
operation like "Quit" then takes place. You can also issue
nonmenu commands by pressing the left Amiga plus a character key. A drawback to this happy arrangement is that you
must memorize specific commands, which vary with the software. But no matter how handy you find the mouse, you are
likely to use the shortcuts from time to time, especially for

menu commands like Quit that arise continually. Shortcuts are the most useful function the Amiga keys perform.

The **arrow keys** are at the lower right of the keyboard. They control movement of the cursor, shifting it a space forward or backward, or a line up or down. These keys are also optional mouse-substitutes, useful for fast typists in general, and for anyone who wants to move the cursor a few letters in either direction. Automatic repeat is a windfall here, since it lets the arrow keys fly across the screen. The nuances of these keys' operation depend on the software.

The **RETURN** key is among the most important of all, and you'll be pressing it constantly. Hence, it is nice and fat, the largest key you'll find. In the broadest sense, pushing RETURN signifies that you have finished your current activity and wish to progress to the next. In some programs, the Amiga waits for this signal before moving on to a new screen, and the key appears in the magnificent role of trigger for all action. In word processing programs, however, its function becomes less exalted, but more revealing. It acts there like the carriage return on a typewriter, dropping the cursor to the left margin of the line below. Likewise, in programming languages such as BASIC, you press RETURN when you finish keying in a command, and the computer accepts the instruction and shifts you down to the next line. In these cases, RETURN also indicates completion, but completion simply has less consequence.

HELP, like the F keys, is a function key. Many programs offer online help in case you get confused, and most of them ask you to press H or some similar key to get it. The Amiga keyboard gives you a special key for this purpose.

The **BACK SPACE** key moves the cursor back one. That's what the left arrow does, and you might therefore think BACK SPACE unnecessary. However, there is an important difference. If you BACK SPACE over text, you delete it. You can keep going and lay waste to all your verbiage. But the left arrow key normally does not delete, since it moves the cursor in mouse fashion, above the text rather than through it. It thus lets you easily backtrack a few letters, insert or delete some characters, then return to where you were. The left arrow is less a replacement for than a helpful adjunct to the mouse, which is at its clumsiest in small maneuvers of this kind.

The **DEL** or delete key reposes at the upper right of the keyboard. Its job also varies with the software. In some programs, it simply moves backwards and vaporizes your prose. Thus, like the arrow keys, TAB, and RETURN, it shifts the cursor. It may also serve to delete whole blocks of text.

The Numeric Keypad

The numeric keypad is the rectangle of keys on the far right which includes the numbers 0–9, a decimal point, a minus sign, and an ENTER key. Since the alphanumeric keyboard already has number keys, the keypad may strike you as pointless. However, some kinds of software, like spreadsheets, demand that you type in a great many numbers, and numeric keypads greatly speed the task. They are like Touch-Tone phones, and let the fingers race.

The numeric keypad also has the ENTER key. ENTER is a ubiquitous command in spreadsheets, where you issue it to signify the end of a number, implant it in the cell, and move on to the next. Placing the ENTER key on the numeric keypad further simplifies data entry, for it prevents the need for recurrent detours to the rest of the keyboard.

The keyboard is your main avenue of communication into the Amiga. But it is not the only one. The mouse is always available for quick and easy screen control. It comes standard with the Amiga, and though you may not absolutely need it, you should find it very useful.

The Mouse

The mouse was invented back in 1964 by Douglas Engelbart, who called it an "X-Y Position Indicator for a Display System" in his patent application. Then a scientist at Stanford Research Institute, Engelbart is a man committed to streamlining technology, making it easy to use, and he thought computer operators should have more control over their screens. His original mouse looked like a small, rounded block of wood with holes for two wheels in the bottom. It went through several incarnations, almost unknown, until it appeared commercially in Apple's Lisa in 1983. In 1984, it attracted widespread and serious attention when it reappeared in the Macintosh, and many other computer companies have adopted it since.

The world is apparently divided into two classes: those who love the mouse and those who don't. Mouse advocates point to the simple pull-down menus and graphics-oriented interface which the mouse ushered in. Instead of memorizing commands like protocol for addressing some electronic grandee, you pick from ones the computer presents you on the silver platter of the interface. They also cite its speed and the feeling of real control it gives you over the machine. Instead of swimming upstream whenever you wish to change your place on the screen, you zip across it at will. You gain speed, power, and simplicity. The computer is tamed.

But keyboard purists raise other points. They say the interface is really separate from the mouse, and the Amiga lets you exploit it with the keyboard alone. In addition, the keyboard is faster. It takes extra time to shift the hand from keyboard to mouse whenever you want to move the cursor or pick a command, and this delay retards your pace and may interrupt the flow of thought.

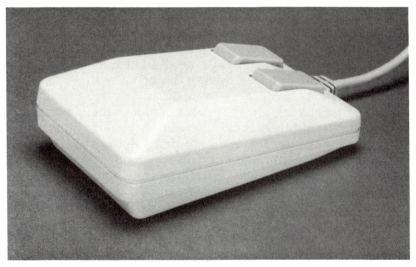

Amiga's Two-Button Mouse

It's probably a matter of taste. The mouse does slow fast typists down, but not that much, and it appears that most people generally favor the comfortable style of the mouse. Moreover, the interface was designed for the mouse, and the keyboard simply does not handle it as adeptly. On the other hand, the keyboard is clearly faster than the mouse with many commands, especially the shortcuts. In any case, the Amiga provides for both camps. You can issue commands with the

CHAPTER
FIVE

keyboard or the mouse as you choose, and you'll probably choose some combination of both.

The Amiga's mouse is about the size of a cigarette pack, though its beveled top—like the first facets of a stone in a jeweler's workshop—gives it a distinctive look. It has two gray bars on top, called *buttons*, as we saw above with the Amiga keys. The right button controls menus, the left one, whatever's left. These two buttons may confuse you at first. However, if you do make a mistake and press one button instead of the other, you almost never cause damage, and you can correct it at once. Moreover, the distinction between them is fairly clear, and with use you'll pick it up quickly.

The Amiga mouse performs three basic functions: pointer movement, menu operations, and nonmenu operations.

Pointer movement. The mouse makes pointer movement both easy and natural. You move the mouse about on a clean, flat surface, and a pointer (arrow, cursor, hand, paintbrush, crosshairs, whatever) reproduces that movement on the display. Keyboard arrow keys can move the pointer only vertically or horizontally. The mouse takes any course you want. It's the difference between driving through city streets and flying over them.

Fluid pointer movement gives the mouse one power the keyboard cannot touch. It can draw lines. Thus, in a graphics program you can use the mouse to pull a dot across the screen and leave a line behind—a curve, a set of loops, your name, whatever you can imagine. The mouse can be a paintbrush.

Menu operations. The mouse controls the menus with the button on the right, the menu button. The menu button is the more limited, less active of the two, dealing entirely with the pull-down menus at the top of the screen. Generally, you use it in three steps.

1. Turn the title bar into the menu bar. To activate the menu bar, which contains the menus, you press the menu button. It's like turning a key in a lock. Since this act always makes the menu bar appear, the menu button is useless for nonmenu work.
2. Roll down a menu. To open a particular menu and see its contents, keep the menu button down and move the pointer to the menu title of your choice, say, Project or Font. The menu automatically unfolds.

3. Choose an offering. To choose a menu item, pull the pointer down to it and release the button. The operation then commences.

The menu button is the specialist of the two. It focuses on one area, the menus, and does not wander away. Its twin is harder to pin down.

Nonmenu operations. For other mouse tasks, you use the left selection button. The selection button is much more of a generalist than the menu button. Its functions are wide-ranging and diverse. Among other things, it lets you do the following:

To **select icons.** You place the tip of the pointer over an icon, press the selection button, and the icon is selected and ready to be acted upon. The icon can represent anything—a disk, program, or project.

You **open icons** by double-clicking with the selection button, that is, clicking twice very rapidly. The pointer then takes a little snooze while the icon opens up. At first, double-clicking may seem like a beat-the-clock kind of challenge, but you soon get a sense of it and it becomes pleasantly automatic.

To **de-select icons.** If you no longer want a particular icon selected, you click the selection button somewhere else on the screen.

The mouse lets you **select several icons** in one swoop. You simply hold the SHIFT key down, click the selection button on the icons you want, then release the SHIFT key.

Placing the cursor. In word processors and spreadsheets, the selection button instantly inserts the cursor wherever you want it, a noble power.

The selection button lets you **drag** the pointer across the screen, a task you will find yourself performing again and again. To drag, you place the pointer at a particular spot, press the selection button, pull the mouse over the screen, and release the button. Among other things, this act transports items, selects areas, and draws lines. If you wish to move an icon to a new position on the screen, for instance, you just drag it to the new locale, release, and the icon hops over. Dragging also lets you select an area. In word processing, if you want to select a whole sentence for, say, deletion, you simply drag the cursor over it. Finally, dragging lets you draw. In graphics programs, you drag a paintbrush across the screen to create a line. Dragging is another maneuver that takes a second to learn and forever to describe.

CHAPTER
FIVE

The mouse is supremely intuitive. You graduate from Mouse University a few moments after you enroll. Your only problem may be keeping the two buttons straight, and even that vanishes quickly, allowing you to exploit the obliging little device to the full.

As hardware, the mouse works in an ingenious way. As you shift it about, the ball on the bottom rolls around. Inside the compartment for the ball are two wheels that touch it and rotate as it moves. The wheels are perpendicular to each other, and a count of their rotations thus indicates the direction and distance the mouse has traveled.

But how does the Amiga actually chalk up the rotations? It's done with light. Each wheel is connected by an axle to a disk inside, and each disk has a circle of tiny rectangular holes punched near its edge. As the disk turns, a photoelectric beam shines at the circle of perforations. Each hole lets the light pass, each intervening disk space stops it. Every time the beam gets through, a sensor registers the fact as an electric impulse. The mouse sends these impulses to the Amiga via a cord, its "tail." The Amiga adds them up, determines the mouse's trajectory, and displays it as position on the screen.

The mouse requires some upkeep, but not much. The main problem you are likely to face is difficulty moving the mouse about, and it can be minimized with a little preventive maintenance. You should find a proper mouse surface: smooth, flat, and clean, though not fine and polished. The device works fine on your danish-oiled mahogany desktop, but the wood doesn't stand up so well. The mouse works on paper, too, but makes a scratchy sound that tries the patience. Cleanliness of the surface is particularly important. Ashes, hairs, eraser particles, and various kinds of dust and dirt can all cling to the ball and wheels, with the result that the mouse moves erratically and the pointer sputters across the screen.

If, despite your efforts, the ball becomes dirty and slow, you can clean it easily. Turn the mouse upside-down. Around the hole for the ball you'll see a small plastic device like a bowl in profile, with two arrows pointing toward the front of the mouse. That's the cover. Place both thumbs on the corrugation below the arrows and push the cover in their direction. It will make a small clack and suddenly feel loose. You can then lift it off. Cup the bottom of the mouse in your hand and turn it right side up again. The ball should drop into your palm.

You should check both the wheels and the ball. The metallic wheels lie in full view in the hollow for the ball. To clean them, rub them with a cotton swab dipped in alcohol or head cleaning fluid. The ball itself demands more delicate treatment. Try blowing on it, or gently wipe it clean with lint-free cloth. (A paper towel or certain cloth rags only replace dirty impediments with cleaner ones.) You can also wash the ball in plain water. Soap, however, gums it up and makes you feel like you are rolling a half-sucked jawbreaker about. Avoid solvents in general, as they may eat right into the ball. To replace it, simply pop it back into the mouse, slip the cover in, and slide it back till it locks.

At the moment, at least two kinds of mouse are commercially available: the *opto-mechanical* and the *optical*. Both cost about the same and run the identical programs, but each has a few advantages and disadvantages. The Amiga mouse is an opto-mechanical one. You can identify this breed by the ball on the underside.

The optical mouse is the same size and shape as the opto-mechanical, but works a little differently. Instead of a ball on the bottom, it has two holes, one for emitting light and the other for receiving it. It also comes with a mousepad, a shiny metallic grid that resembles a finely detailed plaid. You move the mouse about this surface, and a light sensor registers changes in the light it receives. These changes are turned into electrical impulses which can be counted.

Mouse Systems of Santa Clara, California, makes such an item for Apple IIs and Macintoshes. It is called the A+ Mouse, and sells for around $100. (Prices can change overnight in this industry, and they appear in this book mainly to give you an idea of approximate costs. Moreover, the figures are the suggested retail prices, and you can often do better if you hunt around a little.) It has only one button, and so can't be used on the Amiga, but two-button versions may be available soon.

Which is better? The optical mouse has many pluses. It has no moving parts, and thus should last longer than the opto-mechanical. It has its own pad, so you don't have to hunt for a surface. Moreover, it rarely needs cleaning. The pad may occasionally, but it's easier to wash the pad than the ball and wheels. The optical version also demands less arm movement, though this feature may not appeal to those who like free-wheeling mousemanship.

CHAPTER
FIVE

The optical mouse has its drawbacks. For one, the mousepad takes up space on your desk. It's simple to move the opto-mechanical mouse out of the way when you want to jot down notes, but the mousepad is larger and heavier. In addition, since it lacks a ball, the optical mouse encounters more friction and hence moves more slowly. However, you can virtually eliminate drag by operating the mouse just slightly above the pad, like a Hovercraft. The optical mouse works in the air. In any case, don't fret if you have to choose between the two. Both are fine.

There is actually a third kind of mouse, a mouseless mouse. It is an infrared headset. You strap this device to your head like a coal miner's light, and attach two buttons to the lower front of the keyboard. When you press one of these buttons, you can control the position of the pointer on the screen with your head. A small box sits atop the computer to receive these signals and relay them to the computer. Personics Corporation of Concord, Massachusetts, has pioneered this device for the Macintosh, at around $200.

The keyboard may survive without the mouse, but the mouse will never replace the keyboard. It would need a command menu with all the letters of the alphabet, and the mouse would have to scurry back and forth among them, clicking here and clicking there, more like a hen on a pecking-ground than the swallow of the video screen. At the same time, it positions things far better than the keyboard can. The two devices supplement each other, and their resonance enhances the whole machine.

The Trackball
The trackball is essentially an opto-mechanical mouse turned upside-down. Instead of moving the ball against a tabletop, you manipulate it directly with your fingertips. If you are accustomed to a mouse, a trackball can take a little getting used to. You no longer have to move your arms about, just your fingers, and the ball responds more precisely to movement. As a result, some people say it is faster than the mouse. Moreover, it frees up desk space. Though uncommon now, it may eventually be sold as part of the keyboard, so your fingers never have to wander away. Already, a similar device, called a "nudger," is being used by the military.

The Joystick

The first computer games were controlled by paddles. Typically, an army of extraterrestrials would attack from above and the player, using a paddle to guide the blip on the bottom, would fire and jockey left or right to avoid annihilation. However, most software makers now let you substitute keys on the keyboard, such as J and L, for the left and right of the paddle. The keyboard has simply replaced the device. Very few games now require a paddle, and it is going the way of the iceman and the scribe.

But the demise of the paddle stems not only from keyboards like the Amiga's, but also from its own evolution into a better instrument. The original paddle could only move left or right. The new item can move left, right, up, or down, and it also has a firing switch. It is called a *joystick*, after the control lever in small airplanes.

The Amiga keyboard has trouble equaling the fluid maneuverability of the joystick. There are several games that provide a keyboard alternative to the joystick. But they require you to manipulate four to six keys at once, a tricky task in games where speed is crucial. Some games also let the mouse do the work of a joystick, but so far it has also proved lacking. Thus, if you're interested in computer games—and a little diversion doesn't rot the mind or character—you will sooner or later want a joystick.

Ease of use is paramount in selecting a joystick. You want to shift the peg around as swiftly as possible, and naturally quick reflexes should not be thwarted by an uncomfortable joystick. People have hands of different sizes, and you should therefore try out several devices before purchasing one. You can find good ones for under $40. You should, however, check to be sure your joystick has a 9-pin connector and that it will work on the Amiga.

Touch Screens

The touch screen lets you enter information by pressing your fingertip to certain spots on the screen. An assortment of electronic techniques may be used to locate your finger and assimilate the command. Some touch screens can be overlaid on top of existing monitors, and others are built into them.

CHAPTER
FIVE

It sounds grand and futuristic, but in fact the touch screen has practical problems. The oil from your skin can make the screen greasy. Your finger often blocks your view of what you are doing, and is simply too big a pointer to carry out any task much finer than fingerpainting. And finally, the touch screen requires you to hold your arm up quite a bit and can tire you out, especially with applications like word processing. Because of these drawbacks, touch screens are still uncommon, though they do exist for certain personal computers, like the HP 150. But most people probably see them mainly in public arenas. For instance, shopping malls are installing them to replace their directories. You find the name of your destination in a list on the screen, touch it, and the display gives you instructions for getting there. Your finger is small enough, and your arm doesn't grow weary from the job. And many people are tickled by it.

Light Pens

The light pen is an enhancement of the touch screen. You press it to the screen, move it about, and it leaves tracks of light like a magic wand. The device is actually a light sensor rather than, as you might suspect, a light generator. When touching the screen, it detects the electron beam from the cathode ray tube, which completely scans the screen about 60 times per second. A timer tells exactly when in the course of each scan the light pen senses the beam. This information goes to the computer, which can deduce the location of the pen on the screen, and hence the meaning of the command.

The light pen is much cleaner, slimmer, and more precise than a finger, and thus clearly superior to the touch screen. It has a natural feel to it, and gives you a pleasing sense of mastery over the machine. However, it too demands that you hold your arm up to the screen a fair amount, and it must be picked up and put down continually.

Touch Pads

The touch pad is like a second screen, lying flat on your desk. You draw on it with a stylus, as on a piece of paper, and the image immediately appears on the screen. You thus achieve the comfort of the mouse as well as the accuracy of a pencil, and for this reason touch pads are growing increasingly popular. Known variously as the digitizer pad and the graphics tablet, the touch pad is also becoming relatively inexpensive. Koala Technologies of San Jose, California, sells its well-known 4-1/4-inch square Koala Pad for $125, though of course it requires software for the Amiga.

Image Processors

Image processors let the Amiga take snapshots. They typically consist of a piece of converter hardware and software, and requires a video camera and graphics program at extra expense. You point the camera where you like, take the picture, and it shows up on the screen in seconds. You can then alter the image with the graphics program.

It's no surprise that graphic artists are hailing image processors. But they are also becoming popular with such individuals as realtors, security agents, and bankers, since they allow computerized collections of photos—homes, faces, signatures—that can be brought to the screen at once. A realtor, for instance, can instantly call up all photos of the kind of home the client is interested in, and thus increase sales. A security guard at a limited-access area can check individuals against photos of personnel with clearance. A bank can compare signatures on checks.

Image processing works in three steps, only one of which requires the actual image processor:

1. The video camera senses the image; that is, it converts its light into a string of analog or wave-like electrical signals.
2. The image processor translates the analog signals into digital ones—numbers.
3. The picture tube turns the digital data into pictures.

The video camera is the star of the first step. Video cameras require ample light, and so may need well-placed lamps. If you use an image processor frequently, you will do well to set up a permanent "stage," with controlled lighting, a fixture to hold the video camera a few feet above the desk, and a special space for laying documents flat.

The image processor per se does its work in the second step. It samples the analog waves at regular intervals and gives them numbers. The pulse at one sampling point may translate into 7, the next into 8, the next into 2, and so on. These integers usually indicate how gray or what color the corresponding dot on the screen is. For instance, 1 might be completely white and 8 completely black. A number scale from 1 to 16 for each dot would give you finer gradations of color, and one from 1 to 256, finer still.

Step three, making digital data into pictures, takes place inside the picture tube. The operation is exactly like turning digital data from the computer into display on the monitor, and we'll look at it in more depth in the Output chapter.

Some image processors also accept input from VCRs. This capacity, called frame-grabbing, lets you freeze a frame of, say, Robert Mitchum in *The Big Sleep*, then digitize it to your screen. Once in the computer, you can alter it, add sound to it, print it out, and even animate it.

One of the first image processors for the Amiga comes from A-Squared of Oakland, California. It plugs into the Amiga's expansion bus and takes input from video cameras, other computers, laserdisc players, and VCRs. It stores an image in eight shades of gray at the minimal Amiga resolution of 320×200, but the company is also talking about a full upgrade to 16 colors at 640×400. The processor encodes the image to be compatible with the program *Graphicraft*, which you can then use to alter it. It was slated to cost between $250 and $300.

That's about as economical as image processors currently get, but this price does not include the video camera. You also need a lot of storage, and, in fact, you really need an external memory device like a hard disk to take full advantage of an image processor. But it is a joy to play with, and it may be just what you need.

Optical Scanners

Optical scanners, also known as optical character recognizers or OCR's, read in printed pages and can save you a great deal of time at the keyboard. For instance, if someone gives you a typed report to work on, you could feed it into the computer with the optical scanner instead of spending half the day keying it in. Oberon International of Irving, Texas, makes one called the Omni-Reader for $499, an exceptional price. The Omni-Reader looks like a large clipboard with a ruler across it. You move the read-head on the ruler carefully over each line. The read-head emits a tiny beam of light, senses the shape of the reflections, and turns them into ASCII code so the Amiga can work with them. With practice, you can learn to scan each line very quickly, and work two or three times as fast as a competent typist. You must have communications software to run the Omni-Reader on the Amiga, but any communications program will do, and you'll need one anyway if you decide to buy a modem.

Piano Keyboard

A music program like *Musicraft* lets you use the Amiga keyboard to enter notes into the computer. It's a serviceable but somewhat awkward way to play a musical instrument, especially for people used to the feel of a piano keyboard. Hence, Cherry Lane Technologies has introduced a "piano" keyboard especially for the Amiga. When you press a key, it generates electronic sound of a particular pitch. It has 49 keys and a price of $99. If you are serious about using the Amiga for music, this kind of aid is indispensable.

Microphone

Microphones don't strike us as input devices, perhaps because they are so often linked to output. The individual onstage speaks into a mike, and the sound is instantly amplified and sent out to the audience through a speaker. But all the microphone does is take sound waves from the air and turn them into electrical waves. The rest is up to the amplifier and the speaker. The Amiga can use a microphone, and the necessary software to respond to auditory signals. You can therefore play an instrument in its presence, and it will accompany you, sensing your own notes and immediately generating similar ones.

Speech Recognition Devices

Speech recognition devices can understand and act upon spoken words. When fully developed, they will instantly take dictation and display it on the screen, ready to print out. Such "talkwriters" could eliminate typewriters and perhaps even keyboards. However, they face daunting barriers.

The basic problem is the way we speak. Speech recognition essentially involves translating oral sounds into text, and you might think a computer could simply translate the phonemes—the most fundamental sounds—of a word like "going" one-by-one into a phonetic word, then translate that

CHAPTER
FIVE

word into English. But we just don't speak carefully enough for that. On the average, 20 to 30 percent of the words in normal taped conversations cannot be understood at all when played back in random order. We rely on context to understand that the "guh" in "I'm guh go shoppin" means "going," but computers are very slow on this kind of uptake. And that's not all. Human speech varies by individual, region, fluency, health, emotional state, and numerous other factors. And complete systems must be able to handle ambiguous terms ("heel," "heal," or "he'll"), slurred or hasty speech, and run-on expressions like "wanna," "blocka vice," or "a noke tree."

Hence, the current technology is relatively limited. Most speech recognition devices are "speaker-dependent," that is, they must be trained to the voice of every individual who uses them. They must be customized, in a sense. They can also recognize only a small vocabulary of single spoken words, though they can comprehend a few of them strung together, if separated by long enough pauses. The Apricot personal computer, for instance, recognizes up to 16 different words for functions such as RETURN. However, you have to teach it to recognize your own voice, and even then, its manual warns that the voice system sometimes doesn't hear a command or confuses it with another, and thus the manual recommends that you not entrust irreversible functions like DELETE to voice. Speech recognition remains a bit wobbly, and it would be a surprise to the entire industry if it became prevalent before the 1990s.

Input devices are relatively easy to understand because they just convert human signals into electronic states which the Amiga can work with. And they have to be simple to use because they will inevitably fall into the hands of fallible, non-technological individuals who will not tolerate arcane instrumentation. But once the input devices have done their job and your message enters the Amiga, everything changes. You are in the world of the engineers. For most lay people, it is like a cave, where marvelous phenomena with names like "semiconductor" and "integrated circuit" flicker by, and where, once the eyes get accustomed to the darkness, you can see the general contours at least, if not the details. It is here that the protean capacities of the Amiga originate, and the following chapter takes a lantern down into that cave.

The CPU: The Headquarters of the Amiga

W hat happens when the electrical signals from the keyboard or mouse reach the inside of the Amiga? A detailed answer would fill a very large book, but the general scheme is accessible to anyone.

In a nutshell: Your information goes to a master controller, the CPU or microprocessor, a tiny chip of silicon that is, technically, a computer in itself. The CPU stores the data in memory, retrieves it at the right time, acts upon it, and generates output. The Amiga uses a 16/32-bit 68000 microprocessor with a 16-bit data bus, and a trio of special chips to enhance its graphics and audio.

Technical language. What is a *data bus?* What are *bits?* What is a *chip?* What, for that matter, is a computer?

A computer is a logic machine. For most of us, logical analysis is a task that quickly tires and confuses the mind. We simply cannot perform a long string of logical operations with any speed or accuracy. Computers take care of this problem. They execute many, many logical operations far faster than we could ever do, and therein lies their usefulness. It also means that computers are inherently intricate, and we cannot simply glance at their workings and grasp them at once. If we could, we wouldn't need them.

The CPU is the linchpin of the computer. Remove it and all else falls apart. It unites and governs the activities of the other chips as well as of devices like the keyboard and screen. But it is also a complex device itself, and to understand it, we must work our way up through its components. Otherwise, all our talk about it remains helplessly vague.

There are many aspects to a CPU. The most important are:

Logic. The on/off logic provides tiny theoretical models for each discrete operation.

63

Switches. Switches are the basic elements that represent each on and off.

Gates. Gates are collections of switches. Each one executes a single step of logic.

Codes. Codes translate numbers, letters, and instructions into on/off patterns and back from them.

Circuits. A computer circuit is a collection of gates, which can perform complex logical feats and makes the machine possible.

The circuit is perhaps the highest level of unit in the computer. You can make it from many different materials. For instance, you could wire a bunch of gates together across your desk. You could also imprint a circuit on a small piece of semiconductor material, usually silicon, in which case it's called a chip.

Chips can perform numerous functions. They can control keyboard input or hold stored information. But the most complex and important of all chips is the CPU, the heart of the computer and the end point of this discussion.

This overview is like a map of the territory, the condensation of a large area into small but comprehensible shape. It provides the bearings for the following discussion, where, as in any foray to novel lands, new sights will continually pop up. Don't worry about mastering them all. This is a tour bus, not a factory van. Just sit back and take in the view.

The Logic

Most of us are familiar with the classic form of logic, the Aristotelian syllogism. A typical syllogism is "All mountain ranges are beautiful. The Tehachapis are a mountain range. Therefore, the Tehachapis are beautiful." Modern logicians generally spurn the Aristotelian approach as cumbersome and unenlightening. They prefer a system announced back in 1854 by the English academic George Boole.

Boole was a man obsessed. He believed that all human reasoning could be reduced to symbols, and he devoted his life to elucidating these "laws of thought." We can question his success in the underlying mission, for cognitive psychologists today generally ignore him. (The modern field of "fuzzy logic" better approximates human thinking.) But the merit of his Boolean algebra as logic was recognized by contemporaries like Augustus de Morgan and Charles Dodgson (Lewis Carroll), and it influenced successors like Bertrand Russell.

Boole went back to basics. He devised and named a number of statements expressing fundamental logical operations. For instance, he approached the Tehachapi example above with the AND statement. For purposes of generality, we reduce the first two conditions to A and B, and the conclusion to X, thus: If A and B are true, then X is true. Otherwise, X is false. It's a fairly strict relation. Both of the conditions must be true for the conclusion to follow.

Another of his operations was the OR statement. The OR statement is much looser: If A is true or B is true, or if both are true, then X is true. Otherwise, X is false. Here, if we know the truth of either A or B, we don't have to inquire further to determine that X is true. We already know.

A third major type of operation is the NOT statement. The NOT statement is like a very contrary little boy. It takes the truth status of whatever comes its way and reverses it, like this: If A is true then X is false. If A is false then X is true. The operation is simple, but pervasive, and is certainly part of our everyday mental equipment.

Boole devised many other such statements, like the NAND and the XOR, and erected an intricate edifice with them, complete with symbols. There is every evidence that Boole had a grand opinion of his work. For instance, he formulated the argument for God's existence as: $x(1-y)(1-z) + y(1-x)(1-z) + z(1-x)(1-y) = 1$. Yet it seems unlikely that, when he died in 1864 from pneumonia after a walk in the rain, he could possibly have foreseen where it would lead.

Switches

A few nineteenth-century logicians like Charles Peirce realized that you could model Boolean algebra with machines. Indeed, Peirce's student John Marquand actually designed an electrical logic machine, though he never built it. But it was Claude Shannon who made Boolean algebra the blueprint for mechanized logic.

In 1937, Shannon was a graduate student at MIT, designing pioneer computer circuitry. He realized, as Boole had before him, that Boolean algebra reduced all logical operations to *ons* and *offs*, 1's and 0's. Every condition, every conclusion, is either *true* or *false*. You didn't have to worry about more complicated, syllogistic notions like "all" or "only." You just had to think about *on* and *off*.

When we think of on and off, we usually think of switches. Shannon did, too. He saw that he could use switches to carry out all of Boole's logical operations. He followed this thought further and further and eventually created the discipline called switching theory, which lies at the root of modern digital computing.

But how can switches perform computation? Well, they can be turned on to represent true, and off to represent false. And whether they are on or off can have further consequences electrically.

We are used to thinking of switches as causes. We flick a switch and a light goes on. (See Figure 6-1.) But let's turn that perspective around. If we can see the light but not the switch, we can determine whether the switch is on. The light tells us. It does so through the logic of equivalency: If A is on, B is on.

It's a feeble feat, to be sure. But suppose we put two switches on the wire. And suppose we play around with the wiring a bit. If so, we can do a lot more. We can make gates.

Figure 6-1. Switches

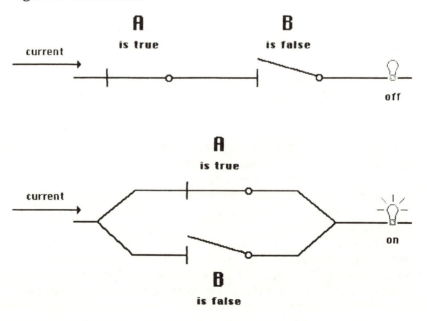

Gates

The gate is the building block of hardware logic, yet it does nothing more than accept electrical input and pass on a result depending on its switches. It acts like a guard at a gate, checking the credentials of all signals that appear and flashing one sign if they're good, another if they're not.

Let's look at the AND gate. The AND gate carries out the AND statement above: "If A is true and B is true, then X is true. Otherwise, X is false." This gate works like a single electric wire with two switches on it. One is A, the other B. Each is closed if true, open if false. If both switches are shut, the wire passes the current along and lights a lamp at the end. Now when we see the lit bulb, we know that A and B are true.

The OR gate is just as straightforward. It carries out the OR statement: "If A is true or B is true, or both are true, X is true. Otherwise, X is false." It works like a wire which forks in two, has a switch on each half, then fuses back together. Again, one switch is A, the other B. But in this case, both switches need not be shut to light the lamp. The current will flow through if either is. The logic is different, and illumination of the light gives us different information.

Of course, we are not restricted to trues and falses. We can just as well think of the on/off states as 1's and 0's. In that case, we see that the OR gate is doing a weird kind of addition. It is saying:

0 + 0 = 0
1 + 0 = 1
0 + 1 = 1
1 + 1 = 1

It's processing information, by evaluating the incoming signals and transforming them to an outgoing one.

You can fuse two gates together. For instance, if you combine an AND gate and a NOT gate, you come up with a NAND gate. The NAND gate is the opposite of the AND, and carries out this arithmetic:

0 + 0 = 1
1 + 0 = 1
0 + 1 = 1
1 + 1 = 0

It looks like a silly performance, but, with clever wiring, NAND gates alone can execute any logical task the Amiga is capable of.

CHAPTER
SIX

One gate is fairly easy to understand. It's also rather useless. But combine them into circuits and they become very useful. With about a dozen gates, you can perform the simplest kind of addition, and with many more, you can do all kinds of calculation. With thousands of AND, OR, NOT, NAND, XOR, and other gates, you can execute a panoply of logical feats, so many so fast that the computer can appear to be thinking.

Of course, the more gates you combine, the more complex and apparently incomprehensible the machine becomes. That's the point. The logic exceeds our immediate capacity. If we could grasp the pattern of a hundred gates at once, we wouldn't need them.

Flipflops. Gates can perform another vital task in computers. They can store information. A long line of them can possess any pattern of 1's and 0's that you want, and hold it until you decide to change it. Such devices are called *flipflops*. The simplest flipflop is two NAND gates entwined in a peculiar way, so that each's output forks and one branch becomes half the other's input. Flipflops cannot generate results, but they are ideal for computer memory.

The Cryptology of Bits

Gates work solely with the ons and offs of Boolean algebra. How then can they perform tasks which are not inherently digital? How can they do word processing or give us videogames? To put it another way, what does it matter if a set of flipflops has a certain pattern of 1's and 0's? By itself, it has no more meaning than a flock of birds on a telephone wire.

It's a good point. In order to make any use of the computer's on/off world, we must be able to code down to it and back up from it. We need a cipher, like Morse code. In fact, there are three such cryptologies, for numbers, letters, and instructions.

The number code. We have seen the limited pseudo-addition a lone gate can carry out. Computers can, of course, perform real calculations with figures like 5,739 and 436,890, but not as they stand. We must first turn them into patterns of 1's and 0's. We call each 1 or 0 a *bit*, short for *binary digit*. We call this method of counting the binary number system.

Here we are in math. For many people, the phrase *binary*

number system produces an instant glazing of the eyes, a mental vacancy that comes from even anticipating that driest of topics: numbers. But hold on. We'll be gliding through this matter quickly, and if math affects you like a sensory deprivation tank, be assured that it won't last long.

Binary numbers are actually simple in concept, simpler than decimal numbers, but we come to them with a bias toward the decimals we use every day. Binaries are unfamiliar and may seem exotic. Moreover, since they challenge popular premises about numbers, they require the mind to reconsider fundamentals, an enterprise some of us resist. In addition, their long strings of 1's and 0's tend to dance before the eye, furthering the illusion of complexity. But it is perhaps proof of their simplicity that any other number system would be very difficult to build a computer around. The Amiga and all other computers love binaries.

Let's see how they work. We can start with a familiar example. In English, words convey meaning through both their symbolic value, that is, their dictionary definition, and their placement in the sentence. "The angry boy killed the bear," for instance, does not mean "The angry bear killed the boy," or "The boy killed the angry bear." The words in each sentence are the same, but their placement tells us their relation to each other, and thus the meaning of the whole sentence.

Decimal numbers express meaning in the same way, through symbol and placement. The symbols, however, are much fewer: the digits 0–9. After we count up to 9 in the decimal system, we run out of new symbols, and so we start combining the old ones. We put a 1 in a column to the left, understanding that any digit which appears there represents ten times itself. Thus 10 equals 1 times 10, plus 0. Likewise, 78 is 7 times 10, plus 8. After 99, we create another column, the 100s, and so on. Thus, the number 143 means something different from 341 or 431. In the decimal system, every digit is understood as its symbolic value times its placement value (a multiple of ten), except the digit on the far right, which is just itself.

The binary system works identically, but with only two symbols—0 and 1. With so few symbols, placement takes on paramount importance. Counting upward, we go from 0 to 1, then run out. To convey two, we start combining. We introduce a column to the left and create the number 10. The

CHAPTER
SIX

digit in the left column here represents two times itself, rather than ten times. Thus, the binary 10 is 1 times 2, plus 0, or 2. Three is 11, or 1 times 2, plus 1. Four requires a third column, and is expressed as 100: 1 times 4, plus 0 times 2, plus 0. The column values increase to the left by powers of two, rather than of ten as in decimal. A number like 18, for instance, is 10010: 1 times 16, plus 0 times 8, plus 0 times 4, plus 1 times 2, plus 0.

Note that the placement values are never multiplied by more than one. Binary can thus be seen as shorthand for a kind of addition. Each digit, except the one on the far right, indicates merely the presence or absence of one of these powers of two. To read a binary number, you can simply add up the placement values of every column that has a 1. Thus, 10010 equals 16 plus 2, or 18.

Each digit in 10010 is a bit, a binary digit. The number requires five bits. The lowest number that needs eight bits is 10000000, or 128 (of course, 00000100 means 4 just as binary 100 means 4). The highest eight-bit number is 11111111, or 255. The computer can thus represent 255 by eight flipflops "on" in a row, and 128 by one "on" and seven more "off."

The letter code. Eight bits can convey more than just numbers. They can represent letters. They simply need a different code. Remember the ASCII system? It gives every symbol on the keyboard a number. For instance, T is 84 and t is 116. In fact, T is 01010100 and t is 01110100, and their coding is not binary and not numerical. We call them binaries and speak of their "numbers" as a shorthand way of summing up their particular pattern. The computer completely ignores this equivalence and uses the ASCII code rather than the binary.

Every time you press a letter on the keyboard, the computer can turn it into ASCII code and store it in memory. Words, sentences, paragraphs can accumulate. We could, if we liked, represent this entire book in ASCII bits, and its sense would be unchanged. You couldn't read it. But a computer could. And, of course, it already has, with a word processing program.

The instruction code. If bits can express numbers and letters, there's no reason why they can't express instructions, too. You just need one more code. It's called *machine language*, and a machine language instruction in the Amiga might look like this: 1011000101110001. The instruction code is in many ways the most important of all, for it is the information we use to program the computer. The number and letter codes generally constitute the raw data we feed in later.

The binary and ASCII codes are standard. Virtually all computers use them. But CPUs differ substantially in their instruction code, so that the Amiga's 68000 cannot, for instance, understand the same machine language as a Z80000 from Zilog. The point is highly significant. It means that programmers must write one set of instructions for the 68000, and an entirely different set to make the Z80000 do the identical task. Ultimately, it has led to compartmentalization of the software field, so that a program will run on some machines and not on others. This problem could have been minimized along the way by using certain tricks, such as standardized intermediary software, but it never happened. Thus, the world of software rather resembles a great continent, with large autonomous zones and snow-capped boundaries between them that require special techniques to cross.

Bits are the alpha and omega of computer data, with nothing else in between. They are the true and false of Boole, the 1 and 0 of binary, the on and off of switches. And they can be combined almost limitlessly. Once you get used to the fact that the clumsy-looking bit-strings zip through the computer in a few microseconds apiece, their real power starts to come clear.

The Search for a Medium

However, attaining such speed was no simple matter. Claude Shannon laid down the principles for designing the gates that computers still use today. But the world awaited a good physical medium to build them with.

Gates made of light switches would not suffice. In 1943, for instance, IBM introduced the Mark 1, a pioneer effort, but one which relied on electromechanical relays. Its switches physically moved, snapping on and off continuously, and the machine emitted an endless clatter. The Mark 1 solved the ballistics problems it was designed for, but it was very shortly made obsolete by a different and far more efficient medium: the vacuum tube.

The vacuum tube was also a switch, with two states: on and off. But since it had no moving parts, it could change states much faster, in a few millionths of a second. Thus, it could perform a thousand times more operations per second than the Mark 1. In 1946, a team headed by John Mauchly and J. Presper Eckert, Jr. built the first vacuum tube computer, known as ENIAC.

It is not surprising that the public looked upon ENIAC and its successors EDVAC and UNIVAC as awesome "electronic brains." The machines were monsters. ENIAC weighed 30 tons. It took up an entire room, contained 18,000 tubes and whole walls of electronic circuitry, and hummed with giant fans and teletypes. According to legend, the lights of Philadelphia dimmed whenever it was turned on. This massive machine could handle a maximum of 20 decimal numbers of 10 digits each.

Vacuum tubes resembled light bulbs, and had all their physical drawbacks. They required large amounts of electricity. They blew out frequently and unpredictably. And worst of all, they gave off heat, so much heat that they were constantly in danger of shutting the computer down. ENIAC emitted 150,000 watts of energy, and despite the rafts of fans, temperatures in the ENIAC room reached a balmy 120 degrees. The heat problem would never be solved, and it meant that vacuum-tube computers could not get much larger than ENIAC itself.

The Transistor

By late 1947, physicists John Bardeen, Walter Brattain, and William Shockley had been working together at Bell Labs for two years, attempting to improve upon the vacuum tube. Bardeen was formulating the theories to guide the effort, while Brattain performed experiments and Shockley aided both. The problem had been tantalizing but exasperating, and often left them feeling like they were wandering in a fog.

But on December 23, they made the breakthrough. In a secret demonstration, they unveiled what has been called "the invention of the century"—the *transistor*. (The word was coined by a colleague at Bell, J. R. Pierce, who collapsed *transfer resistor* into the handier term.) The achievement won them the Nobel Prize in 1956, and deservedly so, for the transistor did everything the vacuum tube did, and far better. It was smaller, used less power, never wore out, and generated much less heat. The transistor quickly replaced the vacuum tube in radios, and—significantly—made them far smaller. Soon

CHAPTER
SIX

America witnessed a proliferation of palm-sized radios, bringing Elvis to the beaches and the high schools.

The transistor is the basic element of the microchip, and therefore of the Amiga. But what is it? The answer involves the ease with which materials move electricity. As we were taught in grade school, some substances, like copper, are excellent pathways for electrical current. We call them conductors. Most of them are metals, because the atoms of metallic elements bond so as to leave a relatively large number of electrons "free" and thus available to assist the current along. Other substances, like rubber, are poor conductors. We call them insulators. They hold electrons more tightly to their molecular structure, so that relatively few of them are "free."

A few substances, like silicon and germanium, are actually halfway between the conductors and the insulators. In their pure state, they do not conduct electricity well, but the addition of just a few impurities—*doping*—can provide the necessary electrons to change them from insulators to conductors. We call these materials *semiconductors.*

To make the first transistor, Bradeen, Brittain, and Shockley doped one tiny piece of germanium with a positive charge and another with a negative charge. Then they brought them into contact and attached a few wires. The new article had a peculiar property: You could control its conductivity. By selectively applying electric current, you could make it a conductor one moment and a nonconductor the next.

The discovery entitled them to almost no space in the press. Who cared? What could you do with it?

Well, you could use it as a switch.

Indeed. As a switch, it was almost magical, and quickly inspired an industry. In 1955, William Shockley started Shockley Semiconductor in Palo Alto, some 30 miles south of San Francisco. Palo Alto was a good place to locate, since it was the home of Stanford University and already had some of the world's best electrical engineers. Soon Fairchild Semiconductor spun out from Shockley, and this notable company in turn emanated giants like Intel Development Corporation. Not all the nation's semiconductor corporations were located around Palo Alto, but so many were that the area came to be called Silicon Valley.

For silicon soon replaced germanium as the transistor medium of choice. Germanium is relatively rare. But silicon is

73

ubiquitous. In fact, after oxygen, it's the most abundant element on the surface of the earth. Whenever you spread a
towel at the beach, you are lying on silicon. When you glance
through a window, you're looking through it. It occurs in
quartz, feldspar, granite, and sand, and we use it in glass,
bricks, and cement. Scientists could hardly have asked for a
more convenient medium.

The Chip

Yet the burgeoning field soon faced a problem. All of the
many transistors that make up a computer—as well as the
other electronic components like resistors and capacitors—had
to be wired together by hand to make a circuit. More parts
were desirable, because they gave the computer greater capacity. But since people had to connect them all, more parts increased the chance of error, and led to less reliable machines.
Human fallibility seemed to be setting an upper limit on computer power. It was an ironic obstacle, and threatened to cap
the early promise of the transistor.

The solution was conceived independently around
1958–59 by two men: Jack Kilby and Robert Noyce. Kilby, a
soft-spoken Kansan in love with pure problem solving,
worked for Texas Instruments and later led the team that invented the pocket calculator. Noyce, a genial extrovert of
boundless curiosity, then worked at Fairchild, later cofounded
Intel, and now sits atop one of Silicon Valley's fabled fortunes.
Both men realized that you could make resistors and capacitors out of silicon also. They wouldn't be quite as efficient as
those made of other materials, but they would certainly do.
And if you could make each element of a circuit out of silicon,
you could make the whole circuit out of it. Countless parts
would suddenly become one part. The new devices were
called integrated circuits or ICs. Because each IC was
"chipped" out of a master wafer in the process of mass manufacture, they also came to be called *chips*.

With heavy funding from NASA, which didn't want to
shoot jumbo computers into space, companies were soon making
chips denser and denser. *Miniaturization* became the password
to progress and fortune. The industry moved from small-scale
integration (up to 100 components) through medium- (up to
1,000) to large-(up to 10,000), and now very-large-scale
integration (VLSI), with as many as 100,000 transistors per

chip. In fact, today we are entering the era of ultra-large-scale integration (ULSI), and, though as yet no one has reached 1,000,000 components, the Japanese have reportedly placed 700,000 on a piece of silicon the size of a thumbtack. ENIAC, recall, had 18,000 tubes.

The process of making these microchips is one of the many wonders of the Amiga, and of the modern world generally, and is worth a brief and much simplified look. It begins with a wafer of silicon about half a millimeter thick and three to five inches across. This wafer goes through a five-stage cycle—heating and coating, printing, etching, doping, and baking—about eight to ten times before all the layers of circuitry have been laid down:

1. The wafer is first heated to 2,000°F and coated with silicon dioxide, and later with a photographic emulsion.
2. An enormous design is greatly reduced in size by camera work and printed on a piece of glass called a mask, about the diameter of the wafer. Workers place the mask atop the wafer and shine a beam of ultraviolet light through it, much as you place a negative over photographic paper to get a contact print. The wafer hardens wherever the light strikes it.
3. The wafer is etched in an acid bath and the soft parts wash away, leaving a configuration of tiny ridges and plateaus only a few microns high.
4. The wafer enters a furnace to be doped, or infused with the necessary metal-oxide impurities.
5. Finally, it returns to the oven to have a skin of aluminum evaporate baked onto it, to form the equivalent of wires between the transistors.

When all the layers are done, a machine automatically cuts the wafer into individual chips, which are tested one by one. Faulty chips are common and normally go straight to the garbage can, though new techniques are salvaging otherwise doomed ICs.

Once manufactured and tested, chips must still be mounted. Each is bonded to a small, domino-like package, quite a bit larger than the chip itself, which protects it from harmful contact with the world. These rectangles have rows of metal pins on each side, often likened to caterpillar legs, which connect them to the circuit board and thus to the other chips in the computer and ultimately to your keyboard and video screen.

CHAPTER
SIX

The Microprocessor

Chips perform many functions. For instance, they store information, handle keyboard input, allocate memory, and control the disk drive. But the master of them all is the microprocessor, or CPU.

The microprocessor made personal computers possible. Before it, computers came either as the truck-sized mainframes or the refrigerator-sized minicomputers, and inhabited sterile, air-conditioned environments tended by a coterie whom today's programmers recall as a "white-frocked priesthood." Programmers would write out their programs as a penciled list of instructions. Data processors would punch these instructions into cards and, when there was time, the computer would read the cards and run the program. If it had an error or bug, as it almost always did, the programmer would go back to the penciled list, study it, alter some of the instructions, and wait for the revised program to wend its way through the data processing center and computer. Programmers stood outside the castle, communicating with it by messenger. Minicomputers were somewhat more accessible, but they existed mostly in research labs and university departments.

In 1969, a team at Intel which included Marcian "Ted" Hoff, Stan Mazer, and Federico Faggin designed a singular chip. First, it was dense. The average chip at that time had about 1,000 transistors. This one had 2,250. More important, it was technically a computer itself, with input, processing, memory, and output. It would accept an instruction as input, act on it, store subresults in a small memory, and generate output. Prior chips were often custom-made to perform specialized tasks. But custom chips were costly, and their proliferation threatened to choke the field. The new chip brought everything together, and could serve almost any purpose. More important, it could be mass produced, and hence made economically. It came to be called a microprocessor. And since it duplicated the function of the multichip Central Processing Unit in mainframes, it was also called a CPU.

The CPU has two faces: a public face and a private one. In its public guise, it directs the activities of the computer. In its private aspect, it turns its back on the computer for a moment and conducts a little business on its own. This latter activity holds the key to the machine, and warrants a little peering into.

The interior of the CPU is complex, but nowhere near as daunting as its mystique might lead you to believe. In fact, we can approach it as if it were a miniature computer. It is mostly a matter of memory, CPU, input, and output.

Memory. The CPU's memory consists of *registers*, a set of flipflops which hold such data as incoming instructions, mathematical subresults, and address locations. This kind of storage is small and very immediate, and resembles your own memory of the series of quotients as 3 goes into 3, then 6, then 9.

The CPU's CPU. The microprocessor has two main parts which stand in relation to it as it does to the computer. The first is the *arithmetic and logic unit* (ALU), which performs calculations and logical operations. The ALU is the high cortex of the machine, an exceedingly complicated area where gates work on data to yield new results. It is the pinnacle of a computer, and resembles your abacus-like mental state when you are dividing 369 by 3.

The second part is the *control unit*, which coordinates procedure for executing a command. It first interprets the instruction, breaking it down into microinstructions, which perform the minute, individual steps required to carry out a whole command. The control unit sends numerous microinstructions and data back and forth among the ALU and the registers in the correct order. It thus acts as you would in first recognizing the formula for division, then deciding to divide 3 into 3, seeing if there is a remainder, deciding to divide 3 into 6, and so on. The ALU does the actual division, while the registers stand on hand to have information shuttled in and out of them, and the control unit pulls the strings.

Input/output. CPU input and output are taken care of by electrical pathways that link the chip to the board immediately around it. These paths enter and leave the chip through its "caterpillar legs." The computer has different networks of such circuitry, serving quite different purposes. One is the *address bus*. It goes from the CPU out to memory, and allows the CPU to tap whatever memory cell it needs. It is one-directional. It simply signals the cell. The cell may respond by sending its contents back to the CPU, in which case it uses the *data bus*. The data bus is generally two-directional, but cannot send data both ways simultaneously. The third important network is the *control bus*. It gives the control unit a special avenue to send orders to the many other chips at its command.

That's it. That's the classic CPU layout. The CPU sits in the middle of the machine like Louis XIV at Versailles, and everything else—memory, keyboard, screen, other chips—revolves around it. And when it needs to take action, it retires, shifts data through the ALU and registers, and re-emerges. It's simple. And it's complicated.

The Motorola 68000

Motorola has had a significant, if unsung, history in the development of CPUs. It introduced one of the earliest in 1974, before the first Altair even appeared. The design of this chip influenced Chuck Peddle's eight-bit 6502, still used in the Commodore 64 and the Apple II, but Motorola itself did not emerge as a force in the CPU world until 1984, when the Macintosh popularized the 68000.

The 68000 is a powerful CPU. It has 70,000 transistors, slightly more than its name implies. It also has a few variations on the classic CPU layout. For instance, it has three ALUs instead of one. Two of the ALUs manipulate address locations and the third, the one we have been concerned with, works on data. In addition, the 68000 has quite a bit of preprogrammed memory, unalterable software which substitutes for gates and simplifies manufacture.

Size. You'll hear the 68000 variously described as a 32-bit chip, a 16/32-bit chip, and a 16-bit chip. The terms seem to say something about the power of the CPU. But what? And which is right? The answer seems to depend on your point of view.

Computer makers like to call the 68000 a 32-bit chip, because it will "work on" 32 bits. That's like calling Boswell a poet because he occasionally turned a winning phrase. It implies maximum capacity is standard capacity. The registers of the 68000 can indeed hold 32 bits, as can the special register called the counter, and the 68000 can therefore operate on instructions as large as 32 bits.

But it can't act on all 32 bits at once. Its ALUs are only 16 bits wide. Thus, it must work on half of a 32-bit instruction at a time, and in practice, 32-bit instructions are not often issued. Moreover, the data bus of the 68000 is also 16 bits wide. Since the CPU is constantly shifting information back and forth along this pathway, its size greatly affects a computer's speed. Even if the ALU could operate on 32 bits at one time, the data bus would remain a major bottleneck. ALU and data bus size are so critical that some people believe that, despite its 32-bit attributes, the 68000 should be called simply a 16-bit chip. Period. There should be no waffling.

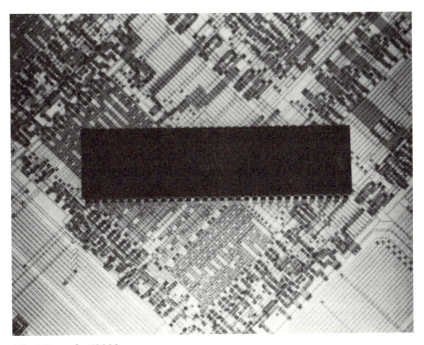

The Motorola 68000

But most observers call it a 16/32-bit chip. Its address bus is betwixt and between, at 24 bits wide, and it is clearly a hybrid overall. Admittedly, the slashed term does not roll merrily off the tongue, and the chip is closer to 16 bits than 32. But for the sake of precision, we'll refer to it a 16/32-bit chip, putting the 16 first. You, of course, can call it anything you like.

Registers. The Motorola 68000 has 18 registers, a boon for programmers. Programmers like registers because they confer great flexibility. Instead of forcing programmers to store and recall data repeatedly from the rest of the computer, they

CHAPTER
SIX

allow immediate manipulation in the heart of the CPU, and let the chip keep more balls in the air at once.

Timing cycle. Intriguingly, the ultimate controller of the CPU—aside from you yourself—is not the control unit at all. It's a clock. And what need, you ask, has the CPU of a timepiece? It needs to know when it can act. The many gates of the CPU must all execute a microinstruction in stride. They must be synchronized. You can think of the clock as a metronome, swinging back and forth, and regularly emitting a tick. At each tick, the gates of the CPU can take some action. The gates need not act at the ticks, but they can act at no other time. The frequency of ticks is called the timing cycle and is measured in megahertz, or MHz, after the nineteenth-century German physicist Heinrich Hertz. One MHz is a million ticks, or cycles, per second. The Amiga works at 7.16 MHz, and can thus execute a maximum of 7,160,000 microinstructions per second. The shortest 68000 machine language instruction— copying from one register to another—requires four cycles. The longest, a division command, takes 170. A speed of 7.16 MHz is pretty fast. By comparison, the 65C02 in the Apple IIc executes at 1.02 MHz, the Intel 8088 in the IBM PC at 4.77 MHz, and the 80287 in the IBM PC AT at 6 MHz.

Instruction set. The instruction set is a measure of the CPU's tone, its class. If we're assessing an automobile, for instance, we care about its speed, but we also care about its comfort and maneuverability. The 68000 is a quality chip. It recognizes over 88 assembly language instructions. As microprocessors go, that's a large and powerful set. Moreover, the instructions are flexible. The MOVE instruction, for instance, comes in a number of different varieties, and a programmer can use the one that is most convenient. Overall, 68000 instructions are also simple, another virtue.

How do instructions actually work, down there in the CPU? Each instruction is a series of electrical pulses, *bits*, coming down a wire. It enters the control unit, which is just waiting, ready to issue its repertoire of microinstructions to the rest of the CPU. The bits of the instruction go funneling through the control unit's gates. Just as some gates can differentiate between a 13 and a 14, so these can distinguish between an ADD and, say, an ADDA. An ADD will cause the control unit to launch one set of microinstructions, an ADDA, another. The proper microinstructions go forth to pick up data and send it through the gates of the ALU. A sum emerges, and is stored. One instruction has been executed, and the control unit awaits the next.

For better or worse, the CPU identifies a computer. The Amiga is a 68000 machine. So is the Macintosh. The PCjr is an 8088 machine. The Commodore 64 is a 6502 machine. The microprocessor does not tell you the worth of any individual computer—that depends on the CPU plus usable software, memory, and many other factors—but it does reveal its central configuration. And the 68000 is so strong and cheap—now around $20—that few new computers will be designed around anything less.

The Amiga's Output Chips

We've been through an everglades of technical information. And now, while you pause you catch your breath, it's time to give the story one more twist.

The CPU doesn't really control everything that occurs in the Amiga. Even in most other computers, there are special chips which act as high-level executives, and control the keyboard, assign memory locations, and so forth. But these chips still come under the direct oversight of the CPU. The Amiga goes further. Its 68000 has three extra chips which amount to full-fledged partners, and process many instructions completely on their own. These are the chips that control most of what you view on the screen or hear through the speakers.

We've seen that the 68000 is swift. Yet perhaps you wondered why, if the Macintosh also has a 68000, the Amiga is so much faster. The answer lies here, in these chips. They are the real secret to the Amiga's zephyr speed, for while the 68000 is impressive, it alone cannot approach the Amiga's pace. The Macintosh forces almost all its instructions through the 68000. The Amiga funnels some through the 68000 and others through these extra chips. Instead of one person painting the house, there are several, and all go home earlier.

But these three chips are not mere handymen, performing any chore that comes their way. They are highly specialized, dedicated to graphics and sound, and this feature makes the Amiga faster still. It also accounts for the machine's remarkable video and audio. They are like experts that the CPU has joined up with, and they have complete control over their own domains.

CHAPTER
SIX

As some chips are devoted to memory, so these are to output, and we will discuss them in more detail in the Output chapter. For now, it is sufficient that you realize they exist, and that they give the Amiga unrivaled power and beauty.

The Future of CPUs

By delegating authority to its three output chips, the Amiga works much faster and gains marvelous plumage. The technique is a true advance in personal computer design, certain to be copied. Where will the next leaps in computer power come from? Current trends, not mutually exclusive, include:

True 32-bit CPUs. True 32-bit chips, like the new Motorola 68020, are just now emerging for personal computers. The 68020 has 32-bit ALUs, 32-bit registers, and 32-bit pathways of all kinds. It uses 200,000 transistors, three times as many as the 68000. Motorola says it also performs about six times faster, and accesses a great deal more memory. Since it is new, it is currently expensive, but mass manufacture always brings chip prices down, and in a few years it may be as economical as the 68000.

64-bit CPUs. Some people think the 64-bit CPU will enter the market near the end of the 1980s. It would seem the natural next step. But the cost of such a CPU is currently unclear, and there are several other routes which may be taken.

Gallium arsenide chips. Instead of using silicon for CPU's, we could use gallium arsenide, a much more efficient semiconductor. However, gallium arsenide is relatively rare and so hard to handle that companies are talking about making these chips in space. Don't hold your breath waiting for them to cost $20.

RISC chips. RISC *(reduced instruction set chips)* chips are based on the austere premise that most CPUs respond to too many commands. If we eliminate less common instructions and hence tighten up on the machine language, chips can be made cheaper and better. By the standards of RISC proponents, the 68000 is bloated.

Circuit-board-on-a-chip. Some people think that larger chips should hold not larger CPUs, but more internal memory. Eventually, according to this line of thought, a single chip could contain an entire circuit board, and lead to incredibly quick, compact computers, perhaps like video slates you could carry around your hand.

CHAPTER
SIX

Parallel processing. The habit of using one CPU originally arose because microprocessors were expensive. Now
they aren't. Thus, instead of making a single CPU bigger and
bigger, engineers could put several CPUs in a single computer.
By coordinating their efforts, we could achieve greater power
with less technological strain. This idea currently enjoys much
favor among industry pundits, and the Amiga makes a little
bow to it.

The fate of these ideas will, of course, affect personal
computing in a primal way. But some of the most exciting
developments in computers are now taking place in another
area altogether: memory.

Memory:
The Amiga as Electronic Storehouse

The Amiga deals with far greater amounts of information than the 32 bits of the 68000. The question then arises: Where is this data when it's not in the CPU? Small amounts of it, almost infinitesimal, are traveling around the buses. But almost all the rest is in memory, awaiting action of some sort. Indeed, the concept of memory pervades the computer. The CPU itself has memory.

Memory is a fundamental measure of a computer, a critical index of its power and usefulness. A computer with expansive memory can scan great amounts of data and juggle it in an impressive and satisfying way. And as the memory increases, it gradually leads to feats of a novel nature. For instance, the Amiga's hefty memory makes possible the iconic interface, the bitmapped screen, and the manipulation of audio.

We tend to think of memory in a narrow, personal way, as a repository of experience or knowledge within our minds that we can call up at will. With regard to computers, the term takes on wider meaning and refers to any record of data, internal or external. In this broad sense, then, a shopping list is memory, as is a book, a movie, a microfilm, and any other device that preserves information. The principal memory instruments in the Amiga are chips, disks, and disk drives. Less common but extremely capacious are hard disks and the intriguing laser discs.

Memory Chips

The CPU does its work at the center of a number of memory chips, from which it continually reaches out to tap data, act on it, and send the results back to memory. Early CPUs acted on information eight bits at a time, and, as we have seen, eight bits is enough to hold one ASCII character. Thus, memory was organized into units of eight bits each, known as memory *words*. A memory word holds one character and has its own address, as it must if the CPU is ever to locate it.

The relationship of CPU to memory is illustrated in the sequence below, which the Amiga might follow to do a simple addition problem:

1. Finds the address of the memory word containing the first number.
2. Moves the contents of that word—the number—to the CPU.
3. Finds the address of the memory word containing the second number.
4. Moves the second number to the CPU and adds it to the number already there.
5. Finds the address of the memory word where the answer is to be stored.
6. Moves the answer to that address.

The eight-bit word quickly became the basic unit upon which the computer acted and therefore the most important unit, period. This eight-bit quantity thus developed a name simpler than memory word. It was called a *byte*.

We measure the amount of a computer's memory in terms of bytes, or rather, since the figure gets high so fast, *kilobytes*. A kilobyte is not actually 1000 bytes, as you might think, but 1024 bytes. (Binary arithmetic creeps in everywhere.) However, it is so close to 1000 that for most nontechnical purposes, it means the same thing. The term *kilobyte* is generally abbreviated to K, so when we say the Amiga has 256K of RAM memory, we mean that it can hold about 256,000 different characters. The advent of mass storage devices like the hard disk is increasing the use of terms for even larger amounts. A *megabyte* (M) is about a million bytes (1,024K, or $1024 \times 1024 = 1,048,576$ bytes). And a *gigabyte* (G) is about a billion (1024M, or about 1,000,000K, or about 1,000,000,000 bytes).

Memory chips come in two varieties: ROM and RAM. In some ways, they are as different as memory devices can get.

ROM is an acronym for Read-Only Memory. You can read it, but you cannot erase it and write over it. There are good reasons for protecting it in this way. In most computers,

CHAPTER SEVEN

ROM contains part of the operating system, instructions computers need to perform common, everyday jobs like handling input from a keyboard or displaying a character on the monitor. They aren't the most glamorous tasks, but a computer without an operating system is about as useful as one without electricity.

For ROM resembles the neuromuscular memory children spend their first few years acquiring. We all must learn to walk, to move our hands, to ride a bicycle. Once we have mastered these challenges, we do them effortlessly, without even thinking about them. Yet they still require memory, as you find out very quickly if you attempt a stunt for which you have no neuromuscular memory, such as a giant slalom. The operating system in ROM takes care of similar tasks in the computer, so you can move on to better things.

Most personal computers store part of their operating systems in ROM chips. ROM chips are memory devices that have been permanently programmed. The software is burned right into the circuitry, and you never need to alter it or think about it. ROM chips have been growing rapidly in size as computers develop larger and better operating systems.

The Amiga has one of the most powerful operating systems even seen on a personal computer. Yet it uses only a small area of ROM to load Kickstart. Routines which reside in ROM on other computers are loaded into a special area of RAM by Kickstart.

You've undoubtedly noticed that when you place Kickstart in the disk drive, it seems to awaken the computer behind a curtain. Some kind of preliminary eye-rubbing goes on back there, but it remains invisible to you. All you know is that after a few seconds the Amiga is ready to accept your software.

In fact, the Amiga is loading the Kickstart's 256K into a part of RAM that is write-protected so that you can't write over it. Once ensconced, the Kickstart acts like ROM and you can proceed with any task you want. When you turn the machine off, it vanishes like RAM.

Why not put this software into ROM chips? It would eliminate the vexation of repeatedly inserting the disk as well as the need to copy it and keep it free from accidental damage. The reason, according to a Commodore spokesperson, is that Kickstart makes it easier for the company to revise the operating system and pass the upgrades on to you. In addition, it lets experts write their own operating systems, so they can turn the Amiga into, say, a special-purpose graphics device. Commodore says that it has no plans to install any ROM chips in the Amiga.

RAM (Random Access Memory) is the second type of memory chip. (The term is not very descriptive, since both RAM and ROM use random access to go directly to an address.) RAM is your desktop, the place where you spread out all your materials to work. If information is not in RAM, the CPU cannot get to it and you must put it there with an input device. Only after it is in RAM can the CPU begin to act on it.

RAM resembles short-term memory in humans. We can remember the events of five minutes ago in much detail, for such memory is essential for our daily interaction with the world. But two weeks from now, we will probably have forgotten them. Only if the events are significant or if we make the effort, do they move over into our long-term memory, where reside our recollections of last year's company picnic, knowledge of state capitals, and most of what we generally consider to be our "memories."

RAM is likewise transient. Every time you turn the Amiga off, you erase RAM completely and forever. The flip-flop transistors in RAM chips require uninterrupted electric current to maintain their data. This fact does not matter much if you are playing a game like *Skyfox*, which is not a receptacle for permanent input. The program is both in RAM and on disk so that erasing RAM does not cause irretrievable loss.

However, the situation is very different if you are keying in your own data, as you do in word processing. In such cases, your work exists for a time only in RAM. Thus, whenever you want to close down the Amiga, you must make certain that you have first saved to disk any information you want to keep.

Unfortunately, you are not the only agency that can shut the Amiga down. Power outages will erase RAM. It is thus a bad idea to work at the computer during high winds or an electrical storm. It is also foolish to risk short circuits by overloading an outlet. But you cannot anticipate all contingencies. You cannot foresee the electrician who turns off the power to your apartment without notice, thinking tenants will simply have to do without TV for a few minutes. Neither can you predict blackouts caused by falling trees or, as at the Los

CHAPTER
SEVEN

Angeles Olympics, balloons released into the sky. Nor the mysterious half- to one-second gaps in current supply that simply erase RAM and leave you staring at an empty screen.

Therefore, experienced computer users save to disk at least every 20 to 30 minutes. It may seem excessive, over-reactive. But the effort needed to save to disk is miniscule— you can do it while you're pausing to form a thought—and the gain in real and psychological security is immense.

If you're like most people, you will probably begin by casually spurning this advice. You will therefore lose data. It is hard to describe the sensation you feel after your brand-new computer vaporizes a document you spent 15 hours touching up. When it happens to you, however, don't blame yourself or conclude that you are a computer klutz. It happens to every-one. Just think of it as your initiation into the personal computer world, like the dunking nineteenth-century travelers took at their first crossing of the equator. And when the power ᴏoes off again, 11 minutes after you have saved to disk, you ᴠill congratulate yourself on your savvy.

RAM is not just row upon row of anonymous chips. Each byte has its own address, like a house in a neighborhood, and for the same reason. When we enter a tract searching for the home of a friend, we depend on street names and house num-bers to get us there. It's the same way in RAM. The CPU goes hunting through RAM to find specific bytes and, like us, it needs their addresses or it wanders endlessly. Unlike us, how-ever, the CPU is restricted in the number of addresses it can cope with at once. This restriction derives from its address bus, whose width determines the number of addresses it can directly call upon. The Amiga's 68000 CPU can access 16M addresses—16,777,216—a vast amount. Its address bus is 24 bits wide and can thus transmit 224 different numbers, or 16,777,216. By comparison, the Apple IIe's 6502 chip can ad-dress only 216 memory locations, or 65,536.

Adding RAM. The size of your RAM limits the amount of information you can have immediately at hand. It's an im-portant factor, for a high-ceiling RAM lets you run larger and better software and handle data in bigger chunks, while a smaller RAM may give you a distinct feeling of confinement.

Technically, the Amiga comes with 512K of RAM, though, since half of it is set aside for Kickstart, we generally say it has 256K of RAM. Moreover, some programs require you to load

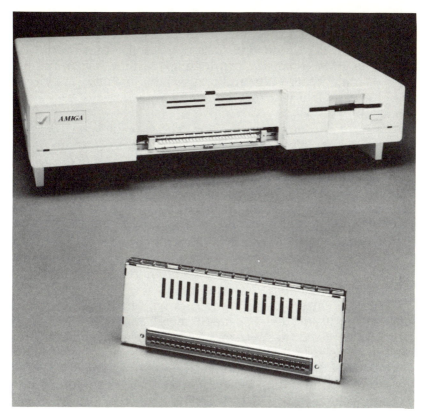

The 1050 Memory Expansion Cartridge

the Workbench in addition, and that can take up another 100K. You can thus be left with about 150K, which is enough for many programs. But others require more, and in any case you'll want extra memory for some of the computer's more impressive feats, particularly the pleasurable multitasking. The Amiga's open architecture make such RAM expansion easy.

Commodore offers a 256K RAM add-on card. It looks rather like a large, metallic harmonica and plugs into the Amiga in the front. You detach the middle third of the front case by squeezing gently on the top and bottom and slowly pulling out. Then you follow the simple directions and plug the extra RAM in. The act instantly doubles your available RAM, to 512K. In contrast, getting 512K on the nonexpandable Macintosh is a significant chore. You have to drive the computer to the shop, where a professional opens its shell, pries RAM chips off the board, and replaces them with larger ones. It takes time and costs more, sometimes much more. The RAM expansion cartridge takes 10 or 15 minutes of work at home, costs $199, and graphically illustrates the virtues of expandability. It may be one of your first add-on purchases.

You can also buy an expansion module called the T-card, from Tecmar of Solon, Ohio. This device snaps on to the right side of the Amiga and comes in three sizes—256K ($799), 512K ($899), and 1M ($999). It also offers a clock/calendar with standby battery, a built-in power supply, and ports for further expansion.

The Amiga's expansion bus will allow up to 8M of RAM, a tremendous amount. You won't need that much RAM to start with, but it may interest you later, and you can be certain that there will be numerous manufacturers ready to sell you memory add-ons when you want them.

Memory chips provide computers with both their most constant needs and their most ephemeral. Kickstart "ROM" is the relatively fixed memory, and RAM the changeable short-term. In the Amiga, both are like desktops, swept clean when you depart in the evening and awaiting replenishment when you arrive next morning. Meanwhile, the Amiga's information stays on disks read by the disk drive.

Disks and the Disk Drive

For many people, the slot in the front of the Amiga is the most troublesome feature it has. Conceptually, at least, it is fairly easy to grasp how a keyboard might generate an electric signal that would become a memory word, or even how the CPU could add 2 + 2 and get 4. Moreover, since you rarely have to deal with the details of these processes, such misconceptions as you have can glow serenely in the mist. But the disk drive takes entire programs and loads them into RAM, where they are ready to go. It is a complex, dramatic act, as it can take the Amiga from blank immobility to vigor in seconds. In addition, this hardware performs the vital tasks of saving information to disk and copying one disk onto another; it can treat you to penalties for little misunderstandings. Finally, the drive requires a special kind of software, a disk operating system, or DOS, whose function is not always well understood, yet whose identity determines the games, spreadsheets, and other applications that you can run on the computer.

If we can analogize the Amiga keyboard to a typewriter and the CPU to an adding machine, then the disk resembles a record album and the disk drive, a record player. The disk and album are platter-shaped and contain coded information. The disk drive and record player have heads that contact them and read and translate that information.

Of course, the two systems work very differently. An album conveys information by its shape. It has tiny hills and valleys pressed into the vinyl grooves, and they actually correspond to the form of the original sound waves. A stylus passes over them, rising and falling as they do, and its ups and downs are turned into variations in the strength, or voltage, of an electrical current. The current flows to a speaker, which transforms the voltage levels into sound.

A disk, on the other hand, conveys information by the pattern of magnetism on its surface. It is a sheet of plastic, usually Mylar, covered with tiny particles of metallic oxide. Magnetized, these particles can represent coded bits—ons and offs. The read/write head of the disk drive is a magnetic sensor. As the disk spins beneath it, it registers the coding and feeds that information into the computer as digital pulses.

The principal difference between them, however, is functional. Since the album has a fixed shape, it is a read-only device, like ROM. Other people have stored data on it, and you merely access it. Without very expensive equipment, you can't alter the hills and valleys and thereby put your own voice on the album.

The disk, however, relies on magnetism, which is easily altered. Hence, the disk drive not only reads the disk, but erases it and writes to it as well. It is a read/write device. Erasability and writability are critical capacities, for they give you control over memory. They let you store information on disks and revise it at your pleasure, again and again. In this regard, the disk drive somewhat resembles a tape recorder, which also uses magnetism.

The visible part of disk operations is simple, yet freighted with certain cautions. When you first turn the Amiga on, you hear the hum of the fan and see blank light on its screen. When the computer warms up, it displays a large picture of a hand inserting the Kickstart disk. You follow the cue and hear a creaky whir as the drive reads the disk. The red disk drive light below and to the right of the slot also goes on. This warning light deserves great respect, for it indicates that the disk drive is engaged or, more specifically, that the read/write head is almost touching the surface of the disk. Never press the eject button while the red light is on, for you could destroy the disk and harm the drive as well. You may find that the red light turns off for a moment or two while the drive is clearly reading the disk. It is, in fact, a little erratic. Just imagine that it's taking a little breath. If you have any doubts, wait to see that the light stays off and, preferably, look for an onscreen signal that the Amiga is ready to proceed. For instance, when the Amiga has read in Kickstart, it displays the hand inserting the Workbench disk. Then you remove Kickstart, feed it either the Workbench or a specific application, and you're on your way.

The Disk

Amiga disks are sometimes called floppy disks, as if they hung down like banana peels. Since the Amiga's 3-1/2-inch disks are plainly rigid, it is not the most evocative name in the world. In fact, it derives from from the older 5-1/4-inch disks, which are in fact slightly flexible, but are also easily ruined by bending. The Amiga runs both kinds of disks, and we'll treat them in turn. They are quite different, but they do have aspects in common.

The main worry with all disks is preserving their software. Software on a disk is like writing in the sand. The magnetic medium is erasable, hence ephemeral, and open to environmental threats that typescript, for example, doesn't face. Because great humidity, cold, and heat can all scramble programs, you should, for example, keep all software out of the direct sunlight. But the most insidious enemy of software is stray magnetism itself. Magnets can instantly sweep away the patterns they have created. And the process is very subtle. If the slight electromagnetism from the read/write head can change the disk, imagine what would happen if you dragged a big horseshoe magnet across it. Moreover, since we can't actually sense magnetism, we don't know when it is near. And the average household contains a number of items which generate magnetic fields, such as the bell of a telephone, hi-fi speakers, electric motors like the one in a refrigerator, and power transformers.

Many office desks also have magnetic paper clip holders. Just one of these clever things can sabotage a program like *Enable*, which costs as much as a good typewriter.

Because of this fragility, you should make backup copies of every disk that matters to you. If a disk is particularly important, make two. A disk can contain information that you have worked on for weeks or months, or that is critical for your business. The philosophy of the backup disk is analogous to that of keeping important papers in a safe deposit box except that disks are less stable than paper. Copying is relatively simple and greatly repays the investment.

3-1/2-inch disks. You will probably use the 3-1/2-inch disk most often, and it is clearly superior to the 5-1/4-inch. First, it is hardier. It comes in a tough plastic shell and stands up well physically to normal use. You don't want to investigate its powers as a Frisbee or doorstop, but otherwise it acquits itself satisfactorily in the world.

The 3-1/2-inch disk also holds more information than the 5-1/4-inch version, even though it is smaller. It gets this capacity from its protective shell. The 5-1/4-inch disk has the notorious oval opening, which exposes the disk surface to the air and makes it susceptible to mishaps of all kinds. Such a disk generally holds no more than the 360K found on IBM PC disks. However, the 3-1/2-inch disk has a metal guard to shield the disk surface. Hence, it is much more reliable and can be trusted with a greater density of data. Protected disks for the Macintosh contain 400K on one side alone. Amiga disks use both sides and boast a behemoth 880K.

Take a look at an Amiga disk. It has the prominent metal guard, which slides left to reveal the glossy gray disk surface through its window. When you insert the disk into the computer, the drive opens the metal guard and begins reading the coding on this surface. It should also shut the guard before ejecting. Make sure it does so completely. If it doesn't, the disk will sit exposed on your desk and slowly gather the dust that will ruin it.

The remainder of the disk has little distinctive geography. Most of it is taken up with space for the label. On the reverse side, up in one corner, you will see the write-enable tab. This feature is a device to protect you from yourself. As long as you leave it at enable, that is, farther away from the corner, the computer will erase and write over anything on the disk that you tell it to. But if you want to preserve the contents of the disk, flip the tab up flush with the corner. This act turns the disk into a read-only device, like a ROM chip.

5-1/4-inch disks. The Amiga will accept an external 5-1/4-inch drive, and so you may find yourself dealing with the older kind of disk, particularly if you run IBM PC programs. As we've indicated, these items are objects of delicacy.

Take a look at the disk in Figure 7-2. It has a large spindle hole in the middle, like a 45 rpm record, which allows the item to spin. It also has a smaller index hole nearby, like a satellite. The disk comes in a black plastic sleeve, and since this sleeve protects the sensitive magnetic surface, you should never remove it. At one end of the sleeve is room for the label. Near one corner of the disk is a square indention called the write-enable notch, which performs the same function as the write-enable tab on the smaller disks. To make the disk a read-only device, you tape over the notch with a special material.

On the other side of the spindle hole from the label lies the oval opening, the shape of a running track. Within this oval you can see the disk itself. This opening has no automatic cover like the metal guard, and so whenever a disk is not in use, you should place it in a sheath called an envelope. Be sure the side with the oval opening is within the envelope. Otherwise, you've done something pointless.

Figure 7-2. The IBM Floppy Disk

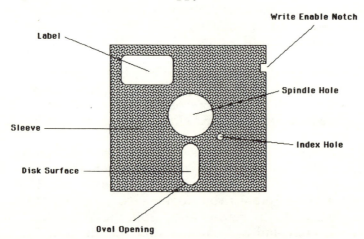

The 5-1/4-inch disks face all the dangers of magnetism, sunlight, and humidity that their 3-1/2-inch counterparts do. But because of the oval opening, they invite perils of their own. Tiny particles, like motes of dust, can obstruct the vital process of reading the disk. Ashes and tar from cigarette smoke seem to have a vile fondness for the surface of the disk, to which they cling like lampreys. Moreover, drops of oil from your fingertips can accumulate there as well. These contaminants can harm not only the disk but the disk drive, since the read/write heads are continually coursing over the disk, a few thousandths of an inch away from it. Thus, a few simple precautions can spare you serious grief:

- Always store the disk in its envelope, with the oval opening on the inside. Do not leave the disk lying around on your desk, even if you require the stimulus of healthy clutter.
- Avoid smoking at the computer if you can.
- Never touch the disk directly through the oval opening. There is plenty of room to handle it on the sleeve. Do not even reach blindly for it, since you will probably pick it up by the opening at exactly the time you are most certain you won't.
- Never attach a label to the disk and then write on it with pencil or ballpoint pen, as you will probably scratch the disk surface through the sleeve and ruin it.

Disks for the IBM PC are double-sided, like those for the Amiga. All disks have magnetic material on both sides, but if only one side is tested, the disk is single-sided. If both sides pass the test, it is double-sided. Do not attempt to use single-sided disks with either the Amiga or the IBM PC drive.

IBM PC disks are also double-density. Disks come in two densities: single and double. The difference lies solely in the stringency of testing—the latter pass stricter tests. Double-density disks store more data per side than single-density ones, but not really twice as much. One side of an Apple IIc single-density disk, for instance, holds 128K, while a side of an IBM PC double-density disk holds 180K.

The Disk Drive

The disk drive "plays" the disk. The Amiga has an internal disk drive, one within the main console. When you insert a disk into the disk drive, it goes in easily most of the way.

Then, at the very end, it requires a little extra pressure. Once it is inside, the two read/write heads come together to clamp it in place. Only one of them reads the disk at a time, but both act to keep it stable.

The Amiga comes with a plastic flat inside the disk drive. Save it. If you ever take the Amiga on a long trip, reinsert it into the disk drive. Movement can cause the upper and lower parts of the disk drive to grind against each other, and the flat prevents this unwelcome contact. If you lose it, use a damaged disk instead or even a new one. A disk costs only a few dollars. A disk drive costs hundreds.

External Disk Drive

The Amiga accepts up to three external disk drives, plugged into each other piggyback-style, and these can be either 3-1/2-inch or 5-1/4-inch. The Amiga already has one drive, and you may wonder whether you need more, especially with the Amiga's great disk capacity. In fact, an external drive is very handy.

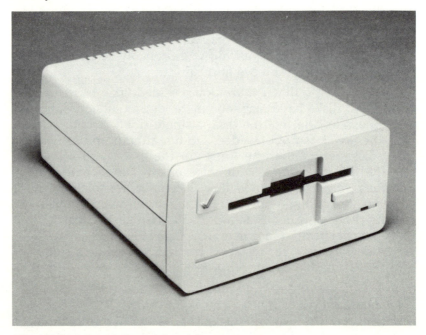

The 1010 3-1/2-Inch External Disk Drive

The 1020 5-1/4-Inch External Disk Drive

A second drive lets the computer communicate with two disks at once. This facility saves much time. Copying, for instance, clearly benefits from an external drive. To copy a disk with a single drive, you must commence a bowing little minuet with the machine, putting one disk it, taking it out, putting the second in, taking it out, putting the first one in, and so on. It's a leisurely pastime. The Amiga is copying part of one disk into RAM, writing it to the other disk, and so on. With a second disk drive, however, you insert both disks at once and the Amiga proceeds on its own, so you can do the same.

Moreover, if you want to run IBM PC software with *The Transformer* program, you will likely need an external 5-1/4-inch drive. Currently, the only such drive that will work with the Amiga is made by Commodore and sells for $395, though others should appear soon.

Before buying such a drive, you should note two facts. First, IBM PC software will run just as well on a 3-1/2-inch disk as a 5-1/4-inch. The computer cares only about the pattern of coding. Most IBM PC software is now sold on 5-1/4-inch disks, but you can easily copy unprotected programs onto the smaller and more capacious disks. Thus, if you know someone with an Amiga 5-1/4-inch drive, you may be able to save money. Second, 5-1/4-inch disks are becoming obsolete. Their shortcomings are just too obvious. Apple recently abandoned them in favor of the 3-1/2-inch entry, and IBM may well do the same. Should IBM software start appearing on 3-1/2-inch disks, your need for the 5-1/4-inch drive will disappear— though, of course, the instrument will remain useful for 5-1/4-inch IBM programs you already have.

If you are interested in IBM emulation, you might also want to consider Commodore's $200 hardware accelerator. This slender device fits onto the expansion bus on the right side of the Amiga. It consists of extra RAM and a Program Assistance Logic (PAL) chip, which together boost the performance of *The Transformer*. The item should be particularly useful for IBM programs that profit from greater speed, such as large spreadsheets.

Hard Disks

A disk can store a fine wad of data, but there are times when it is simply not enough. If we were taking inventory of a museum, for instance, we would need many more bytes than floppy disks could provide. In that case, we would look to mass storage. And today, mass storage generally means a hard disk.

Hard disks are coated aluminum rather than plastic, and they don't bend; hence, they are "hard." They confer two great boons: capacity and speed. Hard disks can store up to 80 times more data than an Amiga floppy and operate 20 times faster. They are either permanently resident in a hard-disk drive, or are removable but cocooned in an airtight plastic cartridge. Sheltered from dust and other foreign matter, they can be extremely reliable. Currently, a single hard disk can hold up to 20M, or 20,000K, and a hard-disk system, with several disks in a drive, can store 70M or more.

Hard disks have drawbacks, however. They are expensive. Though the price is dropping, they start at around $600 and rise rapidly from there. Many cost more than the Amiga itself. In addition, they require backup copies in another medium, such as magnetic tape. Hard-disk crashes are not uncommon and can send whole libraries of information into oblivion.

Tecmar, of Solon, Ohio, has announced a hard disk for the Amiga called the T-disk. This device holds 20M, equal to about 23 Amiga disks, and costs $995. It sits on the "shoulder" of the Amiga console, so it takes up no additional desk space. Tecmar also offers T-tape, its 20M magnetic tape backup system, with lights that show track number and tape direction, as well as read, write, door, and power status. T-tape can be stacked atop T-disk to save further desk room. It costs $595.

Should you buy a hard disk? The answer depends on how you use the computer. If you want to maintain an extensive collection of information, a hard disk is probably indispensable. If you plan to do mainly word processing, a hard disk is nice, but you can get along well with 880K disks. If you just want to play games, you don't need one at all. You should realize, too, that hard disks, despite the tough, back-alley name, are real hothouse flowers and should not be carted around very much. Moreover, the technology is developing rapidly, and prices continue to fall. And, finally, the device may soon—may—find itself in the path of a juggernaut.

Laser Discs

Laser discs are a kind of compact disk and hence are sometimes called CD-ROM. Both laser discs and compact disks use laser beams to write to and read from a platter with a shimmery rainbow sheen. But laser discs are larger. Indeed, they are the mastodons of storage, holding up to 4G, or 4,000M, the equivalent of 180 rolls of microfilm. And since laser disc readers have sold for as low as $200 to $300, and the discs themselves for $20, they are extremely economical.

Unfortunately, they have so far been mainly read-only devices. Like record albums, they convey information by their shape. To write to a laser disc, you aim a strong laser beam at it, and burn in tiny bumps or hollows. To read, you shine a weak laser beam at it. The beam reflects back if it strikes a flat spot on the disk, but scatters where it hits a deformation. A photosensitive device registers every return of a beam, and the computer thereby derives binary information.

Because you create the bumps with a beam of light, you can make them exceptionally small—about a micron across, or 1/25,000 inch. This kind of density makes for vast capacity. However, it is one thing to raise a bump and quite another to smooth it back into a lustrous plane. Once the deformation is there, it stays there. Thus, laser discs have generally served as preprogrammed games or archival reference sources, and as such have not penetrated the mass market.

But many industry observers look upon the laser disc as a giant struggling to get up off its back, for its incredible size could change the entire nature of what computers do. A disc with 4G would hold so much information that programmers could start thinking about completely new classes of computer software. And there is one nascent device that seems to promise writability: the magneto-optical disc.

The *magneto-optical* disc is based on a principle discovered by the nineteenth-century British physicist Michael Faraday: Light changes when it is reflected from a magnetic surface. It turns on its axis slightly. The effect is slight, but modern instruments can detect it easily. Thus, if we magnetize a pattern of tiny dots on a disk, we can aim a laser at them and measure changes in the polarity of the reflection to see which of them have charge and which don't. Again, that's binary data.

But we need some way to magnetize and demagnetize the dots at will, and it must give us dots as small as those on conventional laser discs. The laser's more-than-pinpoint accuracy creates the minuscule bumps on deformation discs. Can a laser also induce magnetism? It happens that it can, through a phenomenon called the Curie effect. When certain metallic material is heated enough in the presence of magnetism, it becomes magnetized. Reheated in the absence of magnetism, it loses its charge. Thus, all we have to do is point a laser at a particular spot in the presence or subsequent absence of magnetism and let the beam heat it to the Curie point. In the United States, IBM and 3M Corporation are avidly pursuing this approach, and reports from Japan also indicate frantic research. The day of the reusable laser disc may come relatively soon.

The Future of Mass Storage

Hard disks are fragile and costly, and read/write laser discs unproven. Though much money and effort are now going into them both, neither has preempted the mass storage market of the future. Two other devices may also prove contenders.

Laser cards are inexpensive plastic items like credit cards, with laser-encoded strips that can hold as much as 2M. They are invulnerable to dirt, X-rays, heat, airport magnetic sensors, and static electricity, and can thus be carried around in a shirt pocket. When slipped into the computer, they are read by a low-power laser. A laser of higher power can write to them. Read-only terminals currently start at $140 to $200, and read/write ones at around $500, a price competitive with disk drives. Drexler Corporation, of Mountain View, California, says it can manufacture these cards in quantity for about $1.50 apiece. Though it is unclear when they will appear, several publishers are already eying them for books and encyclopedias, as they would slash the cost of shipping and storage. Blue Cross of Maryland has adopted them for use by its members, and Wang Labs, NCR, and Honeywell have purchased technology licenses, to develop card-readers and other items about which they choose to remain silent. These durable cards face only one major problem: At the moment, their terminals must be linked to computer systems costing around $10,000.

Stretched-surface recording (SSR) disks are flexible like floppies, but have the storage capacity of hard disks. They are also even more resistant to contamination than hard disks. Developed by 3M Corporation, which hopes to introduce them in 1986, SSR disks will initially hold 5 to 10 megabytes and cost about the same as hard disks. But the company claims they should eventually hold 30 to 50M, partly because they do not need the pristine environment of the hard-disk drive.

Memory is the foundation for the informational work of the computer. It relates to the CPU as a library does to you when you write a research paper. There is thus constant interplay between memory and the CPU, and the results of their exchanges go to output.

Output: The Amiga's Showcase

In the 1950s, the cartoon stereotype had the room-sized computer accepting input on a punched tape or a few cards. It would then hum and buzz, and lights on a panel would flicker on and off to indicate the furious labor within. Finally, the machine would emit a slender tongue of paper, which would contain the answer. This slip was output. Output was the end product of an elaborate process of computation.

Today, output goes on constantly. The Amiga is always giving you feedback on what you have just done, so you can respond with more input. The machine is interactive. Most of this feedback appears on the screen. However, the Amiga also has a speaker, which supplies audio in certain situations. When you do want output in the nature of an end product, you usually want something relatively permanent, and for that you use a printer or, occasionally, a plotter.

Output is satisfying even on the average computer. You punch a key or move the mouse, and the machine displays, it speaks, it prints, and you can sit back and take it as you will. The experience is often all the more pleasurable because you are receiving results rather than putting them together.

That's on the average computer. On the Amiga, of course, output is special. You move up from a pleasant area like the Sierra foothills to a spectacular one like Yosemite. Indeed, the Amiga renders sound and graphics so well that we have devoted all of Part 4 to its capacities in these areas.

Output Chips

The Amiga is distinguished by three custom chips devoted to graphics and sound, which operate independently from the CPU whenever possible. Designed by Jay Miner, they greatly reduce the waiting line for the CPU and make the Amiga much faster than the Macintosh. Moreover, since they are highly specialized, they endow the Amiga with remarkable video and audio.

They originated in the Amiga's early days, when its makers were still thinking of a game computer, and grew from there. During development, the chips bore the proper Victorian names Agnes, Daphne, and Portia (as well as Agnus, Denise, and Paula, and, inevitably, Huey, Dewey, and Louie). Logically, they are a unit, but since their circuitry couldn't fit onto a single chip, they were divided into three.

Agnes, Daphne, Portia, and the 68000 CPU

Agnes. Agnes is the animation custom chip. It contains a mix of things: The Blitter, which quickly draws lines, fills spaces, and manipulates shapes; the Copper, which controls and coordinates the other two chips like a CPU; and a traffic signal that regulates the direct access of memory.

Daphne. Daphne is the graphics custom chip. It manipulates the display on the screen, taking care of two independent screens at once and coordinating movement of the autonomous little items called sprites.

CHAPTER
EIGHT

Portia. Portia not only regulates various ports, but also handles the four sound channels in the Amiga. Officially, it bears the five-footed name of *peripherals/sound custom chip*.

You don't have to know a lot about these chips except that they're the Amiga's resident genies.

The Cathode Ray Tube

Video is the most dramatic and pleasurable of all computer output. It is immediate, detailed, dynamic, and colorful. Video is also a field with its own intricate technology, which we will not try to plumb. Yet we can skim its surface and gain a rudimentary sense of what these devices do, for the basic concepts are not complicated, and it is nice to have some idea of how an item like a television really works.

There are two main video devices for the Amiga: the television set and the monitor. The main ingredient of both is the cathode ray tube, or CRT, more commonly known as the picture tube, whose failure spells requiem for the whole set.

The CRT is really just a complicated light bulb, and its lineage goes back to Thomas Edison's laboratory itself. There, in 1883, scientists were playing with the Wizard's new invention, which was basically a heated filament in a vacuum. In a chance experiment, they noticed that electricity was jumping from the filament to a metal plate within the light bulb. They were stunned. Current was flowing across a vacuum. The textbooks had taught that electricity requires a medium like copper to conduct it, yet here it was, zipping through the void. The discovery led to a revolution.

Soon, Cambridge physicist J. J. Thomson found that you could manipulate this vacuum current with a magnet. The current would veer toward the positive pole. This fact showed that electricity was made of matter, and Thomson later went on to declare it a stream of subatomic particles: electrons. In one stroke, Thomson explained the nature of electricity and destroyed the myth that atoms were indivisible. The achievement earned him the Nobel prize in 1906.

Meanwhile, other scientists had developed an intriguing tool to study the phenomenon. It was a long, narrow tube. At one end, a heated piece of metal gave off electrons, like the filament in a light bulb. They called it a *cathode*. The *cathode ray* then streamed down to the other end, which was coated with phosphor. Wherever electrons struck, the phosphor glowed. The entire apparatus was called, naturally enough, a *cathode ray tube.*

The first person to conceive a wider application for this odd device was the British physicist A. A. Campbell-Swinton. In 1908, he realized that glowing dots at the end could be arranged to form patterns. If the dots were small enough, we wouldn't notice them, but would see instead whole objects.

Campbell-Swinton did not invent television. No single person did—it is a complex machine—but the two best-known individuals battled each other for the honor in the 1920s. One was Vladimir Zworykin, a White Russian exile who worked for David Sarnoff at RCA. The other was Philo T. Farnsworth, a young man from Idaho who insisted on working outside the major labs and thus forfeited much financial backing. Between them, they devised the crucial elements of a TV system: a camera at one end to capture an image and turn it into electrical signals and a CRT at the other to translate signals back into the original image.

The modern CRT doesn't look much like a light bulb or the original tubular device either (though the term *tube* still persists). It is shaped like a funnel, with the screen across the wide, open end and the cathode in the neck. The cathode acts as an electron gun, with the screen as its target. The neck also has the electromagnet, courtesy of J. J. Thomson, which directs the course of the beam.

The cathode shoots electrons at the screen in a very precise way, going across a line of dots at the top, then the line below, and so on, for 200 lines or more, until it hits the bottom. The dots that make up the lines are called *pixels*, short for picture elements, a contraction that actually creates a name with charm. When electrons strike the phosphor screen, the phosphor glows, and the more intense the electron beam, the brighter the glow. An intense beam thus creates white on the screen, while a moderate one gives gray, and no beam at all leaves it black.

By going down the screen line after line, the cathode creates a picture. The pixels are small enough that we tend not to see them separately, but rather fuse them into one large image, as we do with flowers in a pictorial bed at an arboretum or dots in the paintings of Seurat. The mind sees the pattern rather than its constituents.

CHAPTER EIGHT

And, through another optical illusion, the picture appears to move. The eye records a separate image about once every 1/14 second. Thus, when we see a series of images presented every 1/15 second, our eyes blur them together and we see fluid motion, a "motion picture." Dogs dance and people soar out of cannons.

At 15 frames per second, however, we can still detect an irritating "flicker," and so when we watch a movie, the projector shows us 48 frames per second—24 different frames, each shown twice—and the flicker disappears. The CRT works the same way. The cathode gun covers all the lines of the screen in an average of 1/60 second, and often, as in a movie, shows each frame twice. We see 30 different images per second. Our minds fuse them all together and we see clean, steady motion.

Color CRTs

The step from one-color—monochrome—CRTs to full-color ones is much easier to explain than it was to execute. If you spin a top with several distinct patches of color, you'll see still another optical illusion. The hues will blend into a new color altogether. Slices of red and green blur into yellow, those of blue and yellow, white. The colors that strike our eye and seem so robust and independent are, in fact, notorious mixers. It's a trait that makes color CRTs possible.

The main difference between the monochrome and color CRT is the screen. The monochrome is coated uniformly with a phosphor which generates shades of a single color: white in black-and-white TVs, green or amber in certain monitors. A color CRT, however, is speckled with fine dots of three different kinds of phosphor. Each dot generates one of the primary colors of light: red, green, or blue. And every pixel of a color CRT has a trio of dots, one for each color. The electron gun strikes them and from a distance their colors seem to fuse and create a single hue. If the colors of light did not mix, we would need 8, 16, or more dots per pixel, and the enterprise would sink under its own weight.

How many colors can we have? It depends on how many different levels of intensity we can order the electron gun to fire. Each intensity, of course, generates a different color. Bright blue is different from dark blue. Bright blue combined with bright red is different from dark blue combined with dark red. If each dot can have four intensities, then there are $4 \times 4 \times 4$

combinations, or 64 colors. If each can have eight, there are
8 × 8 × 8, or 512.

From a technical standpoint, the trick is to control the
electron gun precisely enough, a task that bedeviled engineers
for many years. The first color TVs tended to break down with
disturbing frequency, and color CRTs are still more elaborate
and expensive than monochrome. But the payoff is brilliance.

Television

The TV set in your living room will make an acceptable video
display. Once you get it hooked up, your TV screen will respond to whatever you do at the keyboard, and you may at
last experience the delicious sensation of wielding power over
the device.

The cable that performs this feat, as we have seen, is
called the RF modulator or converter—RF for radio frequency.
What does the RF modulator convert? Television sets receive
radio signals broadcast over space. These signals pass from the
antenna down into the set, which turns them into video signals. Now, the Amiga emits video signals directly. That would
be fine except that it is hard to link the Amiga up with the in-
nards of the TV. Hence, the RF modulator changes Amiga
video signals into the radio signals the TV is expecting from
the antenna. The TV then reconverts them to video inside.

The television screen, unfortunately, does not permit
high-quality display. One reason is the RF modulator itself.
Every time you change one kind of signal to another, you lose
some of the original accuracy. The information degrades,
much as word-of-mouth degenerates into rumor. And since
TV requires two such conversions—video to radio, then radio
to video—the problem is even worse. A monitor, in contrast,
takes the video signals from the Amiga directly and thus
yields a sharper picture.

The TV screen has another problem, one which involves
the speed with which it can project images. One measure of
this speed is called *bandwidth*. In a simplified way, bandwidth
refers to the amount of electrical information that can be con-
veyed per second. Remember that video devices must be able
to cover the whole screen 60 times per second; otherwise, images will flicker. So if a machine has low bandwidth, if it gets
little information out per second, it cannot reduce the speed at

which the cathode sprays the screen. It must compensate elsewhere. And it does so mainly at the expense of resolution.

Let's take an extreme example. Imagine a cathode gun that strikes 840 dots per second. To achieve flicker-free motion, you would have to give it a screen with only 16 dots, 4 on each side (840/60 = 16). The quality of the picture would be unspeakable, of course, since it would have almost no resolution. Such a CRT would have extremely low bandwidth because it is sending the stark minimum of data. If you increased the bandwidth, you could increase the number of dots and thus refine the resolution, moving up through coarse to grainy and finally to reasonably tolerable.

Bandwidth, like the CPU timing cycle, is measured in megahertz (MHz). (The hertz unit pops up all over, since it measures intervals between any regularly recurring events. Sunsets occur at a rate of 1/86,400 Hz.) Televisions have bandwidths ranging from 3.5 to 4.5 MHz. That's reasonably acceptable, but really not great. It leads to TV's three main limitations: text, color variety, and resolution.

Text. A line of text on TV can be only 60 characters wide, including margins. That is, it is restricted to a 60-column text mode. Since the average line of typed text has about 65 characters, if you are using a TV for word processing, you will not see the full width of a page. In contrast, the Amiga monitor allows both 60- and 80-column text.

Color variety. The pool of colors available for use on television is also slightly reduced. With an RGB monitor, the Amiga offers a total of 4096 colors, the most standard on any personal computer. On a color TV with an RF modulator, it allows 3616. Of course, that's still a fantastic amount.

Resolution. The Amiga offers two basic types of resolution: low and high. TV restricts you to low, while a monitor lets you use high or low. Each type has two subsets of resolution/color capacity: normal and interlaced.

In low resolution, the normal mode is 320 pixels wide by 200 high. If you move up a notch to the interlaced mode, the computer will spray the screen with twice as many lines per second and give a picture 320 pixels wide by 400 high. In both modes, you can select a palette of 32 colors. This number may not seem like much compared with the thousands in the color pool, but in fact it gives you a good deal of diversity, as you'll see if you try naming 32 colors.

Monitors

A monitor is simply a CRT intended for use by a computer. It looks like a TV without a channel tuner. It normally has a much higher bandwidth than TV and hence performs better.

There are three kinds of monitor in general use: monochrome, composite color, and RGB.

Monochrome monitor. A monochrome monitor conveys a picture by shades of one color, like green. A decent monochrome might have a bandwidth of 18 MHz and will show 80-column text as a matter of course. The green phosphor screen is popular, as studies have found that green generates less eye fatigue than black-on-white. Amber screens are also easy on the eyes, and are becoming more and more common, though a few manufacturers are charging slightly more for them. There are a great many monochrome monitors that work well with the Amiga.

A monochrome monitor may be enough if you plan to use the Amiga solely for word processing or other text applications. But if you intend to use it for much else, you will likely want a color monitor.

There are two kinds of color monitor: the composite and the RGB.

Composite monitor. Composite monitors take color, brightness, and synchronizing signals over a single wire, in a "composite" manner. They can therefore plug into the RCA female jack, whereas RGB monitors need the multiple pins of the RGB port. Composite monitors tend to have bandwidths between 10 and 12 MHz, giving more precise color pictures than TV, but less than RGBs. They are also generally incapable of 80-column text. At the same time, they are cheaper than RGBs and may suit your needs better.

RGB monitor. The RGB monitor is the supreme display unit, with a typical bandwidth of over 20 MHz. RGBs use three separate wires to accept the signals for red, green, and blue. Hence the name. These monitors yield excellent graphics and 80-column text, and since Commodore offers a fine RGB monitor at a reasonable price, it will likely be your screen of choice.

The Commodore monitor is a precision instrument that's a pleasure to use. Its screen is 13 inches across diagonally and fairly looms over the console. You turn it on by pushing an inconspicuous squarish button labeled Power, at which the thin horizontal light above it goes on. The screen does not light up till you also switch on the Amiga. Like the computer, it has a host of vents to dissipate heat, and the monitor dies if you block them. A panel along the bottom pulls down to reveal a string of control knobs, which let you adjust brightness, contrast, and other factors.

RGB and the better monochrome monitors permit both low and high resolution. At high resolution, the Amiga grows resplendent. Like low, high has two levels: normal and interlaced. Both allow a palette of 16 colors. Normal is 640 pixels wide × 200 high, and interlaced, 640 pixels wide × 400 high, the finest resolution the Amiga has, and among the finest of any personal computer.

There is actually a third type of resolution, called *hold* and *modify*. Like low resolution, it comes in either 320 × 200 or 320 × 400. However, it lets you put the entire 4096 colors in your palette at once. At the same time, it's more difficult to use and may wind up mainly as a tool for static graphics like paintings.

We'll talk more about resolution and color capacity in Chapter 17. For now, it's sufficient that you get some idea of the differences between televisions and monitors.

Buying a monitor. If you decide not to buy the Amiga RGB, you should realize that shopping for a monitor is worth a little care. The monitor is almost always on while the computer is, and you are thus looking at it constantly. The following steps are helpful in purchasing a decent monitor:

- First, determine the kind you want: monochrome, composite, or RGB. The Amiga is an especially graphics-oriented computer, and an RGB monitor lets it fan all its tail feathers. But if you have no use for color, a monochrome monitor may be the screen you want.
- Visit a retail store and test its monitors on an Amiga. Do not try to judge a monitor on the basis of its performance with another computer. The Amiga is special.
- Fill the screen with lowercase *m*'s. The *m* is a dense letter, hence ideal for assessing image quality. The letters will probably look clear and sharp in midscreen, but if they get fuzzy near the edges, you have an inferior item.
- Check to see that straight lines are actually straight. Sometimes they aren't.
- Look for flicker or smear.

- Be certain that the monitor displays the entire image. Some lose the edges off the screen.
- In the case of color monitors, check how solid, sharp, and appealing the colors are, particularly at the corners of the screen where quality is hardest to attain.
- Finally, consider such subjective factors as size. Ultimately, you should pick the monitor you feel most comfortable with.

By the way, you're not restricted to screens measured in inches. You can, if you like, use your Amiga with projection TVs—those super-wide screens you may have seen in bars, video rental stores, and other establishments. Companies like RCA, Sony, Kloss Video, and Electrohome USA sell these items, from six to ten feet across diagonally. They start at around $3,000.

Video is the source of visual feedback, but not of all feedback. For at the same time the Amiga is showing you pictures, it can be regaling you with sounds as well.

Speakers

As the tune which heralds the Kickstart picture makes clear, the Amiga has audio capabilities. If you purchase an Amiga RGB monitor, you'll find the speaker inside it, with an opening on the lefthand side. You'll also find various audio settings in the front control panel. For instance, on the far right is the knob that increases or decreases the volume.

You are not confined to the speaker in the Amiga monitor. On its left side, unmarked, you'll notice a tiny, white-rimmed opening near the speaker. You can plug 1/8-inch headphones in here, so if people nearby are trying to work, study, or sleep, you can still make music or play a raucous game. At the same time, if you have a video-only monitor or simply want to expand the sound, you can hook the audio ports up to two stereo speakers.

The Amiga comes with a voice synthesis capacity built into its chips, and BASIC lets you make the computer speak easily. You can also vary the speed and pitch of the voice, and change it from male to female. In BASIC, the voice seems to have a weird accent, like the robot Hymie on "Get Smart." But the games maker Electronic Arts has created a demo of a female voice that sounds remarkably authentic, and the Amiga seems destined to speak to us as if it belonged to us.

CHAPTER EIGHT

The Printer

Many applications, particularly word processing, cry out for hardcopies. They aim for a final, polished product that can easily circulate in the world. After all, what good is a letter to Aunt Em if she has to fly hundreds of miles to read it on your Amiga? And word processing is not the only such use. Indeed, almost all applications except games can profit from hard-copies at some point.

Thus, you probably need a printer, whether you know it or not. Printers do not come standard with the Amiga, and you will have to shop for one. The effort is worth a little care. Printers come in different varieties, and one may suit your purposes better than another. They also vary significantly in value per dollar. And printer quality really matters. A good printer is a joy, and a bad one is a geyser of trash.

Here are some of the factors to consider when buying a printer:

• Amiga compatibility
• Cost
• Character quality
• Character versatility
• Graphics capability
• Color capability
• Noise
• Speed
• Size of printer

The fundamental concern involves harmony. The Amiga and the printer must be able to communicate with each other. As it happens, it's not much of a problem. The manual specifies 11 printers the Amiga can use:

• *Daisywheel.* Alphacom Alphapro 101, Brother HR-15XL, Qume LetterPro 20, Diablo Advantage D25, and Diablo 630.
• *Dot-matrix.* Commodore MPS 1000, Epson FX-80, Epson RX-80, and Epson JX-80 (color).
• *Thermal-transfer.* Okimate 20 (color).
• *Ink-jet.* Diablo C-150 (color).

And you are not restricted to these.

For compatibility is largely a matter of software. Printers differ in the way they interpret signals from the computer. One printer can need a particular instruction for, say, boldface, and another a different one entirely. Your software may perform a kaleidoscope of feats, but if it cannot send the right signals to the printer, you will never see hardcopies. The software that performs this task is called a printer driver. The Amiga comes with drivers for the 11 printers above. But other printer companies may also issue drivers, and these should give you the printer of your choice.

There are two basic kinds of printer: the daisywheel and the dot-matrix. Less common are the thermal-transfer, ink-jet, and laser printers. Each has virtues and drawbacks, though the laser printer has almost no flaw but breathtaking cost, and even that is falling fast.

Daisywheel

The daisywheel printer most resembles an actual typewriter. It gets its name from the shape of its printing element—the metal object which contains the bossed numbers and letters of the alphabet and prints by driving an inked ribbon against paper. In an IBM Selectric, for instance, the element is a small globe. In a daisywheel printer, it is a hub with flat spokes radiating out—like a daisy. Each spoke has a raised character on it. To print, say, a *B*, a hammer strikes the B spoke, which in turn presses the ribbon against the paper. The "daisywheel" can also have its spokes bent upward into a cup, in which case we call it a thimble.

The daisywheel has several significant advantages over most other printers. One is quality of output. Since it prints by direct impact, it creates solid characters, as sharp as those from the best typewriters. For this reason, it is sometimes called a letter-quality printer or a formed-character printer. It can also use the once-through-only carbon ribbon, which further enhances clarity. Moreover, you can change the element at will, snapping it out and replacing it with another that has, for example, italic lettering. Most daisywheel elements cost between $10 and $20, and so you can accumulate quite a few; when one wears out, you can simply buy another. If you plan to use the Amiga mainly for correspondence or documents that must look professional, you should consider a daisywheel printer seriously.

However, the daisywheel has its shortcomings. It is much slower than the dot-matrix. The most expensive will tap out

CHAPTER
EIGHT

about 55 characters per second (cps), and the cheapest around
12, that is, about one page every two and a half minutes. A
pace like this can be highly annoying, although since the
Amiga lets you address other projects during printout, it no
longer breaks the back of the workday. Daisywheels also make
quite a racket, and they render graphics poorly since their
bossed spokes print fixed shapes. They cost from around $400
to $3,000.

The five daisywheels initially available for the Amiga are
the Alphacom Alphapro 101, the Brother HR-15XL, the Qume
LetterPro 20, the Diablo Advantage D25, and the Diablo 630.
The first four are all rather similar. The Alphapro 101 is the
least expensive, at around $400. It's also fairly small and com-
pact, but prints at 18 cps. The Brother HR-15XL is slightly more
expensive, at $600, and prints at 20 cps. The Qume LetterPro
20 does 22 cps and costs $795. The Diablo Advantage D25 is
still faster, printing at 25 cps and selling for about $745.

Diablo, owned by Xerox, has an excellent reputation for
quality, and its Diablo 630 is easily the most substantial daisywheel for the Amiga. It can print 200 different type styles at
40 cps, and each element is capable of 192 different characters. The printer costs $2,095, and is something of a standard
in the computer world.

Dot-Matrix

Dot-matrix printers differ fundamentally from daisywheels.
Consider that the daisywheel has an assortment of solid
characters, all immutable. In contrast, the dot-matrix has
essentially one character, a dot, which can multiply into any
character. If you break the space occupied by a character down
into a grid, or matrix, and fill the matrix with an array of dots,
you can reproduce whatever character you like simply by
darkening the right dots. The trick is exactly the same as that
used to display letters on a video screen: The dots fuse into
letters from a distance.

The matrix is an abstract rather than a physical entity. The
actual printhead is a not a matrix but a column of 7, 9, or, recently, 24 pins, each poised to press the ribbon against the paper and form one dot. As the head travels quickly down the
line, a microchip tells the pins exactly when to strike. Obvi-
ously, the pins must move in very rapid sequence to create a
string of legible characters. But total movement is far less in a

114

dot-matrix—which only strikes—than in a daisywheel—which both strikes and rotates the element. Hence, the dot-matrix is much faster, with speeds between 50 and 450 characters per second.

The dot-matrix has other notable features. It is very versatile. A good dot-matrix can easily print boldface or gothic lettering without your so much as touching it. Some even allow you to design your own typefaces. The capacity to adorn your prose with, for example, italics, or create your own letterhead, is a major advantage over both typewriters and daisywheels, and puts a print shop at your fingertips. The dot-matrix also produces excellent graphics, since the pins in the printhead can generate many shapes other than letters and numbers. But if you're interested in graphics, be sure that the dot-matrix you're considering will actually render them. Some cheap printers come with alphabetic and numeric character patterns stored in chip memory and can produce nothing else. If you are in doubt, ask for printers that are all-points addressable or have dot-addressable graphics. These synonymous phrases mean that the printer will place a single dot wherever the computer tells it to.

The main drawback of the dot-matrix has involved its letter quality. If the printer places dots too widely apart, the characters seem pale and porous, with a Sunday-comics look about them. The dots in such printout are actually visible, and the trick lies awkwardly exposed, like a poor magician's sleight of hand. The dot-matrix has historically been thought unfit for correspondence.

But this complaint is disappearing. Many dot-matrix printers are now achieving sharper, more solid characters by making two passes over a line. The first prints out a regular line of type, and the second, shifted just a bit, fills in most of the gaps. However, the second pass greatly slows the speed of the printer; thus, most such machines let you choose between letter- and draft-quality output. Even so, the caliber of print, called *near letter quality*, is still recognizably dot-matrix.

The new 24-pin printers may change all that. Their pins are very small, about twice the size of a human hair. Hence, while a 9-pin printer can give you resolution of 72 dots per inch, a 24-pin machine offers 180 dots per inch. The dots that make up its characters are completely indistinguishable except, on close examination, in the curves of letters like *C* and *S*.

Such machines do *virtual letter quality*, which easily suffices for most business correspondence. And, as if their quality were not enough, they need only one pass, and hence are much faster than their 9-pin cousins. Printers with 24-pin heads include the Brother 2024L, Toshiba P351, Daisywriter 24, and Epson LQ-1500. They sell for around $1,300 to $1,600, about the price of a good daisywheel.

Four dot-matrix printers were initially announced for the Amiga: the Commodore MPS 1000, Epson FX-80, Epson RX-80, and the color Epson JX-80. But the Commodore MPS 1000 had not appeared by press time, and according to a company spokesperson, work was not proceeding on it.

The other three printers come from Epson, a corporation with an outstanding reputation. The FX-80 costs about $500 and is a fine, reliable machine. The Epson RX-80 is versatile and fast, with a speed of around 100 cps. It is easy to set up and use, with documentation anyone can understand—rather unusual for a printer. It costs about $600, a very reasonable price, and of course has the Epson backing.

Finally, there is one Amiga dot-matrix that can do color— the Epson JX-80. It is hard to work with the Amiga for any length of time without yearning to print its glorious screen on the page. The computer almost demands hardcopies in color.

However, there are several things to remember about color printers. The first is that printing color graphics can involve a lot of issuing commands and setting DIP switches, not the most amusing pastime, though the Okimate 20 for one has greatly eased this task. The second is that color printers tend to be slow and their ribbons expensive. Thus, the best way to run off a few hundred color reports is usually to print out one and feed it into a color photocopier. But since color copiers aren't yet common in the office, color printers have not proliferated either. The third thing is that few color printers will give you the Amiga screen in all its richness, though some do fairly well. The world awaits a color laser printer, but in the meantime other kinds of printer can still be satisfying.

If you've ever used a typewriter ribbon that was half-black and half-red, you've got an idea how color dot-matrix printers work. The Epson JX-80, for instance, uses ribbons with red, yellow, and blue stripes. The printer shifts the ribbon up or down in front of the pinhead so that the pins hit the right color. For instance, if you wanted red, the printer would place the red stripe before the pinhead. To achieve a composite color like orange, the pin strikes first yellow, then red. The Epson JX-80 has nine pins, prints seven colors (black, red, orange, yellow, green, blue, and violet), and sells for about $700.

The dot-matrix is easily the bestselling kind of printer on the market. But others are appearing all the time.

Thermal-Transfer

The thermal-transfer printer derives from the moribund thermal printer. The plain thermal, like the dot-matrix, creates characters from pins in the printhead. But the pins, instead of striking the page, are momentarily heated. They warm spots on a special paper, the spots darken, and characters appear. This printer was quiet and inexpensive, but it required a special paper that had a slick, chemical feel to it and could even smell bad. It was hard to photocopy and tended to fade and curl with age. For most people, these drawbacks were sufficient. There was not much point in creating a gorgeous document if you couldn't stand to hold it in your hands.

The thermal-transfer is a clear improvement. It, too, heats pins to make dots. But instead of transferring heat directly to the paper, the hot pins touch a special ribbon, whose waxy ink then melts onto the page. The thermal-transfer is almost silent. It works so quietly that at first you hardly think it's working at all, especially if you're used to an impact printer. It is thus well-suited to offices and other environments where roaring whines are not appreciated. Moreover, its wax-based ribbons give you color that fairly glows, and its resolution can be impressive as well. Finally, it is economical, selling for from $200 to $300.

The Okidata Okimate 20 is the thermal-transfer that works with the Amiga. It boasts a very low cost, around $265, though to use it with the Amiga, you must also buy a special cartridge designed to link it to the parallel port of an IBM PC. Its printhead has 24 tiny heat elements, so its quality is outstanding. It gives you black and seven colors, and about 100 shades. It prints any kind of text or graphics, at either 80 cps or 40 cps. It also comes with a special disk that makes controlling the printer very simple, and this is a prize.

What's wrong with the thermal-transfer? Well, the wholesale shifting of wax to the page depletes ribbons very quickly so that even a black-and-white ribbon wears out after 75 pages of text. Since graphics uses more ink than text, and since color often needs several passes, color ribbons can become useless after 8–15 pages. With a six-dollar ribbon, then, you can expect to pay a minimum of 8 cents per page for text, 40 cents per page for color graphics. In addition, though they do not require the odious paper of the thermal, they do best with paper that is smooth and shiny. You can try feeding bond or rag-content paper into the printer, but you'll get a very uneven product.

Ink-Jet

Ink-jet printers bear some resemblance to thermal-transfers. As the name suggests, ink-jets fire tiny bursts of ink at the paper to make dots. They are silent, often swift, and capable of remarkable graphics. They can easily render color, through jets filled with different colors of ink. They also last long, since they have fewer moving parts. However, they can cost up to $6,000, though low-end prices have recently plunged to around $500. Moreover, the jets can get clogged if you fail to use the printer for a while, since the ink in them tends to dry and harden.

The Amiga will work with the Diablo C-150 color ink-jet. This machine is a trim device weighing about 24 pounds and costing about $1,300. It yields brilliant quality, but it will probably be used mainly for graphics. It prints text at a painful 20 cps, as slow as a daisywheel. The printer also requires special paper, and setting it up can be an intricate business, though documentation is very clear. The Diablo C-150 is extremely quiet, and you have to listen to it carefully to detect any noise at all.

Laser

Laser printers are the dream machine. They work quite differently from the printers mentioned so far. A laser burns a pattern into a metallic drum, and the drum generates printout in a manner similar to photocopying. These instruments have extreme virtues: lightning speed, complete silence, superb characters, stunning graphics, and extraordinary versatility. But their prices currently start around $3,500, where the Hewlett-Packard LaserJet and several other machines now hover. Higher up the scale is Apple's LaserWriter, which costs $7,000 and is probably worth more. This impressive item prints eight pages a minute, yields resolution of 300 dots per inch, and has 512K of ROM and 1.5M of RAM, far more than most personal computers. It will run easily on the Amiga, since it was designed to be fully compatible with the Diablo 630 daisywheel. Prices for other laser printers extend up to $20,000, and the device in general is not something to buy on the spur of the moment. But engineers are working hard to bring the cost down, and laser printers may soon appear with price tags that are tempting and perhaps even compelling.

The type of printer clearly determines its most important properties, but you should give a little thought to its size as well. The machines take different sizes of paper. Most accept paper 8-1/2 inches wide, which can hold 80 columns and handle the standard 8-1/2 × 11 inch page. This size is fine for almost all applications you are likely to use. Occasionally, however, as with spreadsheets or some graphics, you may want a wider carriage. Printers are available up to 14 inches across, capable of 132 columns. These devices cost a bit more, however, and occupy more space, so you will do well not to purchase them unless you foresee actual use for them.

A decent printer can take you far toward realizing the potential of your Amiga, and a mediocre one can actually obstruct you. The decision may be difficult, but if you are teetering between a cheaper and a better, more expensive model, go for the more expensive one. You'll probably find it was worth it.

Controlling the Printer

Every peripheral requires software to control it, and the printer does, too. We've seen that the Amiga comes with software for 11 different printers. But it also lets you specify how each of them will work. It does so with the second and third screens of *Preferences.*

The second screen, the *Printer Requester,* takes care of the basics. You use it to sign the printer in and announce the central attributes of printout.

First, you must get the Amiga to communicate with the printer, that is, tell it which printer driver to use. The box in the upper right has the names of the chosen 11. You select the name of yours by clicking the up or down arrow until it appears in the middle, where it is highlighted. If your printer

CHAPTER
EIGHT

isn't listed in Preferences, yet you have the proper software, click the arrows till *Custom* is in the center, then click the box to the right of the words *Custom Printer Name.* A cursor appears. Type in the official name of the printer driver and press RETURN. At printout, the Amiga will look that file up and use it to talk to the printer.

It is also essential to tell the Amiga which port to send its signals to. The printer can be plugged into either the parallel or serial port, according to its nature, and there is a picture in the upper-left corner for each. You just click the right one.

The Printer Requester screen also lets you select the properties of printout. You can choose page size, margin size, number of characters per inch (pitch), and number of lines per inch (spacing). In addition, you can set print quality. *Draft* is fast but coarse, while *Letter* is slow but comely. Finally, you can indicate your paper type. *Fanfold* is continuous-feed, while *Single* is individual sheets.

Once past the Printer Requester, you can move onto the third screen, the *Printer Graphics Requester.* Here you can enjoy yourself, for this screen lets you play with the image before it reaches the printer.

For instance, *Shade* lets you choose among printing in color; in gray-scale, which renders colors as shades of gray, like a black-and-white TV; and in black-and-white, the either/or choice, which prints colors as black or white according to their brightness level.

You can control the reductive black-and-white option and gain interesting effects. The *Threshold* scale across the top of the screen is your key to this feature. It lets you determine exactly how dark a color must be to print as black. The scale runs from 1 to 15, with each number a brightness level. The lower numbers are the darker, and the darkest, 1, is on the left. The printer will print as black every level to the left of your setting. Hence, if your threshold is 14, you'll get midnight in the Sahara. If it's 3, you'll get streaks, patches, or perhaps nothing at all.

The *Image* option affects only gray-scale and black-and-white printing. It lets you reverse the onscreen image to obtain the effect of a photographic negative. To get it, you click *Negative.* If you leave this setting at *Positive*, you receive the ordinary screen.

Finally, *Aspect* lets you print sideways. The top of the
onscreen page appears at the side of the printed one. It sounds
like a circus stunt, but in fact this feature is very useful for
printing out spreadsheets and other documents wider than one
page across.

You won't use the options of the Printer Graphics Requester every day. But it's pleasing to know that the Amiga
makes them available to you. And—who knows?—by the time
one or two harvest moons have passed, you may have printed
more than one document on its end.

The Color Plotter

There is one final output device, a specialty printer called a
color plotter. The plotter draws directly on paper with one or
more pens, so its lines are solid. Directed by software, an arm
of the plotter can pull a pen straight in one direction, while at
the same time the device itself moves the paper in another.
The plotter works with exceptional precision and is excellent
for graphs, charts, technical drawing, and many other visuals.

Prices generally range from $500 for the Heath ET-500,
which has one pen, to around $2,300 for the Houston In-
strument DMP-29, which has eight pens, resolution of 1/1000
inch, and the incredible speed of 22 inches per second. The industry standards are Hewlett-Packard and Houston Instruments; most software tends to run with these machines or
their compatibles.

You probably won't need a plotter for your home, but for
businesses that pay to have graphics done by outside services,
these machines can be economical.

PART THREE
Software

The city of Sophronia is made up of two half-cities. In one, there is the great roller coaster with its steep humps, the carousel with its chain spokes, the Ferris wheel of spinning cages, the death-ride with crouching motorcyclists, the big top with the clump of trapezes hanging in the middle. The other half-city is of stone and marble and cement, with the bank, the factories, the palaces, the slaughterhouse, the school, and all the rest. One of the half-cities is permanent, the other temporary, and when the period of its sojourn is over, they uproot it, dismantle it, and take it off, transplanting it to the vacant lots of another half-city.

Italo Calvino
Invisible Cities

The Software Pyramid

Software is really an unfortunate name. It conjures up a notion of strange, drooping technology, like a Dali watch draped over a table edge. Software isn't soft. It's not even tangible. You might better think of it as "commandware," for it is really just instructions that define the computer's job. These instructions are translated within the computer into bit patterns, on/off electrical states, which physically cause it to alter other bit patterns and thereby manipulate data.

Software is essential, vital. It's the blueprint which the Amiga transforms magically into structure. The computer's hardware merely confers possibilities. The software realizes them.

But what kinds of things can software do? There are certain well-marked functions that dominate the software market:

- *Programming.* If no commercial program does exactly what you want, or if you simply want to work one-on-one with the Amiga, you can buy a programming language like Pascal and write your own software.
- *Word processing.* The Amiga can let you type in words and edit them as much as you like before printing them out.
- *Spreadsheets.* The Amiga can give you a numerical worksheet, a grid on which you can alter one figure and immediately see the effect on all other entries. You can use it for financial planning as well as baseball statistics or tax computation.
- *Databases.* The Amiga can house information like a file and let you access it instantly by a variety of criteria.
- *Games.* The Amiga runs an assortment of recreational programs, from space-monster laser fights to more cerebral games like chess.
- *Graphics.* The Amiga lets you easily create pictures and graphs of stunning quality.
- *Music.* You can compose, alter, and play back music on the Amiga.

125

CHAPTER NINE

But these categories scarcely exhaust the range of software that will be written for the Amiga. It will also run educational programs for both children and adults, and perform many other functions not easily categorized, such as showing bio-feedback signals on the screen.

Except for programming languages, all of these programs are applications, that is, software with a specialized purpose. Many of them are serious, expensive items, and you should take your time about purchasing them.

How to Buy Applications

There are several reasons for caution when buying applications. Many poorly designed programs repose on the shelves, and you don't want to get stuck with one. Yet the quality of software is much harder for a buyer to assess than, say, the quality of fruit, or even of books. Stores sell it in bright, cellophane-wrapped packages that tell you nothing except that the software company hired a marketing expert. Prices vary and are often an unreliable guide to caliber. And software salespeople are, well, salespeople. They're interested in the bottom line, and their recommendations mean, at best, that they like the program, and at worst, that they just want to move the product.

There are several ways to avoid strolling into a store and walking out with a piece of junk after a two-minute chat with a salesperson. Here are some:

• Size up your own needs. You have a particular purpose for the software you are seeking. If you're looking for a word processor, for instance, you may want it only for occasional home use, or for prolonged work on books or reports. If you're looking for a game, you will want one that suits your taste, not your neighbor's or your salesperson's. Programs differ in orientation, and if you know what you want, you're more likely to get it.

• Be sure the program runs on your hardware. It must first of all run on the Amiga itself. But some games also require joysticks. Databases commonly demand a second disk drive. Other programs need an 80-column display. Know the limits of your hardware.

• Comparison-shop. Once a program is written, the cost of manufacture is low. Programs can vary widely in price, and

you should take the suggested retail price as the high-water mark only. If you look around, you may find real bargains.
• Talk to friends with computers. Find out what software they use and how it works. Have them demonstrate it for you. You might also consider visiting or becoming involved in a user group. User groups can be excellent sources of information.
• Read reviews in computer publications. There are many magazines and some books which review software, and their assessments are generally impartial and informed.
• Ask questions in stores. Ask, ask, ask. A store should be willing to let you sit down with a program and test it out before you buy it. Some will even let you take it home for a week's trial.

In sum: Be informed, about the software and about yourself.

Applications represent the peaks of the software hierarchy, in many ways the islands above the sea. You may never need to plunge down beneath them and see what they rest on, but it is nonetheless very useful to understand the software structure. The concepts involved appear again and again in computer literature, and without some knowledge of them, you're likely to feel left out, landbound amid a party of skin divers.

The Pyramid

The island-like structure of software in the Amiga or any personal computer is basically a pyramid of instructions. It is a power hierarchy which exists for the convenience of you, the person at the top, and it lets you issue commands to specialist programs that possess much "knowledge," rather than having to instruct the CPU in every little detail down to the base. Much of the hierarchy is therefore invisible to you, and it helps to approach it with an analogy.

Suppose you wanted to build a swimming pool. You could structure the task in several different ways. First, you could hire a crew of untutored laborers and explain every step of the process to them. This approach would demand a lot of time and knowledge on your part, as you would have to design the project and direct every worker yourself, yet it could result in exactly the pool you want. Second, you could hire a series of

CHAPTER
NINE

subcontractors—plumbers, plasterers, landscapers, and so forth. You yourself would require less time and expertise. You would still have to design the pool, but you could give more general instructions to the subcontractors, who would supervise workers in the specifics of construction. Third, you could simply retain a pool contractor, a specialist in the task, who would assume responsibility for pool design and construction. This approach would take little time or knowledge on your part at all, since you would merely specify the general features of the pool you wanted, such as depth and location. It would cost more and you would have far less control over the details of the creation, but the contractor would probably build it better than you could yourself.

Finally, let's say you live in a large mansion with extensive grounds. You would want a handyman to let the crew in the gate in the morning, obtain various tools for them, carry messages, and perform other routine but essential jobs so they could concentrate on the pool itself.

This situation roughly corresponds to the levels of software (see Figure 9-1) available for the Amiga:

- *Handyman.* The handyman is the operating system, which quickly and silently takes care of routine chores the crew would otherwise have to carry out. These chores generally involve interaction with the hardware rather than the particular task at hand.
- *Laborers.* The individuals who do the step-by-step physical work on the pool resemble machine language and assembly language. They are near the bottom of the pyramid, yet indispensable. If used alone, they also require the most detailed instruction.
- *Subcontractors.* The subcontractors are higher-level languages, which can bundle several machine language instructions into single commands and are thus easier to use.
- *Contractor.* The contractor is an application program, which provides a design for the task and supervises its execution, saving you vast amounts of time.

Let's look at these types of software more closely.

Figure 9-1. The Software Pyramid

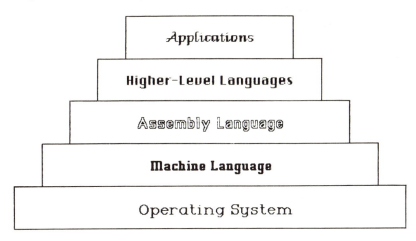

Operating System

The operating system takes care of everyday functions within the hardware itself. For instance, it translates between the computer and the peripherals around it, such as the keyboard and video screen. It deciphers the meaning of every keyboard character you press, and sends an image of it to the screen. The operating system also helps other software enter and leave the computer.

By taking care of such repeatedly needed tasks, it fills in chunks in all software written for the machine. Without it, programmers would have to include operating system functions in every program.

Yet this software is also rather detached and may even seem transparent. For instance, the keyboard appears to be pure Amiga hardware, but is controlled by the operating system. Pull-down menus seem a part of applications, but they are created by the operating system. Because of its pervasiveness, the operating system is probably the most important software a machine can have.

CHAPTER
NINE

Machine Language

The operating system responds to and integrates itself with the instructions you issue. The most basic level of these instructions is called machine language. No matter what software you have, it ultimately conveys its orders down to machine language, which carries out each particular you need. As a laborer acts on the material world with a spade or trowel, so machine language acts on the chip circuitry.

We've seen machine language before. It's the on/off code for instructions to the CPU. The computer translates a machine language command like 1101001101001001 into a corresponding series of electrical pulses, which go to the control unit in the CPU. The control unit identifies the instruction and sends a flurry of microinstructions to the arithmetic/logic unit and registers. A new result emerges, and the computer has processed data.

You can write programs in machine language if you want. The enterprise is a marvel of tedium. Suppose you want to add 5 to 1,048,560 and store the sum at an address in memory. A simple program to perform this task on the 68000 chip would be:

0111001000000101
0000011010000001
0000000000001111
1111111111110000
0010001010000001

The first instruction says, "Load 5 into the CPU." The second, third, and fourth—actually one very long instruction—say, "Load 1,048,560 into the CPU and add it to 5." The last says, "Store the sum at a specific address."

Consider the difficulties of working with such a program. To write it, you have had to memorize around 90 complex instructions whose appearance bears no relation to their meanings. Then you have to type this program in. You enter nothing but ones and zeros, over and over again. The digits tend to swim together, and it becomes very easy to make a typo. But the computer demands total accuracy. A one placed where a zero belongs creates a different instruction and throws the entire program awry. And finally, when you look back over the code, the trance-inducing pattern makes it very hard to identify the errant instruction.

Machine language is a slow, unpleasant, and inefficient way for people to give the computer its electrical signals. But the machine will read nothing else. Therefore, we use a variety of intermediary programs, both to translate more human commands into machine language and to give us greater power per command.

Getting to Machine Language

Since machine language is essential, every computer program must be translated into it. Now, translation requires three elements: statements in one language, a translator, and new statements in another language. In the case of computers, each of these stages is represented by a program. Whereas machine language requires only one program in the computer, all other languages need at least three. Let's look at them.

The first is called the *source* program, since it initiates the action. It is written in a computer language, a collection of symbols the translator will recognize. In BASIC, for instance, the source program is written in instructions like PEEK and GOSUB, that is, in the BASIC language.

The second program is the *translator*, in this case the BASIC translator. The BASIC translator is often called either "BASIC" or the "BASIC program." These terms can be very confusing, since they refer to other things as well. Both the BASIC translator and the BASIC language are known as "BASIC," and both the BASIC translator and the BASIC source program, which you or someone else writes, are known as the "BASIC program." This problem is not peculiar to BASIC, but occurs with all the higher-level languages. Unfortunately, sometimes only the context will tell you what the speaker means in these cases.

The third program is in machine language and is called the *object* program, as it is the goal of translation. Since the source and object programs just state the same instructions in different languages, sometimes the source program will be erased when the object program is attained. The translator program differs from them, changing one into the other but otherwise remaining aloof. (See Figures 9-2 and 9-3.)

You will hear translators referred to as either *interpreters* or *compilers*. Both turn source into object code, but the distinction between them tends to generate confusion among beginners. It's actually quite simple. When the computer receives a source program, it can either alternate between translating and executing instructions, or it can translate them all first, then execute them.

Figure 9-2. The Two BASICs

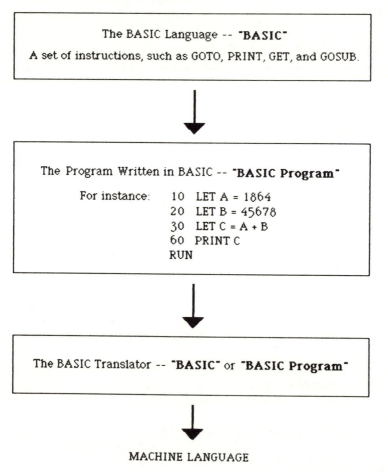

The BASIC Language -- **"BASIC"**

A set of instructions, such as GOTO, PRINT, GET, and GOSUB.

The Program Written in BASIC -- **"BASIC Program"**

For instance:　　10　LET A = 1864
　　　　　　　　　20　LET B = 45678
　　　　　　　　　30　LET C = A + B
　　　　　　　　　60　PRINT C
　　　　　　　　　RUN

The BASIC Translator -- **"BASIC"** or **"BASIC Program"**

MACHINE LANGUAGE

Interpreters translate and execute, translate and execute, over and over again, with the result that source program and action become interlayered. They very much resemble human interpreters. If you're dictating through a translator to a foreign scribe, you would probably utter one statement, hear it translated, watch it written down, then utter your next. A software interpreter works the same way. It translates one instruction, the computer carries it out, it translates another, and so on, until the program ends.

Compilers translate all instructions before executing any, with the result that source program and action become sequentially distinct. They resemble human book translators, who render all sentences into another tongue before you read any of them, and who are never called "interpreters." Compilers create the entire object program, and the computer then zips down it.

Compilers are generally preferable, if you can get them. They are much faster than interpreters, because they aren't continually shuttling back and forth from one language to another. This speed can be important in games and other applications. But compilers may demand more memory and make source programs harder to write and debug—that is, remove errors or bugs from. An interpreted program can be written and tested in fragments. A compiled one cannot be looked at until the whole program is ready to run.

Figure 9-3. Getting to Machine Language

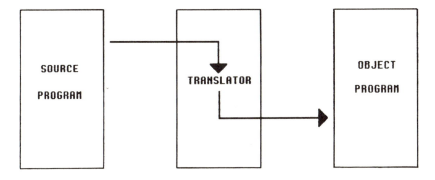

Assembly Language

Machine language is dizzying to read and arduous to program in the necessary detail. We can solve the first problem with a simple one-to-one translator. Suppose that, instead of binary numbers, we use their decimal equivalents. An elementary decimal-binary translator could convert the code into machine

CHAPTER
NINE

language. Since decimal numbers are much shorter and easier to read than binary, we could write and debug source programs far more effectively. Where each source instruction corresponds to a single machine instruction, we have an *assembly language*. We call the translator program an *assembler*.

But why have an assembly language made up of decimals? Why not use, say, abbreviated verbal commands, which have the extra advantage of self-description? For instance, instead of the machine language program above, we can write:

```
MOVEQ    5,D1
ADDI.L   $FFFF0,D1
MOVE.L   D1,(A1)
```

The first instruction loads the number 5 into the CPU, the second adds 1,048,560 to it, and the third stores the sum. It's not exactly self-evident, but you can see what's going on. And in fact 68000 assembly language is written in just this way.

The benefits of assembly language over machine language are clear. But it also has advantages over higher-level translators. First, the assembler takes up less space in memory, sometimes 1/8 the amount. Second, assembly language creates shorter machine language programs. It lets you write code with greater precision, thus saving even more memory. Third, and consequently, it runs faster—at least twice as fast as higher-level languages and a thousand times faster than some interpreted programs. If you want to delve deeply into computers, it makes sense to learn assembly language.

But assembly language still demands painstaking detail. You have to feed every CPU instruction into the machine yourself, and the process takes time and increases your chance of error. You can reduce this problem by moving up a level in the pyramid (see Figure 9-4).

Higher-Level Languages

Higher-level languages do two things: They translate English-like commands into machine language, and they turn each higher-level command into a whole set of machine instructions. This second function sharply distinguishes them from assembly language. It gives them power.

BASIC is one well-known higher-level language. Let's look at how it handles our addition program:

```
LET A = 5 + 1048560
```

134

Figure 9-4. BASIC, Assembly, and Machine Language

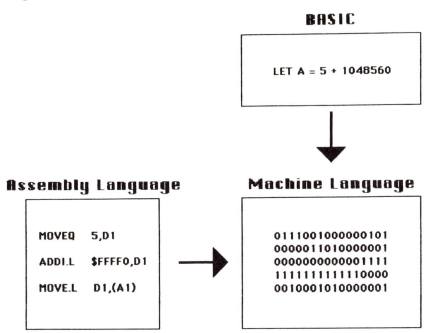

A single instruction loads 5 and 1,048,560, adds them, and sends the sum to A—everything the two previous programs did. A higher-level language is more than just a translator. It's a packager as well.

Two versions of BASIC are available for the Amiga, MetaComCo and Microsoft. BASIC may be the first higher-level language you come into contact with. But it's not the only one there is. There are several other higher-level languages—like Logo, Forth, C, and Pascal—which have their own distinct personalities and therefore their own virtues and fans.

You may also have heard of two older higher-level languages: COBOL and FORTRAN. COBOL (COmmon Business-Oriented Language) is a wordy code which is used mainly in business. FORTRAN (FORmula TRANslator) is much more compact and primarily does mathematics. These languages had their heyday on the large mainframes several years ago and are now waning. You may find versions of them for the

CHAPTER
NINE

Amiga, but BASIC, Logo, and other languages are now far more popular.

Higher-level languages make programming generally feasible and interesting. Programming has several benefits. It's economical. It lets you adapt the computer to your own needs and carry out a panoply of tasks. It brings you into closer contact with the machine.

But there are drawbacks as well. Programs take time to write and debug, and virtually all programs have to be debugged. Moreover, commercial software will generally outperform anything you could have devised yourself. For instance, few people will go through the labor of writing their own word processor with so many good ones already on the market. Most of us prefer to pay for the work of specialists.

Applications

Applications stand at the peak of the pyramid. They are programs, like the BASIC translator, but they perform highly specific tasks. They turn Turing's universal machine into a special-purpose one. *Archon*, for instance, turns the Amiga into a game. *Enable/Calc* turns it into a spreadsheet-type calculator. The source program you write in BASIC may also be an application, if other people can use it to manipulate their own data. In fact, applications are commonly written in BASIC and other higher-level languages.

Applications are characterized by their built-in knowledge. Since they presume you have a relatively narrow purpose— you want a word processor to help you write, for instance— they can anticipate many of your desires and either satisfy them outright or make them very easy to fulfill. A decent word processor, for instance, will perform carriage returns automatically, since it is reasonable to assume that you want this function. A good spreadsheet will contain many commonly used financial formulas. Applications generally reduce your own input to the raw data and immediate instructions needed for your particular goal.

And there can even be levels among applications. For instance, spreadsheets require you to lay them out to fit your task. If you want to figure out your taxes, say, but don't want to spend the time and effort to design the optimum layout, you can buy a tax program that will work with the spreadsheet. Such programs are examples of specialization within specialization.

Applications do it all. They are like the contractor who simply takes responsibility for the entire job. But even the contractor relies on the special knowledge and power of the handyman, who unlocks the gate in the morning, assists in little ways throughout the day, and locks up again at night. Before we go any further, we must therefore take a good look at the Amiga's operating system.

The Amiga Operating System

The operating system, sometimes abbreviated OS, is the software that binds the hardware together. It becomes part of every program a computer runs, performing the standard, repetitive chores that programmers do not want to bother with. Yet since it can do these chores with varying power, thoroughness, and grace, it goes far toward determining the "personality" of the machine.

The operating system is actually a collection of programs, itself arrayed in a hierarchy. For most purposes, it can be divided into two parts: nondisk and disk.

The first part does everything but control the disk drive. It is made up of programs like the monitor—not to be confused with the hardware monitor—which continually checks input devices like the keyboard to see if signals are coming in and channels them into the CPU and memory, and out to the screen. Since we deal with it directly only when we insert Kickstart, we hardly ever think about it, and it almost seems part of the hardware itself.

The second part regulates the disk drive. This software is sometimes called the disk operating system, or DOS. It gets a great deal of attention. It gets so much, in fact, that it is widely referred to as the operating system itself. Hence, most full commercial OSs call themselves DOSs, and the term *DOS* has apparently driven *OS* into the ground.

So much fanfare surrounds the disk drive because that's where you insert purchased programs. A DOS must be able to read their contents and store them in memory. It is like the handyman meeting the crew at the gate. If the crew can't communicate with him, he'll leave them outside. Thus, software authors write for a particular DOS as well as for a particular computer, and a program for, say, AmigaDOS will not run on a computer with a different operating system.

138

The Structure of the Amiga's DOS

The Amiga's operating system has an OS and a DOS, like most other operating systems. Its OS is Intuition. Its DOS is AmigaDOS. AmigaDOS is unusual because it has two different interfaces, which you can choose between. The normal interface, the one almost everyone will use, is the Workbench, with its pointer, icons, and menus. The other one, buried a bit beneath the Workbench, is the Command Line Interface, or CLI.

Intuition is the basic OS. It comes on the Kickstart disk, which you insert to get the Amiga going, and it resembles the ROM software of other computers. It controls the fundamental hardware operations of the machine. Software writers can make calls to its many subroutines and thereby use them to control the Amiga. Intuition has particularly powerful graphics utilities, and this feature makes it simple for software authors to use the pointer, icons, menus, and Amiga's graphics in general. Hence, the Amiga interface is often called the Intuition interface. In general, however, you don't have to worry about it.

AmigaDOS is the DOS, and controls disk operations. It performs some functions that you rarely have to think about, such as allocating memory, but it also takes care of others that require your cooperation, such as naming disks, saving to disk, and copying disks. You can participate at the level of either the Workbench or the CLI.

Normally, you'll use the Workbench, the glossy front for AmigaDOS. It carries out only part of the CLI's functions, but it makes them seem so effortless that it appears a completely different system. The tradeoff is classic: power for simplicity.

But before we get into the DOS, let's first look at disk operations themselves. What, exactly, do we need a DOS to do?

Controlling Disks

When a DOS is on a program disk, the first task of the disk is to get its DOS into the machine. After you insert a disk into the drive, the Amiga immediately looks for the DOS and starts reading it into RAM. Once in memory, the DOS reads the rest of the disk, a process called *booting*. In effect, a small part of the disk shinnies up into the computer and then hauls the rest of it in.

Let's look at the physical disk itself, the item which will store your data. It is a thin platter coated with magnetic material. A blank disk holds no information. Its stray magnetic charges are as patternless as the craters on the moon. Thus, when you want to copy data from RAM onto a blank disk, the first thing the DOS must do is impose a framework on it. It needs a means of recording data in sequence, or that data will never be recovered. The DOS must create an addressable structure. Therefore, you must format or initialize a blank disk before it can do anything else.

Initialization takes place in two steps. First, the DOS divides the disk into concentric rings called *tracks*. You can't see them, even if you open the metal guard, but they are magnetically distinct, and the read/write head of the disk drive recognizes them at once. The Amiga lays out 80 tracks per side, for a total of 160. Second, the DOS partitions the disk into wedges like pie slices. This act subdivides each track into a number of arcs, which are called *sectors*. AmigaDOS creates 11 sectors per track.

The 11 sectors on the outermost track are much larger than the 11 on the innermost. Nonetheless, each holds the same amount of information: 512 bytes. Since each formatted disk has 1760 sectors (11 sectors per track × 160 tracks), the entire disk can hold 901,120 bytes (512 bytes per sector × 1760 sectors), or about 880K.

If you bought an Amiga early, you must beware of a hazardous quirk in the disk drive light during initialization. It will go out for about one to ten seconds in the middle of the process. The drive continues to initialize, even though the light is off, so if you try to remove the disk at this time, you'll probably damage it. Wait till it comes on and goes off a second time before removing it.

Once you've initialized the disk, you begin storing information on disk. Separate storage units are generally called *files*. And, in order to get to your files, you must give each a distinct name. Thenceforth, you can refer to it in commands, open or close it, and generally manipulate it to your ends.

The computer also requires a listing of the files and programs on the disk. It needs to know what it has. This catalog is called a *directory*. The DOS tells the computer where to look for the directory on the disk and how to find the items listed. The directory is analogous to a telephone book or the card catalog in a library, though far smaller.

Workbench Operations

The Workbench makes disk management so simple you rarely have to think about it. It's even easy to explain.

Copying disks. To copy a disk, you open the System drawer and click the Diskcopy icon, which shows two disks with an arrow from one to the other. The Amiga then issues a series of instructions in requesters on the screen, and you follow them. The Diskcopy routine also initializes the blank disk, a timesaving step.

Always make a backup copy of important disks, starting with Kickstart and the Workbench. As we stated earlier, disks are fragile and anything can happen to them. Think of it as a shrewd insurance policy. A blank disk costs only a few dollars, and you can always reuse it. A commercial program may cost hundreds, and a disk with your work on it can be invaluable.

Initializing. To format a blank disk, you open the System drawer and click the Initialize icon, a disk with an *E* on the left, an *F* on the right, and something like Krakatoa in the middle. The disk drive will then format the disk.

Naming and renaming. Often enough, we decide to change the name of a file, perhaps to make it more appropriate or informative. To name or rename any icon, you first select it by clicking it once. Then you hold down the right mouse button, pull down the Workbench menu, and release at Rename. A window appears onscreen with the current name of the icon. You move the pointer to the window and click the left button once. Then use the DEL key to erase the existing name. Type in the new one, press RETURN, and the icon now has a different name.

Opening files. To open a file, you double-click its icon. The disk drive whirs, the computer reads from the disk into RAM, and soon the file window opens up.

Deleting files. To delete a file, you drag its icon into the Trashcan and click Empty Trash from the Disk menu.

Directory. Where is the Workbench directory? It's right before you, the display of icons on the screen. Or, let's say, it's arguably right before you. It is really unworthy of the name, since it doesn't begin to indicate the real number of files in AmigaDOS. But it does show you those with Workbench icons.

The Workbench is meant to be almost automatic to use: intuitive. But the easy way is not always the most instructive, and you may want to open the box and peer into what's really happening. For that, you enter the CLI.

The Command Line Interface

The Amiga Tutor gives you a simulation of the Command Line Interface, and in fact you've probably already seen the real thing. Soon after you load the Workbench, you see a list of lines labeled AmigaDOS and suggesting that you set the clock. That's the CLI. The Workbench itself is the last part of AmigaDOS to appear.

As we've seen, Commodore correctly anticipated that most people won't want to poke around the AmigaDOS edifice. Hence, you have to take active measures to get in. You open Preferences, select CLI ON, and click SAVE. Then you open the System drawer, which will now have a new icon: a cube with *1>* on it and the label *CLI*. Click that, and the world of the CLI opens up to you.

What's it like? Well, the first thing you see is a window with the legend *New Cli Window* and the prompt *1>*. The rest is blank. The CLI is awaiting an instruction, and that's what it's like. You have to know what commands to type in, or it will wait forever.

One interesting instruction to enter at the outset is NEWCLI (or newcli—the CLI doesn't care about case). Press RETURN, and a second CLI window appears, with the legend *New CLI task 2* and the prompt *2>*. Type NEWCLI again, and you get a third window, with *New CLI task 3* and the prompt *3>*. You can keep going on. The operating system is multitasking itself. AmigaDOS is one of the few operating systems that can perform this feat, though you'll find that you can enter commands into only one CLI at a time. You select the CLI you want to use by clicking on its window. The other CLIs on the screen then dim. To close each window, type ENDCLI and press RETURN.

Let's look at how the CLI performs the tasks we outlined above with the Workbench.

Directory. To see the CLI's directory, type DIR. A host of items will spill out very quickly and race up the screen out of sight. Unless you've made the window very large, you'll lose most of them, for the CLI window has no scroll bars. But you should be able to see that they are divided into two categories.

Some have *(dir)* after them, like *Demos (dir)*, and others *.info*, like *Demos.info*. That's because all programs on the Workbench have at least two files. The one with *(dir)* after it holds the actual file contents, while the one with *.info* contains data about the icon. The legend *(dir)* also indicates that the file is a subdirectory, with other files within it. If you want to see the directory of a disk other than the Workbench, you have two choices. If the disk is in another drive, type DIR *[disk drive name]*. If you have only one drive, type: DIR *[disk name]*.

Copying disks. The CLI has preset names for Amiga disk drives. The internal drive is DF0:, while the first external drive is DF1:, and the next two are DF2: and DF3:, in the order they are attached. Hence, if you have an external disk drive, you can copy to it by simply issuing this command:

DISKCOPY DF0: TO DF1:

If you want to copy from the external drive to the internal, you just switch DF1: with DF0:. But what if you have only an internal drive? You type in:

DISKCOPY DF0: TO DF0:

A requester appears on the screen, and you commence swapping disks. There are two things in particular to note here. First, the colons. Don't forget them. They are flags which tell the Amiga that you have named a hardware device, a disk drive or disk, not a software file. Second, the 0 in DF0 is a zero, not a capital *O*. It may look the same on the screen, but it's a different binary pattern within.

Initializing. To initialize a blank disk, you type in a somewhat more complex command: FORMAT DRIVE *[drive name]* NAME *[disk name]*. For instance, to initialize a disk in an external disk drive and give it the name DATA2, you enter:

FORMAT DRIVE DF1: NAME DATA2:

The disk gets a format and a christening. *Remember, formatting a disk erases any data that might be on the disk.* You should format only new disks or disks which have information you no longer want.

Renaming files. To rename files in the CLI, type RE-NAME FROM *[current name]* TO *[new name]*. Instead of TO, you can also type AS. In fact, the FROM, TO, and AS are all optional, but they help you orient yourself in the command.

CHAPTER
TEN

Thus, to change a file's name from PRETZELS to SAUER-KRAUT, you enter:

RENAME FROM PRETZELS TO SAUERKRAUT

Simple. Unfortunately, we're just starting. The names of files on most computers are subject to certain rules, and the Amiga is no exception. First, the name should not exceed 30 characters. Second, it can't contain a colon (:) or a slash (/) since these symbols have special meaning to the Amiga. Third, you can use the space, equal sign (=), plus sign (+), and quotation mark (") only if you enclose the entire name in quotation marks, so it's best to avoid them. Fourth, if you have more than one drive operating, you add the disk drive name plus a colon to the filename, like DF1:PRETZELS. Fifth, if the file belongs to a subdirectory, you also add the sub-directory's name plus a slash, like DF1:PICNIC/PRETZELS. Because a name like this essentially constitutes a set of direc-tions to the file, it is also called a *pathname*.

Opening files. You can open a file from the CLI by typ-ing in its name, for example, CLOCK. But you must be careful not to let the new file override the CLI. To make sure the CLI holds the reins, type RUN before the filename. RUN initiates multitasking, so the Amiga keeps both the CLI and the file go-ing simultaneously. If you type RUN CLOCK, the clock will appear in a window, and you can click its close gadget to ter-minate it.

Deleting files. To erase files, type DELETE *[filename]*. Again, if you have more than one disk drive and are deleting a file in another subdirectory, you have to type in the path-name. For instance, if the file PRETZELS were in the current directory and the internal drive, you could simply type DE-LETE PRETZELS. But if it were in an external drive under the subdirectory PICNIC, you'd have to type:

DELETE DF1:PICNIC/PRETZELS

Be careful with this command. It isn't forgiving like the Trashcan. It deletes immediately.

After these functions, the Workbench nears the end of its capacities. The powerful CLI, however, has just begun. It per-forms many other tasks and even lets you write elementary programs called batch files. Its full range is beyond the scope of this book, but if you like tinkering with the mechanism, you should definitely explore it.

Other Operating Systems

AmigaDOS is one of at least a hundred different operating systems available today. Not all of them are widespread or important. But you will hear about some repeatedly, either because of their horde of programs or their vanguard position. Those below are the most likely to catch your ear.

CP/M. CP/M has been around for a long time. Invented by Gary Kildall of Digital Research and first marketed in 1975, it quickly became a standard for computers with eight-bit CPUs, since it worked well on the popular 8080 and Z80 chips. A vast library of over 3000 programs has grown up around it, including such standards as *WordStar* and *dBase II.*

MS-DOS. MS-DOS is the standard among 16-bit computers, mainly because IBM chose it for the PC. Microsoft, the giant Bellevue, Washington, software house, markets this operating system, whose name is simply an abbreviation of Microsoft DOS. (IBM calls it PC-DOS.) MS-DOS resembles CP/M in many ways, and both have affinities to the CLI. For instance, all demand that the user memorize special commands rather than pick options from a menu. MS-DOS is mainly restricted to Intel's 8088 and 8086 chips.

Unix. Unix was developed in the Bell Labs at a time when AT&T was legally forbidden to enter the computer field. Now that the fetters are gone, it is actively promoting its Unix Version V, and its coffers guarantee that Unix will become more significant. Unix has several excellent features lacking in CP/M and MS-DOS. It is portable, runs on a variety of computers, and has gained acceptance through its widespread use in universities. It has a powerful file structure and a plethora of utility programs, which enhance the software author's job. But Unix exists in several incompatible versions, and each of them demands that you learn countless commands. In addition, it occupies large tracts of memory, though denser ROM chips and cheaper hard disks could mitigate this problem.

Pick. Pick, named after its developer Dick Pick, resembles Unix in its complexity, power, and size. It is, however, quite easy to use. It is mainly an information system, good for businesses but not as suited to scientific work as some other operating systems. It also lacks the tremendous backing behind Unix, and its future is thus harder to foretell.

CHAPTER
TEN

Apple ProDOS. The Apple II line of computers uses a simple, straightforward operating system called, in its most recent version, ProDOS. A great many educational programs and games have been written for this DOS, which runs on the 6502 and 65C02 eight-bit chips.

Macintosh. Apple's Macintosh and Lisa computers have the operating system whose interface most resembles the Workbench. Though programmers find it large and complicated, users love it. Since it employs a mouse to point to icons and pull-down menu items, a complete novice can run it competently almost from the outset. If imitation is flattery, then AmigaDOS has paid a compliment to this DOS.

An operating system takes care of the routine so that programmers can focus on the specific. It contributes to programs of every kind, from those you write in machine language to the most expensive applications. The DOS is discrete and often invisible, so we are not prone to think of it as a portion of *Marble Madness* and *Graphicraft*. But it works together with them all.

Programming

A 1983 market survey by Apple Computer, Inc., indicated that many new computer buyers are curious about programming because they think it necessary to operate the machine. In fact, it's necessary that someone program the Amiga, but that person does not have to be you. Programming requires the time to break a problem down into its logical parts, and the patience to puzzle out the bugs that afflict the first stages of almost every program. You may well prefer to buy your software from professionals.

But if programming appeals to you, don't hesitate. It isn't that complicated, and it can challenge your ingenuity and satisfy your creative urges. It also gives you real control over the computer. Moreover, you don't have to be a logician, or even have a logical mind, to enjoy it. Don't be daunted by the initial hours of learning a programming language, when everything appears gnarled and foreign, and new instructions seem to tumble out of the void without end. Languages, both human and computer, are enclosed and intradependent systems, and the first words you learn in them always make you sense how much you need the rest. You cannot see the structure and feel the mastery until you have simply plowed on for a while. But you eventually do, and at that point you simultaneously gain a sense of accomplishment and wonder why others cannot see what is so obvious to you.

You can program in 68000 assembly language if you like. It'll give you an excellent feel for the computer. But most Amiga owners will probably want to start with the higher-level languages. With them, you don't have to keep track of registers or memory addresses, but instead can think in terms of variables and formulas. Since your instructions each represent a group of machine commands, you can concentrate more intently on the problem at hand, and your task is thus greatly simplified.

The higher-level languages described below currently dominate the field. BASIC is the best known and most convenient for Amiga owners, since a version of it comes with the computer. But the others are worth looking at, for they may suit your needs as well or better.

BASIC

BASIC is short for Beginner's All-purpose Symbolic Instruction Code—another case of an acronym invented before the words it supposedly abbreviates. It was devised in 1964 by two professors at Dartmouth College, John Kemeny and Thomas Kurtz, who wished to make computers more accessible to non-science majors. At that time, of course, it ran only on the large mainframes, since there were no other computers around. When the Altair came out in 1975, two young men named Bill Gates and Paul Allen helped devise a BASIC translator for it, and soon founded a company, Microsoft, on the market strength of this program.

Microsoft BASIC remains the industry standard, but the Microsoft company no longer owns the rights to it. Commodore does. Hence, unless you bought your Amiga within the first weeks of its introduction, you get a free copy of Microsoft BASIC with the machine. This BASIC has been specially enhanced for the Amiga. It contains not only the typical BASIC instructions—GET, PRINT, GOSUB, and so forth—but also many that take advantage of the Amiga's sterling virtues. For instance, its numerous graphics instructions let you generate images on the screen without a graphics program. It also has audio commands. The TRANSLATE$ and SAY instructions will turn a typed English statement into a vocal utterance, whose pitch, volume, and other attributes you can then toy with. There is a Macintosh application that performs this feat, and it costs over $100.

In all, Microsoft BASIC has over 200 reserved words, far more than conventional BASICs. Don't let this richness scare you away. You don't have to learn all of them, or even the majority of them, to do almost everything you'll want. The unlearned commands will simply wait, eager courtiers with special skills, until the day you need them.

Microsoft BASIC is not only powerful, but flexible and easy to use. It places many instructions in pull-down menus, so you can simply select them rather than type them in. And, when you do type commands, it lets you enter them in either uppercase or lowercase. This may not seem like much, but some BASICs demand that you enter instructions solely in capital letters, a throwback to the days when personal computers had no lowercase.

The language is also rather simple to learn. Essentially, it consists of lines of commands. You type in these lines one at a time, and pretty soon you have programmed the computer. And most lines in BASIC have two simple parts: command and operand.

Commands. The commands are short English or semi-English words like RUN or GOTO, or arithmetic operators like plus (+) and minus (−). Microsoft BASIC's 200 words would be a minute amount for a human language. But human languages seek to describe the universe, and so are immense. Computer languages are different. They are instructions for a machine, and 200 of them can make the Amiga perform acrobatic stunts indeed.

Operands. The operands are the numbers or letter-strings the commands act upon. Not all commands have operands, just as not all English verbs have objects. But one or more operands per command are common. Operands come in two types: constants and variables.

Constants are specified pieces of data, like 5 or "The cat watched the frog." You know what they are, and you expect them to stay that way.

Variables are names pinned to changeable values, like the x's and y's in high school algebra. To the computer, a constant is straight data, but a variable is the address of a memory location. Whenever you issue a command with a variable, the machine reads it in, checks its registry of address names, and acts upon whatever is stored at the address.

Naming variables demands a little discretion. Not a lot, but some. Variable names can have up to 40 characters. Variable names must begin with a letter and can include only letters, numbers, and decimal points, so if you want to call a variable RIO BRAVO, you have to resort to some expedient like RIO.BRAVO or RIOBRAVO. Moreover, you cannot use any of BASIC's reserved words, that is, its commands or keywords. The keywords are words modifying commands, much as adverbs alter verbs in phrases like "put over" and "open up." Among the keywords are AT, INVERSE, USING, ON, STEP, CURSOR, MOUSE, RGB, and FN.

The Amiga's Microsoft BASIC was not ready when the first machines were shipped, so Commodore included a version called ABasiC instead. ABasiC is almost identical to Microsoft BASIC, except it fails to use the pull-down menus. You type everything in. Otherwise, ABasiC is just as powerful.

Is BASIC the language for you? It does have several advantages. It's free and convenient. It's not hard to learn. It's an interpreted language, so you can make and test corrections immediately. Its loose structure makes it easy to alter or enhance your programs midway through writing them. And it's as close to a standard as you can get among higher-level languages.

However, BASIC has detractors. The severity of their criticism may stem partly from simple partisanship. Serious programmers like to think they have chosen the correct language to work in, and enjoy stressing flaws in its rivals. And the eminence of BASIC makes it a target for everyone. Nonetheless, its shortcomings are real enough. First, its loose structure is an aid only for short programs. When you start writing longer ones, it leads to confusion in debugging. Moreover, if you start off with BASIC and get accustomed to its relaxed, permissive style, you will find it harder to go on to languages like Forth which do not tolerate any giggling on the bus. In addition, in its interpreted version, BASIC is probably slower than any other higher-level language the Amiga can use.

Ultimately, your decision in this matter should depend on your attitude toward programming itself. If you find it mildly engaging, but of no lasting interest to you, then perhaps you should simply stay with BASIC. If, on the other hand, you wish to teach programming to your kids or write a lot of programs yourself, you should probably consider the languages below.

Logo

Logo is another simple language, but one very different from BASIC. Developed in the late 1960s by Wallace Feurzeig, Daniel Bobrow, and Seymour Papert at Cambridge, Massachusetts, Logo makes extensive use of graphics. A little "turtle" shuttles across the screen drawing lines and patterns as you command. Instead of keying in a list of logical instructions, you are scooting around the display.

Logo is fun, and the turtle is only one reason why it is widely deemed the best language for children to learn. There are many others. For instance, in Logo you can see the results of your instructions as soon as you issue them. The language thereby conquers the attention-span problem. In addition, it lets you create programs by adding relatively small building blocks together. A program can thus expand in various directions as you and/or a child choose, and you can also easily add enhancements to it. It has great flexibility.

But Logo is hardly just a child's toy. One of its most powerful features lets you define your own commands. You can thereby wrap a set of Logo instructions into one big, new function. For instance, if you wanted a command to draw a triangle, you could type in:

TO TRIANGLE
REPEAT 3 [FORWARD 40, RIGHT 60]
END

Henceforth, whenever you issue the instruction TRIANGLE, the turtle will move forward 40 units and turn right 60 degrees, three times, thus forming an equilateral triangle. Note that the program has learned. You have taught it something.

Logo is not limited to graphics. It can carry out virtually any program that BASIC can. Moreover, the language induces good programming skills, enabling you to move on to a tightly structured language without difficulty.

What's wrong with Logo? Well, it's still an interpreted language, so it's relatively slow. It's also not as compact in memory as some of the other languages. These are drawbacks if you wish to write and publish your own programs. If you do, you'll probably want to look at Pascal, Forth, or C.

Pascal

Pascal—named after the seventeenth-century mathematician and philosopher Blaise Pascal, who contrived a mechanical calculator as a teenager—was invented by Nicklaus Wirth in 1969, both to show that a good language did not have to be elephantine and to provide one that would teach students how to write clean, efficient programs.

The Pascal programming language is structured. Structured languages aim at widespread comprehensibility. Essentially, the idea is that anyone should be able to pick up the Pascal program you have written and understand it. BASIC programs can be like certain people's handwriting—distinctive and legible to them alone. Program readability is not just an esthetic goal. Often, several individuals work on commercial programs, and if two people inadvertently create the same variable name, like HOUSE, madness ensues. Even in a solo effort, you can make this mistake if you return to a program you haven't worked on for a while.

Pascal has several features which enhance its clarity. It simply reads down the list from top to bottom, thus creating a more standard format. Moreover, it demands strict definition of variables, usually in one place at the head of the program, so you can see at a glance which variables you have and which you don't. (Pascal programmers get used to the nagging "undeclared variable" message on the screen.)

Furthermore, it facilitates the creation of modules, that is, independent subroutines which carry out discrete little tasks, and which can have variables that won't be recognized outside the module. Modularity is a great aid to program portability, that is, to adapting the same program to different operating systems. For instance, if you want to run a program on two computers with the same CPU, but with different operating systems, like the Apple IIe and the Commodore 64, modules make the job easy. You build separate modules into the program to handle all communication with the DOS. You then go ahead and write the main body of your software, calling the DOS subroutines only when needed. To shift the program to the new DOS, you rewrite only the DOS modules. Without such modules, you might have to rewrite everything.

A simple Pascal program to add the numbers from 1 through 150 might look like this:

```
PROGRAM ADDUP ;
   VAR TOTAL :      INTEGER
   VAR NUMBER :  INTEGER
 BEGIN
   TOTAL := 0
   FOR NUMBER := 1 TO 150 DO
     TOTAL := NUMBER + TOTAL
   END;
```

The first section specifically defines variable types, here both integer. The second section details the instructions. It sets the variable TOTAL at 0 to start. It then gives NUMBER the successive values of 1 through 150, and adds each value to the ever increasing TOTAL. After NUMBER reaches 150, the program has performed its task, and it ends.

Pascal has relatively few basic concepts, but it requires that you follow its rules of syntax without deviation. It simply forces you to think out your programs clearly. (Well—it doesn't really force you to. Like BASIC, it has a GOTO command, which lets the Amiga jump around the program like a keno light. However, Pascal purists condemn excessive use of this instruction, and indeed if you aim for a software gem, you will use GOTO only as a last resort.)

Pascal is not for everyone. It is harder to learn than Logo, say, and its rigor may irk you if you are programming for yourself. Moreover, you may not need it if you are writing mainly small programs. On the other hand, a certain prestige accrues to mastery of Pascal, and you may find that the language makes you a better programmer as well.

Forth

Of all the languages mentioned so far, Forth is the most unusual and inspires some of the fiercest loyalty. Invented around 1969 by Charles H. Moore and first used to control telescopes, Forth is distinguished by its reverse Polish notation (RPN), a type of coding which can be intimidating to the neophyte. For instance, look at this line from BASIC:

IF A=B THEN PRINT "Success"

Here it is in Forth:

: SUCCESS
 A B =
IF ." Success" THEN ;

It appears as though someone has been playing 52 Pickup with the BASIC statement. But the strangeness tends to recede when you learn a little about the rules of reverse Polish notation. In it, operations tend to be expressed after the items they operate on, much like German verbs. Thus, the BASIC A=B becomes the Forth A B =. In addition, Forth uses punctuation marks as commands, adding to its eerie façade. For instance, a period followed by a quotation mark (.") means PRINT, and a semicolon (;) indicates the end of a definition.

Like a proper goblin, Forth has power. Among other things, it can create its own commands, as Logo can. In the example above, for instance, the program brings the command SUCCESS into existence. Henceforth, whenever you issue it, the program will check A and B to see if they're equal, and print "Success" if they are.

A conspicuous drawback to Forth, of course, is that you must learn to think in reverse Polish notation. Forth proponents claim that the language is much simpler than it looks, and that at the same time it does not ignore flexibility in the authorship process. Forth programs can easily be altered to run on many different computer makes, and have proved particularly useful with robots. Though not everyone is persuaded, such strengths have made Forth the language of choice among numerous software writers.

C

C was designed by Dennis Ritchie in 1972 to run on the Unix operating system, and has since been adapted to numerous other DOSs. This language is rapidly becoming very common, for a number of reasons. It retains the association with Unix and grows in popularity with it. Though simple, it attains power by combining discrete elements. It is fast, portable, compact in memory, and rather enjoyable to use.

C is actually halfway between assembly language and the higher-level languages. It lets you write close, step-by-step logic, yet can shield you from offensive contact with the machine's architecture. Dennis Ritchie specialized in writing systems software, that is, operating systems, language translators, and the like, and many programmers now favor C for this use. AmigaDOS itself is written in C. If it were written in machine or assembly language, it would take up less memory and run faster. But currently, with the ample capacity of the 68000, programmers are choosing ease of creation over economy of result.

C is another structured language, but one not quite as strict as Pascal. It resembles Pascal, however, and its crisp notation actually makes it look stricter, like a lowercase shorthand speckled with curved brackets. Terse as it is, it looks far less threatening than Forth, and it is in fact rather easy to learn. Here is how our Pascal example would look in C:

```
main ( )
  int TOTAL = 0;
  int NUMBER = 0;
  {
  while (NUMBER < 150)
    {
    ++NUMBER;
    TOTAL = TOTAL + NUMBER;
    }
  }
}
```

Note that, again, we commence by declaring TOTAL and NUMBER to be integers. But, unlike in Pascal, we don't have to announce formally that they are variables. The language assumes it. Then we move on to the active part of the program, a simple loop. The counter—++NUMBER—adds 1 to NUMBER, and the next command adds the new NUMBER to TOTAL. The loop then repeats. After NUMBER reaches 150, the loop ends. We have added every number between 1 and 150, and we have our figure.

C is not just being used in systems software. Lotus *1-2-3* is written in it, as are the programs of Microsoft and such other well-known software as *dBase III* and *WordStar 2000*. The name, by the way, derives from the fact that it is a successor language to B, also developed at Bell Labs.

Other Languages

There are several other languages which you will hear of from time to time, such as Modula-2, Ada, LISP, and Prolog. While you may never buy them for your Amiga, it is pleasing to have some acquaintance with them.

Modula-2. Modula-2 is the latest effort from Nicklaus Wirth, and even more rigorous than its Pascal forebear. Like Pascal, Modula-2 demands that you provide first a header, then an area for declaration, then the main executing instructions, the "verbs." But Modula-2, as its name suggests, differs from Pascal in its greater capacity to support modules, and has attracted the attention of many serious programmers.

Ada. Ada was developed for the U.S. Department of Defense, which was looking for a super-language to use in "embedded computer systems," that is, computers inside other devices like nuclear missiles. It is a costly, lumbering, complicated language, and it is so large that few versions of it have yet appeared on personal computers. But its size makes it extremely versatile, so it can do almost anything without special enhancements. Ada is worth watching since, as it is refined, it should improve and come down in price.

LISP. LISP (for *List Processing*) was developed by John McCarthy at MIT in 1960. It has gained attention through its suitability to artificial intelligence, that is, planning, general reasoning, and use of knowledge by computers. It has become especially prominent in expert systems, programs which reproduce the decision-making process of experts. For instance, an expert system currently exists for diagnosing patients. It questions them about their symptoms and reaches a diagnosis, which may be all the more accurate because people will confide things to a machine that they would hide from a doctor. LISP comes in a bewildering variety of dialects.

Prolog. Prolog is a declarative language. It requires you to declare a separate name for every different variable you come up with. This does not sound onerous until you realize how often programmers use little counting tricks such as $X=X+1$, repeated until $X=50$, to perform some action 50 times. With Prolog, each new amount needs its own variable name. Why would anyone want this cumbersome feature? The reason is parallel processing—using several CPUs instead of one. Parallel processing demands careful coordination among operations in all the CPUs. Yet, in $X=X+1$, the value of X depends on where you are in the program, and so if you blindly shuttle X back and forth among the CPUs, you get weird and disastrous results. Advocates of parallel processing are very keen on Prolog and its cousin languages, Hope and FP.

Programming gives you control, but it also takes time and effort. In any case, whether you decide to do it or not, you will be buying applications software. You can't program everything, and there are a great many attractive applications available.

Word Processing

In 1976, soon after the Altair appeared, a former filmmaker named Michael Shrayer completed a program to help people write software. He then sat down to type the documentation for it, and a sense of inappropriateness overcame him. Why should he clatter away at the typewriter when he should be able to write the documentation on the computer itself? He looked around for programs to perform this task, found none, and wrote one himself. It was *Electric Pencil*, the first word processor, and it appeared in early 1977.

Since then, word processing has become one of the classic applications, and personal computers are turning up on secretaries' desks for the sole purpose of using this software. The term *word processing* is rather mundane, smacking less of Parnassus than, say, pump-top cheese, but the actual technique is a swift and even enjoyable way to prepare sentences for the page.

If you have never used a word processor, you may wonder exactly what sets it apart from a typewriter. Primarily, word processors interject a temporary transition zone between your thoughts and the paper. With a typewriter, you must form sentences in your head before setting them down, and the expression that seems luminous in the mind may prove pallid on the page. With a word processor, you enter sentences into the computer and study them on the screen. You can look your prose over, spruce it up, pare it down, and generally fine-tune it before committing it to hardcopy. You gain a playground for second thoughts.

Word processors let you make corrections cleanly, easily, and almost instantly. You can not only delete and insert words, paragraphs, and pages at will, but move chunks of prose from one spot to another. Some word processors also let you change the spelling of a certain word throughout the text in a flash.

The effect of instant correctability on your way of writing is marked. Instead of working sentence by sentence in a linear way and waiting until the entire first draft is complete before

CHAPTER
TWELVE

making corrections, you find yourself amending sentences you have just composed, jumping back and forth from place to place as ideas strike you. You are removed to a height, as though from a plain to a peak, where you can look down, target revisions, and watch the lightning flow from your fingertips. This shift has inspired confidence in many people whose anxiety over their prose had formerly made it even worse, and thus it has led to happier and better writers.

Moreover, the version of your document in the Amiga can act as a master stencil, from which you can make as many copies as you like. If you use a typewriter, you must find a photocopy machine or resort to carbon paper to perform this feat. But with a word processor and a printer—and you absolutely must have a printer for word processing—you can make as many copies as you like, and the first will look as good as the last.

The temporary transition zone is like a pedestal for the rest of the word processor. Since word processors are applications, they come with special knowledge about their jobs, and take care of an assortment of little tasks that free you from the mechanics of writing and promote your concentration. For instance, a good electric typewriter will have a power-return, so you can return the carriage with a single keystroke, and a power-space, so you can move right as far as you want by holding one key down. But most word processors perform the following functions.

Automatic carriage return. When you near the end of a line, the software tests the words to see when they no longer fit. At that point, it moves the text down to the next line. This feature is called *wraparound.* It relieves you of one more chore, and anyone who has written on a typewriter knows the slight but perceptible annoyance of having to interrupt a racing, intricate thought to end a line, perhaps hyphenate a word, and return the carriage. Of course, word processors still require you to press RETURN at the end of a paragraph. The program that anticipates paragraph endings will be the one that takes over the world.

Paging. Word processors can wrap around from one page to the next. Instead of removing a sheet of bond, threading in another, and adjusting it to the horizontal, you continue writing and maintain your train of thought. The software silently shifts you to the next page, and often automatically numbers it.

CHAPTER
TWELVE

Margins. Word processors can set your margins and keep them there, so you never again have the problem of bell-bottom text, with one-inch margins at the top and quarter-inch margins at the bottom. Moreover, you can set them before writing and alter them at any time afterward.

Justification. Word processors can perform the trick of aligning your prose to the left margin, right margin, or center. If you justify both left and right, you can generate neatly squared pages like those in books. Center justification simply centers every line, and saves you the trouble of counting characters when typing titles and other heads.

The features listed above were enough to make word processors a triumph in the marketplace. But the Amiga gives these programs even greater powers:

Mobility. The mouse lets you move instantly across your text. You may take the mouse for granted, but without it, editing can be like crawling back and forth on a scaffold.

Fonts. Because the Amiga has a bitmapped screen, it can represent letters in myriad shapes. You can therefore write in a variety of fonts—airy, blocklike, tendriled, whatever. A font is a kind of design, and may even be copyrighted.

Styles. The Amiga can also display styles of type, such as italic, boldface, or outline. Styles differ from fonts. Fonts are the fundamental character patterns and involve features like the presence or absence of serifs. Fonts are not generalizable, that is, they don't interact with other fonts. Styles do. They are the means of playing with fonts, as by slanting or thickening them, and so you can have Helvetica italic or Times Roman boldface. Styles can also combine with each other, yielding, for instance, italic boldface.

Sizes. You can also write in various type sizes. Many word processors let you choose from the tiny 9 point through 12, 14, 18, 24, 36, all the way up to the grand 72 point size. Others let you expand or condense your print to any size in-between. Watch out for poor letter quality at the larger sizes, where some programs render curves with pronounced steps.

Print replication. Because the screen is bitmapped, you can print out exactly what you see on it. This feature frees you forever from the bare, sticklike font of the typewriter, and lets you undertake print shop tasks like creating quality letterhead.

Word processors have a final virtue which does not occur to most people: silence. The noise alone from a typewriter can

CHAPTER
TWELVE

fray the nerves after a long stint of writing. A word processor is quiet as the sunrise.

Textcraft
Commodore-Amiga, Inc.
1200 Wilson Drive
West Chester, PA 19380
215-431-9100 ext. 9707
$99.00

The Amiga's first word processor was *Textcraft*, developed by Arktronics Corporation of Ann Arbor, Michigan, and marketed by Commodore itself. *Textcraft* is a decent word processor, relatively inexpensive and easy to learn. It isn't top caliber, for it fails to use many of the Amiga's most pleasing features, but it is certainly adequate for most casual work.

Textcraft is so simple to master that you can probably do it without looking at the documentation. Its Help menu gives you three fast starters. First, the Quick Reminder explains the meaning of the editing icons across the top. Second, the Keyboard Reference shows you the effect of pressing particular keys. And third, the 21 different "One Minute Tutorials" detail almost any function you might wish to try.

Textcraft has the normal complement of formatting features. It offers single- or double-spacing and right, left, center, and flush justification. It automatically numbers pages, letting you set the number on top or on the bottom, and in a variety of styles, including roman numerals. It also allows headers and footers, legends the computer will print at the top or bottom of every page.

Textcraft displays 60 or 75 columns on the screen. But it's not limited to this amount. If you set your margins wide enough, some of the text on the left will disappear as the cursor approaches the right edge of the screen. All the text is still there. The document is simply larger than the screen window, and the software is shifting the window so that you can see it. How wide can a *Textcraft* document get? If you pull the box in the bottom scroll bar all the way to the right, you'll see it can have lines of 225 characters across.

The program has six icons across the top, which depict its editing powers. To carry out any one of them, you click it—or press the shortcut function keys—and the pointer changes shape. You then select the text you wish to work on, the operation occurs, and you click another icon to get back where you were before.

The icon you'll use most often is the *Pencil,* which lets you move the cursor. If you want to make changes while in Pencil, you can easily delete with the DEL or BACK SPACE key, and add with numerous others. But occasionally you'll want to cut or move a whole block of text. When that happens, you call on the *Scissors* icon.

When you click Scissors, the pointer turns into a pair of shears. You drag it across the unwanted text, and it vanishes the moment you lift the button. You can then return to Pencil and continue writing. But what if you accidentally vaporize the wrong paragraph? You click the *Pastepot* icon—it looks more like a bottle of glue—and the pointer turns into a pastepot. You click the Pastepot wherever you want the prose to reappear, and it returns at once. Hence, the Scissors do not irretrievably delete, but rather remove, your prose to a holding area. Since you can click the Pastepot anywhere, you can use it and the Scissors to move blocks of text from one spot to any other.

The *Camera* is the copying icon. Click it and the pointer turns into a camera. You drag it across a block of prose and release. It will look like nothing has happened. But if you now use the Pastepot icon, you can paste in the prose you selected with the camera.

The remaining two icons are brushes. The *Alignment Brush* is a broad roller, and lets you change text format. You click the icon, select the area to reformat, then choose your new format, for example, double-space instead of single-space. The *Style Brush* looks like a paintbrush, and lets you select a type style from among plain, boldface, italic, underline, superscript, and subscript. Again, you click the icon, select the prose, and choose the new style. After it appears, you click back to your former icon.

Textcraft can carry out string searches, that is, hunts for particular words or phrases. It will also instantly replace one phrase with another of your choosing, very helpful if, for instance, you are writing a report on the Colombian eruption and realize you have throughout spelled *Nevado del Ruiz* as *Nevada del Ruiz,* or, for that matter, *Colombia* as *Columbia.*

This word processor has a final feature that is quite distinctive. It comes with six ready-made forms for business letters, résumés, title pages of term papers, memoranda, technical reports, and business reports. These forms are a beginning, not an end. You can use them as they are or revise them as you like.

Textcraft has virtues, but also, for an Amiga program, surprising limitations. The prerelease version had neither fonts nor different type sizes, a clear indication that the software is ignoring the wealth. Even the notepad has these features. In addition, the software lacks the modestly heroic Undo command, which can rescue deleted prose and save you much time and agony. Finally, its editing procedure is inelegant. There's simply no reason for you to be clicking icons all the time to get new pointers for every different job. One pointer could easily select text for all. You could then pick a command, watch it executed, and continue writing at once, without clicking back into Pencil again.

Unless it's revised and enhanced, *Textcraft* will not be the principal word processor for the Amiga. The program is disappointing, like a world traveler who returns with nothing but tourist gimcracks and tales of the heat. *Textcraft* is serviceable, but for a complete word processor, you may want to turn to *Enable/Write*.

Enable/Write, from The Software Group, of Ballston Lake, New York, looks to be a superb piece of work. It will have every attribute of *Textcraft* except the forms. Moreover, the company says, it will offer different fonts and type sizes, automatic footnoting, automatic indexing and table of contents, scrolling in half- or full-page increments, and a built-in calculator, a very handy extra. *Enable/Write* will do search-and-replace with "wild card matching," that is, with the capacity to search out parts of words, so that if you typed in *Amiga*, it would pick up not just *Amiga*, but *Amiga's* and *Amigas*. It will also have a command to transpose characters so that if you accidentally type *shotr*, for instance, you can place the cursor after the *r*, issue the instruction, and watch the two letters instantly reverse. Finally, it will offer a multiple-column copy-and-move capacity to help you format pages for newsletters. There's not too much more you can ask of a word processor.

Writing Accessories

Word processors are not the only software for writers. There are several other kinds, and if they are not yet available for the Amiga, they probably will be soon.

Outline processors. Outline processors help organize rough drafts. You type in topics that come to mind, notes, citations, whatever seems relevant, and the program helps put it all in order. Of course, this software is useful mainly if you are in the habit of outlining in the first place.

Font programs. Some programs consist of nothing but fonts you can load into your word processor. These can dramatically extend the esthetic range of your work. Fonts are not mere gingerbread. They impart a tone to your prose. The right font can make a business report seem more authoritative, a brochure more futuristic, a newsletter more distinctive. Moreover, anyone who spends much time in front of a video screen will understand the importance of pleasant text. It's the difference between overlooking a park and a vacant lot.

Spelling checkers. A spelling checker examines each word you type, compares it against the words in its dictionary, and flags it if it isn't recognized. It thus catches not just ordinary misspellings, but typos as well, though it won't notice mistakes which form other legitimate words, like *affect* for *effect* or *strobe* for *strove*. Proper nouns *(Abu Dhabi)* and rare words *(caoutchouc)* may be absent from the program's dictionary, in which case you can usually add them. A good dictionary can have as many as 50,000 words.

Layout programs. Layout programs are useful for newsletters and other small publications. They let you arrange copy, headlines, and pictures on the page. Most word processors have a crude layout capacity, letting you array prose on the page in a certain way. But few of them allow you to do such things as setting prose into columns or turning a headline on end. If you want to use the Amiga to produce a publication, particularly with a laser printer, you may find a layout program very handy.

Boilerplate programs. Some professionals, like lawyers, come in contact with boilerplate all the time. They deal with documents like pleadings or standard contracts which have a certain basic form, but which normally require alteration to fit the circumstances. Boilerplate programs provide such forms.

CHAPTER
TWELVE

Indeed, all of us require forms at certain times, and the ready-
mades of *Textcraft* constitute an elementary boilerplate
capacity.

Word processing is perhaps the most common computer
application of all. It is a great aid to most people, and professional authors are turning to it at a steady clip. Journalists
use it constantly, and writers of science fiction have embraced
it en masse. No matter what your needs, this software will
likely loom up along the road at some point or other.

Spreadsheets

In 1978, Dan Bricklin had an idea. Why not write a program to do financial forecasting? He was an ex-programmer attending Harvard Business School, and he thought it might be useful in real estate. He took the idea to a professor, who laughed at it. The notions students had. But Bricklin was determined, so the professor put him in touch with Daniel Fylstra, a former student who had researched the market for similar fluff.

Fylstra liked the concept and passed it on to Bob Frankston, a math prodigy interested in computers since he was 13. Frankston and Bricklin soon founded a company, and over the snowy winter Frankston labored on the program at night in an attic. By spring it was ready. They called it *VisiCalc*. It was a spreadsheet. Nothing like it had ever been seen before, on mainframe or micro.

Fylstra took the product to Apple Computer, Inc. Executives looked at it politely, and some expressed the opinion that it was simply a checkbook balancing program. But when released in October, 1979, *VisiCalc* proved an instant success. Fylstra first suggested a price of $100, but it sold so quickly that he raised it to $150, and then even higher. Businesses were clambering over each other to get the software. By 1981, it was selling 12,000 copies a month. And since for the first year it ran only on the Apple II, it spurred sales of that computer and opened many doors for it into the business world.

What is a spreadsheet? Why were business people so anxious to get one?

A spreadsheet is a table that does calculations. It has the shape of a grid, like the mileage chart on a road map. It can therefore replicate budgets, accounts receivable, balance sheets, and almost any other financial table. You can enter figures directly from the table on the page to the table on the screen, and everything looks the same. But one thing is different. You can now add formulas, and have the table calculate and display results automatically.

It's a big difference.

CHAPTER
THIRTEEN

Let's look more closely at a spreadsheet matrix. Like any other grid, it has a series of adjacent vertical towers—columns—and horizontal layers—rows. Normally, each column has a letter at its top, and each row has a number to its left. These letters and numbers give names to the columns and rows.

Each column intersects each row in a flattish rectangle called a cell. Cells are the building blocks of a spreadsheet. They have addresses, or cell names, made up of their row and column coordinates, such as C3 or W51. Cells hold the contents of a spreadsheet.

Since you need to place information in specific cells, you must have a way of selecting them. You use a cursor. In spreadsheets, a cursor is a brick of light or darkness that fills the cell and opens it for data entry. Cursor movement is easy with the mouse, but on older computers it entailed endless little treks and was not a source of joy.

Cells can contain labels, that is, words. Labels set up the framework for your spreadsheet. Suppose, for instance, that you are making a table of month-by-month household expenses for the past year. You have two variables: kind of expense and month. You can therefore begin by typing in labels for the kind of expense down the left, and for month of the year across the top. Each will intersect the other only once, and you will have cells for, say, Rent in August and Electricity in May.

Cells can also contain values, that is, numbers. Values form the meat of a spreadsheet. In our household expense table, you would enter dollar amounts at such intersections as Rent in August, and these values would fill the bulk of the grid.

So far, we have an ordinary table. But now we introduce the formulas and transform everything. Like a label or value, a formula can be entered into a cell, and it enables the value of one cell to depend on that of another, or several others. For instance, suppose you wanted to include monthly totals in your budget. You could enter an addition formula beneath each column of figures, and the spreadsheet would calculate the sum automatically. And if you went back and changed the amount of any of the expenses, the total at the bottom would instantly change to reflect it. This feature turns a spreadsheet from a mere record into a speculative tool.

A table with only a few cells in each direction would not need much computer assistance. But some tables can be enormous. Many businesses, for instance, have large budgets with hundreds of categories of expense. To accommodate them, spreadsheets are also huge. In fact, they are always much larger than the display on the screen. The screen acts like a window onto a vast document below. To gain access to the whole record, you can scroll that document up, down, or across the window, much as turning a knob will scroll a microfilm. The size of spreadsheets not only makes possible mammoth tables, but also lets you put several related budgets on the same sheet for cross-referencing.

It can all get remarkably intricate. Imagine that your company has a budget 50 columns wide and 100 rows deep, and you are planning your expenses for next year. Each outlay affects the bottom line, of course, but may also affect many other figures in this 5000-cell document—subtotals, averages, percentages, as well as perhaps other outlays and the calculations that depend on them. You will, of course, want to play around with the expenses to see which can be most satisfactorily reduced or increased. If you want to cut the amount in cell AF133, for example, and don't have a spreadsheet, it may take a lot of time to determine all the ramifications of this move. Indeed, the consequences could well be so complex that, for purposes of inquiry, calculation would not be worth the effort. With a spreadsheet, however, you can determine them at once, by pressing a few keys. Spreadsheets can thus make financial planning faster, cheaper, easier, more flexible, and more exact.

And not just financial planning. Spreadsheets can perform a multitude of tasks, probably more than people have yet dreamed up. They are not only useful for altering projections, but also for keeping records that change very rapidly, like batting averages, or for making tabular computations of some complexity, like statistics in certain fields of psychology. As an instant, multidimensional adding machine, however, the spreadsheet still finds its major applications in business.

A spreadsheet program does require that you devise your own table. The effort may take a little time, and sometimes your design will be less than optimal. Some software companies offer templates, predesigned spreadsheets for specific tasks, with all the labels, formulas, and special information you need. Templates work together with spreadsheet programs and can be very useful. A tax preparation program, for instance, may contain the forms you require as well as the latest tax tables and the capacity to let you see at once how various financial maneuvers will affect your tax.

Once you have a spreadsheet in final form, you may want a hardcopy of it. But how do you print out a document that's 20 columns across if only 8 columns fit on a page? It seems an awkward situation. With other computers, you either print in segments and paste them together or buy a sideways printer program, which directs the printer to turn the document on end and print it vertically. But the Amiga comes with a sideways printer program free. It's in *Preferences*, on its third screen. You open Preferences, then click Change Printer and Graphic Select to leaf down there. Under the heading Aspect, you click Vertical. When you print out, the top of the spreadsheet will line up along one side of the paper, and you will have a more manageable document.

Spreadsheets, like word processors, are one of the major software applications, and they have tamed computation in a way their predecessors, the electronic calculators, could scarcely approach.

In general, a spreadsheet should be powerful enough for your needs, yet easy to use. There are several qualities to look for when shopping for one:

Size. The program should be big enough to handle every chore you foresee for it. Most spreadsheets are substantial indeed, and your major limitation will not usually be the software. It will be RAM. If you have 256K of RAM, you may not be able to use all the 16,002 cells in a garden-variety 254 × 63 spreadsheet. In addition, as you approach satiation, operations will take longer and longer, and you will almost hear the computer groaning under the load.

Speed. The speed at which a spreadsheet calculates is sometimes hard to assess, yet it becomes very important the larger your table becomes. The most powerful spreadsheets will minimize the finger tapping.

Formatting. A good spreadsheet will contain a number of special formatting features. It will let you expand or shrink columns to fit their roles. For instance, a column listing the names of customers should be wider than one that lists dates. The spreadsheet should also allow you to express numbers as integers, decimals, or dollar amounts, and should make it easy to insert blank lines or columns, label features, and move items about.

Windows. Many spreadsheets will let you break the screen into two or more parts—windows—so that you can examine different parts of the spreadsheet at one time. This feature is particularly useful for large spreadsheets or for related ones on the same grid.

Automatic repeat. Often you have to enter the same name, figure, or formula in a number of different cells. Instead of typing in each one, you should be able to issue a command and have the computer enter them for you.

Relative cell references. Formulas must refer to other cells, for they operate on cell contents. The program can structure these references in two ways. One is *absolute cell reference*. It can require the exact name of each cell, such as AG135. The other, the more flexible, is *relative cell reference*. Relative cell reference indicates cells by means of directions from the cell with the formula. Why is this feature useful? Suppose you have 24 columns of numbers, each 50 cells high, and you want to add each column up. With absolute cell reference, you would have to enter a new formula at the bottom of each column, since the names of the cells to be added will change each time. With relative cell reference, however, you can enter one formula and copy it right across the row. You move the formula from the first row, where it refers to "the 50 numbers above," to the second row, where it still refers to "the 50 numbers above." Since the formula remains the same, you save time and sidestep ennui.

Preset formulas. Most spreadsheets come with numerous formulas already configured for your use. They may include mathematical formulas such as logarithms, statistical formulas such as standard deviations, financial formulas such as for compound interest, logical formulas such as IF-THEN, and trigonometric formulas such as sine and cotangent. The number and utility of these formulas is one index of the program's power.

Compatibility with other programs. Often you'll want to move the contents of a spreadsheet into a word processing document to show in a report or into a business graphics program to generate a graph. A spreadsheet compatible with other such software, like *Enable/Calc*, makes these transfers

CHAPTER
THIRTEEN

smooth. (Spreadsheets sometimes come prepacked with sibling programs, like the famed Lotus *1-2-3* for the IBM PC. Such packages are called *integrated software* and fall into a special category.)

Good documentation. Spreadsheets aren't hard to learn, but they aren't *Pac-Man* either. A spreadsheet should come with lucid documentation to launch you onto the gently rolling waters of the spreadsheet. It should also have a reference section that's clear and comprehensive.

Protection. Certain spreadsheets will let you hide the contents of specified cells, so they appear blank on the screen as you work. Normally, you use a password to conceal or reveal these cells.

Multitasking. Some Amiga spreadsheets, like *CalCraft*, are making good use of multitasking. It's the kind of feature that lifts the Amiga above the flock.

CalCraft, from Synapse Software of Richmond, California, was one of the first spreadsheets available for the Amiga. At the time this book was being written, late 1985, *CalCraft* was to be a 256 × 256 program which used multitasking to display up to four spreadsheets on the screen at once. Moreover, the spreadsheets could be linked. That is, in a business "what if" situation with each spreadsheet representing a different scenario, you could change a figure in one and it would change in all four, allowing instant comparison. The spreadsheets could be as large as the screen or as small as 2 × 2, the definitional limit. *CalCraft* was also to have gadgets for most of the common formatting operations, such as rendering numbers in dollar or decimal format, and in general to make full use of pull-down menus and the mouse interface.

Spreadsheet Accessories

The Amiga will attract numerous templates, especially once certain spreadsheets establish themselves as standards. The following are often important aids to spreadsheet work:

• Tax programs
• Financial analysis programs
• Home finance programs
• Accounting programs

One of the best-known and most popular small-business accounting programs is *Rags to Riches*, from Chang Labs of

San Jose, California. It's not actually a template, since it doesn't run atop another spreadsheet, but rather a specialized spreadsheet, designed for a particular purpose. Chang Labs planned to release its general ledger, accounts receivable, and accounts payable software soon after the Amiga appeared, and its sales register program shortly after that.

Spreadsheets are dynamic software. Press a button and their rows and columns can flicker all over with computational changes. Indeed, they can even be considered very high level languages, since each cell can embody enough formulas on top of formulas to constitute a small program in itself. In contrast, the third important type of software is more static, more like an electronic archives. It is the database.

Databases

Whenever you get a piece of junk mail, you know your name and address are in the data bank of a computer somewhere. Giant machines keep track of our credit ratings, and government mainframes reportedly hold extensive records of our lives. They also contain massive quantities of data on military, economic, academic, and other affairs. As everyone knows, computers store information.

The Amiga can, too. All it needs is a program called a *database.*

Of course, a database does not just store information. Piles of data are worthless without some quick way to get at the facts you want. Imagine a library without a card catalog or an encyclopedia in random order. They would both abound with information, but the chaos would render them inaccessible. A database must therefore organize the information it holds.

Even so, an organized database alone is little different from a file cabinet. But a database has electronic powers. Like a word processor or a spreadsheet, it can direct the computer to scan its contents and act on them immediately. With a large bank of data, such a program can thus sort and retrieve information by the criteria you select. That is, a database can perform instant research.

Instant research means informational muscle. It gives you lightning control over inventories, personnel files, invoices, and many other business records. It lets you check patterns in your daily exercise, peruse collections that have grown past human memory, and inspect relationships in your genealogy. Because you can sort through this information so quickly, you get what you want in moments. For instance, if you are a cook, you might maintain a database of recipes. If you came home one day to leftover mushrooms and chicken and wanted to make a meal of them, you could simply search the database by ingredients, and it would flash the choices. The alternative, paging through cookbooks, is no alternative at all.

The larger the database, the greater the benefit from instant research. Thus, a hard disk system will let you maintain a much more powerful database than floppy disks. And a mainframe can hold the largest databases of all. Into these can go reports, newspaper and magazine articles, judicial opinions, movie reviews, and documents of all kinds. For a small fee, you can tap into them with a modem, a device which hooks your Amiga up to telephone wires and enables it to communicate with other computers all over the world. Thus, you could, within minutes, check all the references to Antarctica in the past two years of the New York *Times* and display them on your screen. This kind of database resembles a card catalog as a spacecraft resembles a donkey cart.

Database programs for the Amiga, though not so huge, can still be very useful. Like the spreadsheet, they require you to create a structure for them. The process of using a database can be broken down into four steps.

Formatting. You start by designing a form, which gives structure to your database. Typically, this task entails listing the categories of the data you want to access. For instance, if you wished to compile a database of information on your coin collection, you might want to create such categories as denomination, date, mint mark, condition, price at purchase, and current price.

Data entry. After devising an architecture, you must then type in the information itself. This task is extremely pleasant, like dragging the blocks up to make the Pyramids. Once it's done, however, it's over, except for relatively painless updates. Be sure to make backup copies of your database. Otherwise, you might have to enter the data all over again.

Retrieval. Retrieval is the true fun and glory of a database. With the coin collection, for instance, you could list your silver dollars, your nineteenth-century dimes, your nickels now worth over five dollars, and, with some databases, calculate the percentage increase in value of your coins. Retrieval lets you master the collection, no matter how large it is.

Printing. Sometimes you will want to print out parts of your database, perhaps in a certain order, and the printing faculty lets you arrange your output in a manner pleasing and satisfactory to you.

CHAPTER FOURTEEN

Database Jargon

Like the other major applications, databases have their own peculiar vocabulary. The meanings of the terms below, unfortunately, are not intuitively obvious. Moreover, in their everyday English senses they somewhat overlap. Finally, as so often happens in the personal computer lexicon, some have burst the bounds of strict definition and are spreading out to conquer new territory. It is worth the effort to keep them straight (see Figure 14-1).

An *entry* is a single unit of information. In the coin database, for instance, the date of a particular penny would be an entry, as would its condition or current price.

A *field* is a group of similar entries. In the standard database layout, with titles across the top and lines of data below, fields form columns beneath the titles. Denomination, mint mark, and price at purchase would be fields. (Some people use *field* to mean a single entry. It's an odd usage, since *field* is a collective noun, but you will see it.)

A *record* is the set of entries related to one item, like planets revolving around a sun. In the standard layout, it forms a row across the fields. For each coin, the entries in its fields—mint mark, condition, and so forth—would constitute together the record.

A *file* is your entire database. It is not, however, your database program, which creates many files and stores them on data disks.

These concepts form the framework of almost all databases. The database file is composed of individual entries as the spreadsheet is composed of cells. You can group entries with those of similar type, as a field, and with those having the same reference point, as a record. Using this pattern, you can then search, sort, retrieve, and print, all in a variety of time-saving ways.

Simple and Complex

Most of the databases you're likely to see on personal computers fall into two categories: file managers and true relational databases.

File managers, or file management programs, are the simpler. They are easy to use and relatively inexpensive. However, they are generally limited to list management, and even there are somewhat awkward. While a more complex database

Figure 14-1. Structure of Databases

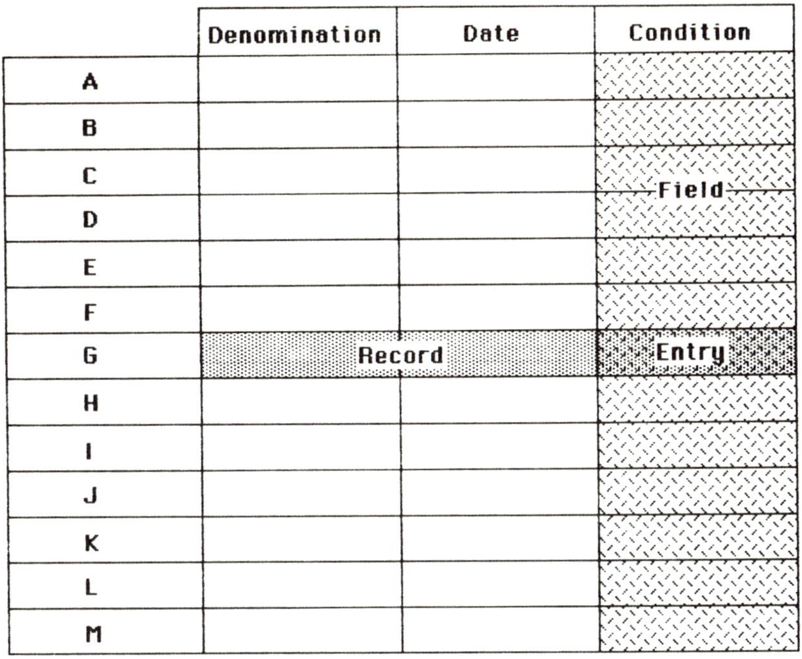

	Denomination	Date	Condition
A			
B			
C			~Field~
D			
E			
F			
G	Record		Entry
H			
I			
J			
K			
L			
M			

will let you access more than one file at a time and sort several fields simultaneously, a file manager normally restricts you to one file and, often, to sorting one field at a time. Moreover, while the more powerful databases may allow extensive calculations, so that certain fields can even depend mathematically on others in the manner of a spreadsheet, file managers have a much more limited capacity for computation.

A true *relational database* is more complete. By definition, it allows at least these five major operations: adding records, deleting records, searching records, searching fields, and joining records from two files into one new file.

The first two are self-explanatory. Searching records, as we've seen, lets you pluck them out by specific criteria, for instance, all nickels minted before 1930. You can also search fields, hence, records and fields, simultaneously. For example, if your database held a customer list, you could instantly obtain the address and phone number of customer Stephen D'Amato without getting the rest of the record on him.

CHAPTER
FOURTEEN

A good relational database might search by at least 20 different criteria, including range of entries (for example, everyone from 25 to 30 years old), parts of entries (everyone with a last name ending in *-son*), OR functions (everyone with a degree in biology *or* art history), and AND functions (everyone with degrees in both biology *and* art history).

The fifth operation, joining files, simply combines smaller files into larger ones. It can be quite useful, but it also usually takes the computer a long time to complete, as much as several hours with a very large file.

Of course, a database is not judged solely on these qualities. It should handle a large amount of data, say, 1M to 5M or more, with many fields, themselves ample. It should also be able to sort several fields at once. (A sort is different from a search. A sort rearranges the order of lists, while a search tracks down records by criteria and displays them.) It should also have computational capacities and password protection for sensitive information.

And it should have lucid documentation. A database can be elaborate, and the manual must make it clear to you. Often, database manuals are very large, and such girth is commendable, as it is better to explain things fully than to omit explanations on the grounds that they might bore the user. But a decent manual will also commence with a brief overview of the chapters so that you don't start wading in with no sense of how deep the water gets or when it will end. Online tutorials are also very welcome.

Informational Databases

The normal database, like the spreadsheet, comes empty and ready for you to load with information. However, some companies sell databases with many or all the blanks filled in. These programs are computerized reference works, and their range is large. There are programs with recipes, maps, horoscopes, astronomical charts which display the sky on any given night, and many more. If you find such a compendium benefits from computer power, the software may be useful to you. But if the program gives you no more capacity than a book, you are probably better off buying the book.

Integration and Emulation

This chapter title sounds as if it were taken from a sociology text—one of those enormously entertaining adventures into abstraction. In fact, it is an attempt to deal in one chunk with software that goes beyond the model of one program for one specific computer. Both integration and emulation greatly increase the range of the Amiga, the one by providing a set of programs which can interact with each other, the other by providing a pipeline to the wider software world. Integration is the packaging of two or more programs which do different things, but which nonetheless communicate with each other. Emulation is the capacity to run software written for different machines entirely.

Integrated Software

The word processors, spreadsheets, and databases that we have looked at so far each perform only one kind of task. A word processing program handles text, but cannot find co-tangents. A spreadsheet does computations, but cannot move paragraphs around. However, frequently you may want to combine such powers. For instance, a good business report may require spreadsheet figures and graphs in addition to word processing. For that, you want integrated software. Programmers began developing such packages with the advent of 16-bit computers like the IBM PC, and the software is becoming available for the Amiga at a very rapid clip. Integrated software must be approached with some caution, however, for it has both special virtues and potential drawbacks.

A traditional benefit has been the common user interface, that is, the standardized commands across the programs. For instance, if the instruction to delete is the same in the word processor as in the spreadsheet, all the programs are easier to learn. Integrated software packages like Lotus *1-2-3* have thus appealed to busy professionals, who don't want to waste valuable time puzzling over software. However, the Amiga makes all programs more or less easy to learn. Since, in addition, all Amiga programs share the same basic command structure, this boon is divested of meaning.

The second traditional advantage has been speedy transfer of information back and forth among the programs. If you want a spreadsheet to appear in a letter you are writing, for instance, you simply shift it over to the word processing program. If you want an instant graph of the spreadsheet, you so indicate to the business graphics program.

The Amiga's multitasking should greatly enhance this capacity. Not only will you be able to transfer material quickly and easily, but you'll be able to see both programs at once. Moreover, multitasking also enables Amiga integrated software to run not just a word processor and spreadsheet at once, but also two or more word processors. You should thus be able to shift information fluidly from one report to another.

However, buying integrated software is a little like buying prewrapped bags of fruit. You take the good along with the bad. Instead of selecting a word processor from one company and a database from another, you must accept all your programs from one source. And for an integrated package to be good, each of its parts has to be good.

This concern is especially important with the Amiga, since its multitasking lets you run any two programs together. If you buy a good word processor, spreadsheet, and business graphics program from different companies, you can still run them at once. The only thing missing is the cut-and-paste capacity, and even that should be easy to provide.

Perhaps because multitasking so easily improves the general caliber of integration, a number of integrated packages appeared for the Amiga very fast. Integrated software is often the last kind to come out, and the emergence of these programs is an interesting phenomenon indeed. One of the first packets expected, *Enable,* was delayed because of renewed negotiations with Commodore about its contents, but at least two others were quickly available: *VIP Professional* and *Maximillian.*

VIP Professional comes from VIP Technologies of Santa Barbara, California. It claims total fidelity to the standard of the renowned Lotus *1-2-3.* The Lotus product is one of the great success stories in modern business, and it pervades Fortune 500 offices. But it's expensive, selling for as much as $500. *VIP Professional* was to cost $200. In addition to providing the same spreadsheet, database, and business graphics as *1-2-3*, as well as the same features and commands, *VIP Professional* offered use of the mouse and pull-down menus. In addition, the company states that the files created on *VIP Professional* can be used on Lotus *1-2-3* itself.

Maximillian, from Tardis Software of Pebble Beach, California, comprises word processor, spreadsheet, business graphics, and communications program. The company also offers its *Maxi+* upgrades for each function to help you customize the package. For instance, if you were satisfied with the word processor, but wanted a more powerful spreadsheet, you could purchase *MaxiCalc+* and fit it right into the integrated program. Again, *Maximillian* was intended to sell for around $200.

You should be aware that some people are predicting the death of integrated software. The Amiga may kill it. If it can shift data easily back and forth among completely different programs, there would seem little reason to buy integrated software at all, unless it came at a bargain rate. And in that case, you are just ordering in bulk.

Emulation

Prior to the Amiga's introduction on July 23, 1985, it was common knowledge that it would emulate the IBM PC by hardware. The device even had a name—the Trump Card. At the personal computer level, hardware has been the traditional means of emulation. Companies put two or more CPUs inside one computer, and thereby expand the range of software it runs. The Commodore 128, for instance, has both a 6502 chip like the Commodore 64 and a Z80 like CP/M machines. At the Amiga's introduction, however, spectators at Lincoln Center saw it emulate with a software program, *The Transformer.* There was general amazement.

Emulation by software is common on mainframes, whose great capacity makes it easy. One man who had had experience with mainframe software emulation was Bill Teal of tiny Simile Research, Inc., in New Jersey, and he thought he could do it with the Amiga, too. Teal approached Commodore with the idea and the company told him to make the attempt.

CHAPTER
FIFTEEN

As his success grew apparent, Commodore abandoned plans for the hardware unit and concentrated solely on the software. However, the initial commitment to hardware, plus the difficulty of software emulation, plus Commodore's poker face, fooled almost everyone into thinking the company was making hardware.

How does a software emulator like *The Transformer* work? Well, it mimics the CPU. That is, it reads a command written for the IBM PC's 8086, translates it into Amiga signals, has the Amiga's 68000 and its special chips execute it, and returns for the next instruction. This procedure takes quite a bit more time than going directly through a CPU. Hence, if the Amiga and the IBM PC both worked at the same speed, emulation would be a sluggish business indeed. In fact, the Amiga's 68000's speed of 7.18 megahertz clearly outstrips the IBM PC's 4 megahertz. Even so, by itself, it's not enough. But the ever-helpful Agnes, Daphne, and Portia boost the Amiga to even greater speed, and it is they who ultimately enable the Amiga to carry out all the extra steps in time.

To use the $99 *Transformer* you insert the 3-1/2-inch disk into the Amiga and soon see the MS-DOS screen, which presents various menu offerings. You then insert either another 3-1/2-inch disk into the Amiga's internal drive, or a 5-1/4-inch disk into an external drive. At this point, the Amiga essentially loses its identity. It becomes an IBM PC. In exchange for running PC software, you forfeit the Amiga's graphics, audio, multitasking, and other bounties.

The Transformer does not give you a 100 percent complete IBM PC, at least not yet. Its first version was incompatible with programs requiring the IBM graphics upgrade card, though its second version, due out before 1986, was to fix this problem. In general, Commodore has not specified how compatible *The Transformer* will be, beyond saying that it will work with the 25 bestselling PC programs. That's a lot, and for most people compatibility should not be a serious concern.

How fast is *The Transformer*? It's the key question. Currently, it seems to run IBM software at around 60 percent of speed. Its disk access is about the same as the IBM's, but certain other features like graphics are about half as fast. If you want to emulate word processing on the IBM PC, you shouldn't notice much difference, since this application doesn't depend on high velocity. On the other hand, if you plan to use large spreadsheets and do a great deal of calculation, the Amiga will bog down quite a bit.

Commodore is offering a $200 hardware accelerator, which should perk up even these applications. It plugs into the expansion bus on the right side of the Amiga, and Commodore says it thinks this device will enable the Amiga to equal or even exceed the speed of the IBM PC on most operations, including intense calculation.

Integration and emulation are horizon techniques. They aim to reach far out and bring back great possibilities to your doorstep. Or, rather, to one of your doorsteps. The multi-dimensional Amiga has several, each opening onto new worlds, new horizons, rather like an Escher print. Graphics and audio are two such worlds, and where they overlap, you find the most playful application of all.

Games

In 1975 and 1976, the forest primeval of the personal computer industry, one kind of application dominated all others: games. The hobbyists who developed the machine wanted to have fun with it, and game software turned the computer into a fount of recreation. And the power and fascination of such diversions struck society with force a few years later, when videogames appeared everywhere from arcades to ice cream parlors, and a multimillion dollar industry sprang up around them.

Game programs remain a hot-selling application. They somewhat resemble conventional games like Monopoly, but with certain notable differences. For one, they give immediate feedback—crackle and flash to respond to your every move. For another, they generally let you play alone, not solitaire-style but in competition against the computer itself. In *Skyfox,* for instance, you vie against the program, not another person. This quality means that you can play a computer game whenever you want and for as long as you want, whether other people are available or not.

The Amiga was originally designed as a game machine, and it retains a tremendous talent in this field. Its speed, graphics, and audio permit games unimaginable on other computers, even in the arcade. Its speed allows quicksilver animation, while its graphics leads to brilliant simulation, and its audio creates sounds so rich and engaging that they make the beeps and whistles of other games seem quaint. The Amiga's voice capacity alone should transform computer games.

There are many different kinds of games, but they can generally be placed into four categories, according to their primary thrust:

Arcade games. Arcade games test manual dexterity, and normally come with sparkling graphics and nonstop action. These affairs often have a paranoid martial air—you've to get Them before They can get you—and no one has ever claimed they ennoble the mind. However, they can be captivating, and some of them demand much more strategic thought than most people realize. And since the software comes without the voracious coin slot, owning it can save you a great deal of money. Almost all successful video-parlor games have been converted to run on personal computers, but most forfeit screen resolution in the transition and thus have never won the hearts of arcade purists. It will be interesting to see if the Amiga mutes this complaint.

Simulations. Simulations reproduce lifelike situations on the screen, the more precisely the better. For instance, flight simulators on larger computers teach pilots how to land, and on the Amiga can give you the experience of soaring over the countryside. Another simulation, *MacSlots* on the Macintosh, replicates the face of a slot machine so well you can almost feel the chips in your hand. The Amiga's audiovisual abilities are ideal for simulation and should lead to the most realistic games ever seen on personal computers.

Adventure games. Adventure games focus on text rather than graphics, and challenge you to solve mysterious puzzles or negotiate strange worlds. They are like detective novels, but instead of watching the protagonist figure out clues, you struggle with them yourself.

Strategic games. Most games involve strategy, but some emphasize it so strongly that they deserve a category of their own. Chess programs, for instance, are highly strategic, as are good poker programs. There are also global strategy games, where you pretend you are master of America or Russia and attempt to achieve some political feat.

Let's first look at some of the games out for the Amiga, and some of the others that may be adapted in the future. It is perhaps perilous to base descriptions of these games on pre-Amiga versions, but in most cases the framework will remain the same, even if the exterior blazes.

Arcade Games

Several arcade games were due around launch, including four from the eminent game maker Electronic Arts of Menlo Park, California. One, *Arcticfox,* puts you at the helm of a supertank in the frozen north. Another, *Marble Madness,* is a well-known video parlor game in which marbles race down chutes afflicted with hazards like ice and acid. The other two, *Skyfox* and *One-*

on-One, merit more extended looks, for they are representative of broad classes of software.

Skyfox is a classic jet fighter game. You sit in the cockpit of a flying death machine, a twenty-second-century super-technological torpedo like that piloted by Clint Eastwood in the film *Firefox*. It has a rapid-fire laser cannon, heat-seeking and radar-guided missiles, a special deflection shield, and, through links to the computer back at base, tactical maps, co-ordinate layouts, autopilot, and numerous other instruments to aid you in your task.

What is that task? Well, a retinue of loathsome motherships has just landed, and you are being sent out to protect the Federation from destruction by their tanks and jets. It's not a pleasant job, for the enemy is ruthless, remorseless, and apparently endless. Yet you can keep from being over-whelmed, at least while you're learning, by setting their aggressiveness at five different levels, and playing against 15 different combinations of their tanks and planes. You can also enjoy the wild and exhilarating sense of flight.

For *Skyfox* is a game filled with action, and one of its highlights, even on the Commodore 64, is its flight simulation. From your seat in the cockpit, you can see the instrument panel, the windows in its nose, and through them, tanks, clouds, planes, mountains, and sky. You hurtle forward, and the ground races up under you, turning as you turn and reced-ing as you kite up for an aerial view of the world. *Skyfox* is essentially a flight simulator combined with an extraterrestrial combat game, and it has the thrills of both.

The sports action game is a very different type of arcade game, and *One-on-One*, also from Electronic Arts, is perhaps the most famous example of it. The program offers a match-up between two of the reigning kings of basketball: Julius Erving, better known as Dr. J, and Larry Bird. Like kids on a play-ground, these athletes face off on the half court. You control one with a joystick, and play against the Amiga or a friend who controls the other.

Erving and Bird are not just tags hung on stock figures. The programmer consulted with both of them as he designed the game, and as a result each onscreen player resembles the real-life superstar. Erving can float and twist through the air for eternal seconds while Bird is a tough defender, a strong re-bounder, and a sharp outside shooter.

You can choose from four levels of difficulty: park and rec, varsity, college, and pro. As you progress up the ranks, the referee calls more fouls and the computer plays tighter defense. Throughout, you follow regular basketball rules, and the program recognizes three-pointers and gives you foul shots.

The court has a 24-second clock and a glass backboard. Sound effects include the *thunk* of the dribbled ball and the roar of the crowd when you score a basket. If you try a slam dunk, you may shatter the backboard. In that case, a maintenance man emerges to sweep up the glass and mumble something you probably don't want to understand.

Simulations

All games are simulations, to some extent, and few are solely simulations. Rather, most employ some simulation, as *Skyfox* does. This classification thus occupies a shadowy, twilight sort of realm, somewhere between an aspect of other categories and a full-blown category in its own right. Yet it has proved very useful in describing games, particularly those which specialize in either the audiovisual sense of you-are-there, or the modeling of a complex societal activity.

MacSlots is perhaps as pure an example of the audiovisual type as you'll see. It's a computer slot machine. You insert your coins, pull the lever, and await your fate. It involved no action or hand/eye coordination, and so is not an arcade game. It has no text, and is not an adventure game. And it certainly requires no strategy. Yet it has its own peculiar fascination, for it renders the slot-machine experience with eerie fidelity. The wheels click into place one by one. The knob on the lever has a tiny gleam to it. When you win, "coins" clank out onto the tray. The program even offers you drinks. As a result, this software seems to hypnotize people, and they play it for hours on end—again, much like the real thing.

Another interesting simulation is *Pinball Construction Set*, from Electronic Arts. This software comes with several pinball games ready to play, but, as the name suggests, it also lets you contrive your own. The pinball game itself occupies the left hand of the screen. On the right are game components and icons for commands. The mouse moves the cursor, a hand with a pointing finger, to the components: slingshots, flippers (two sizes), polygons, bumpers, kickers, launchers, a magnet, lanes, rollovers, and knife-edge targets. You point at the object

CHAPTER
SIXTEEN

you want, click, and drag the object over to the pinball game, where you situate it. You will quickly find that it takes practice to invent a game that is both fun and esthetically pleasing.

Once you've built a game, you will eventually need to see how it would work on Jupiter or one of the asteroids. This program makes it easy. You point and click at the World icon, and bring to life the following menu: Gravity, Speed, Kick, and Elasticity. You can increase or decrease any of these qualities. Thus, you can multiply the gravity so much that the ball will drop to the bottom like pig iron, or, indeed, that it won't shoot into play at all. Alternatively, you can make it float through the game like down after a pillow fight.

The second kind of simulation involves replication of intricate human endeavors, usually commercial. For instance, *Millionaire* is a game in which you play the stock market. You study the financial news each week, assess the trajectory of your investments, then buy or sell and move on to the next week. In the end, the program counts your money and tells you how rich you are. This game does not present the stock market to you visually, but rather gives you the factors involved in making investment decisions. It simulates a model rather than an experience.

Adventure Games
Despite the power of simulations to compel our attention, some of the best computer games have no dazzling graphics, stirring sound, or other pyrotechnics. They are called adventure games.

The first adventure game was written on a mainframe computer in the sixties. Since then, many of them have been dull, interactive mazes, the kind laboratory rats would be playing if they could work keyboards. But today there are dozens of adventure games, many significantly better than simple mazes. Some even make effective use of graphics, like Penguin Software's *Transylvania*.

But the premier maker of adventure games is a Cambridge, Massachusetts, company called Infocom, which issued most of its bestsellers for the Amiga shortly after launch. Infocom programs are literary works as much as games and support the company's motto that the graphics are all in your head. For instance, the introduction to the game *Infidel* sets up this scene:

> You slowly awake in your tent, half-senseless with a hangover, and suddenly realize all is quiet outside. Your workers have deserted you. You had handled them tactlessly, feeding them little, paying them less, and making them dig in the dirt on their holy days, and now they've left you to face the scorching desert alone. As you arise, you pray enough supplies remain for you to continue your desperate quest for the lost pyramid. Outside, you hear a plane....

Not exactly lunch in Beverly Hills. And that's just the beginning. The prose sets you down firmly in an exotic scene of abandonment and peril, and you start roaming the desert, looking for fabulous treasure, trying to survive, and meeting much agony. It takes time to make progress through an Infocom game. The program monitors your score and gives you a rating based on how far you get before you die.

Not all Infocom software pits you alone against a hostile world. In some games, you make the acquaintance of other characters and engage in friendly dialogue with them. In *Planetfall*, for instance, you are a bumbling ensign and explore an alien world with the help of a robot named Floyd.

Infocom packages often come with documents inside. *Infidel* includes a map of the Nile River Valley, and *Planetfall* presents you with official papers from the Stellar Patrol of the Third Galactic Union. It's a good idea to read these documents, since they'll help move you through the game.

Other good Infocom adventures are *Zork III*, *Deadline*, and *Enchanter*. To succeed in any of them, it helps to chart out the adventure as you move through it. An accurate map will help you keep track of your discoveries in case you have to start over. You will. Otherwise, it wouldn't be an adventure.

Strategic Games

Games of high strategy have long commanded respect, and great players of chess, bridge, and poker have been lionized as masters. On computers, too, strategic games form the loftiest tier of the genre, and they are in many ways the most intriguing.

Chess is the classic computer strategy game, and the best chess games now available are *Sargon III* and *Psion*. *Sargon III* is a challenging, complete, fully recommended program that has achieved the pinnacle of repute in the field. *Psion* is a newer program for the Macintosh that has many virtues, but perhaps the most notable is that it displays the chessboard in three dimensions. While *Sargon III* gives you a stylized over-

CHAPTER
SIXTEEN

head view, the kind you see in chess columns, *Psion* shows the pieces as if you were there. Good Amiga chess programs will probably do the same.

One of the first strategic games will be *Archon* from Electronic Arts. *Archon* looks like a chess game between wizards and dragons except that when you land on another's square, the resident piece does not automatically succumb. Instead, it fights. This program also has a good reputation and should shine on the Amiga.

The casinos at Las Vegas and Atlantic City have for several years now offered computerized poker machines, where you slip a coin into the slot and win money according to the absolute contents of your hand. More realistic poker software has appeared on personal computers, and one of the best is *Real Poker*. *Real Poker* lets you pull up a chair at a game in a Western saloon, where you play against onscreen individuals with distinctive traits. Only the relative contents of your hand matter here, and you must adjust your betting to the known characteristics of fellow players. Such a program, adapted for the Amiga, could go even further. For instance, your opponent could place his or her bet orally, forcing you to respond to nuances of voice exactly as you do in a real poker game.

Another good strategy game is *Balance of Power*, from Mindscape of Northbrook, Illinois. This game involves the ultimate in strategic facedowns, thermonuclear brinksmanship, and gives you the satisfaction of sitting atop the power structure of the United States or Soviet Union. From there, you manipulate the nations, hotspots, and events of the globe like chess pieces. It's a very pragmatic game. You can take either an offensive stance, destabilizing unfriendly governments, or a defensive one, propping up friendly ones. The program presents you with complex issues of policy and demands hard choices. If your opponent makes a foray into your zone of influence, for instance, you can either issue a Challenge, in which case the world moves one step closer to annihilation, or back down, in which case you lose prestige. It's an engrossing pastime, one you will not quickly tire of.

We've seen that the Amiga can be an electronic typewriter, calculator, file cabinet, and toy. We've also seen how its special attributes can expand and brighten these common computer functions. It's now time to delve into the heart of the attributes. It's time to look at what the Amiga can do with pictures and sound.

PART FOUR

Light
and Sound

Merely in arrangement of colours and texture of plumage this little bird was a gem of the first water.

Alfred Russel Wallace
The Malay Archipelago

Behind the Screen

The CRT appears to create the Amiga's video, but it's really just the front for the real power, which lies in the Amiga itself. The CRT is the tool of the Amiga, its electron gun a swiftly moving paintbrush for the computer. Even the level of resolution depends mainly on the Amiga, and to understand its video at all, we have to get beneath the surface and look at the source of things.

First, however, let's go back a bit and refresh our memories about the basic video concepts. We've seen that color monitors work by spraying a screen coated with phosphor. They have an electron gun—often three of them—which directs a beam of electrons at the screen. The gun can vary the density of electrons in this beam. At one moment it can shoot a lot of electrons, in which case we say it has high intensity. At the next, it can shoot few electrons, giving low intensity.

Since the beam is composed of electrons, it has no color itself. The color arises only when it strikes the screen. The screen has three kinds of phosphor dots, which glow red, green, or blue when hit. The dots respond to the beam's intensity with different levels of luminance. A green dot, for instance, reacts to a high-intensity beam with a bright, whitish green, and to a low-intensity beam with a dark green. The Amiga can fire the gun at 16 intensities; hence, each dot can appear in 16 different shades.

If that were all, the Amiga could generate only 48 colors. But red, green, and blue fuse together to create still other hues. For instance, dark blue and dark red yield violet, while dark blue and bright red create light purple. In fact, each pixel on the screen draws on three dots for its color. Since the Amiga can create 16 different hues of each primary color, and since each hue can mix with any two others to produce a new color, an Amiga pixel is capable of $16 \times 16 \times 16$ colors, or 4096. It's a vast amount. It appears as an almost unbroken spectrum, and gives artists a remarkable color pool.

The Amiga achieves its range in an interesting way, which sheds light on all its graphics capacities. To understand

CHAPTER
SEVENTEEN

it, we have to venture down into the memory edifice and see where it stores its signals for color and how it uses them to build the screen.

The Source of Color

John Donne once wrote, "Why grass is green, or why our blood is red/Are mysteries which none have reach'd into." The Amiga's 4096-color screen is not so elusive. Its colors come from a set of 32 memory registers.

The Amiga screen is bitmapped. That is, each pixel has its own memory location, and the binary contents of that location dictate its color. It's an excellent way to do graphics, for it gives programmers great control over the screen. It resembles the way a dot-matrix printer, by breaking the elements of printed characters down to pins, achieves a versatility impossible in a daisywheel.

But how do we get the pixel memory to indicate the color? What kind of code do we use?

One approach is to give each of the 4096 colors a number and store it in binary. Each pixel address would then hold the number of a color, which would be, in effect, a command to the CRT to shoot the electron gun at a certain combination of intensities. However, you need 12 bits to convey 4096 numbers. That's a byte and a half per pixel, and means this method demands a wide swath of memory. And memory is precious.

The designers of the Amiga took a different tack. Instead, they set up 32 color registers, each 12 bits wide. At this size, each can hold 4096 numbers and hence access any hue in the color pool. Now if instead of directly ordering a color, a pixel address simply orders the color of a register, it will need far less memory space. For instance, suppose pixel address 1 holds a binary 19. The computer will go to register 19 and examine its contents. If it has the code for turquoise, turquoise appears onscreen at pixel 1. If it has the code for black, black appears. Each pixel memory location now needs only 32 different numbers, and it can indicate them with five bits. Hence, this method lops off seven/twelfths of the previous bitmap, a great savings. It's called color indirection.

There's an obvious price for it. Color indirection limits us to 32 colors onscreen at any one time. We can load any color we want into a particular register, and so pick and choose among the 4096, but we cannot get more than 32 at once. Yet 32 is more than most computers allow and should really not hinder your enjoyment of the machine. Moreover, color indirection is not just a space saver. It is also a performer.

Because of color indirection, if you change the hue in one register, you instantly change it everywhere it appears on the screen. It cannot be otherwise, since every pixel that refers to that register must take on the new color. That's a significant power and makes for fast color changes. You can see a fine example of it in Preferences, where you can select one of the four colors that make up the Workbench, then move three sliders—for red, green, and blue—left or right till you get the new color you want. As you move the sliders, you'll see how the different combinations affect the color square and get an idea of the wealth in the pot. And when you finally select the new color, you'll find it changed at once throughout the Workbench.

Color indirection also makes it easy to draw single lines in multicolored segments. You arrange for the paintbrush to refer to one register for, say, two seconds, then to another for two seconds, and so on, so that as you pull it across the screen, it changes hue systematically and leaves a trail of many colors.

Moreover, once you get the colors on the screen, the technique lets you juggle them in rapid sequence. You can arrange to move the contents of register 1 into register 2, and 2 into 3, and so on, like musical chairs, all the way around to moving register 32 into register 1. You can make these wholesale shifts once a second or faster, and the colors on the screen will cycle rapidly. The effect can be stunning. For instance, you can alter the colors of concentric circles so that they seem to be expanding. Or, if you have previously drawn a line with serial colors in the above manner, you can create the impression that each color segment is in motion, traveling down the line. It will remind you of the phi phenomenon, whereby light bulbs in a rectangle flash so as to suggest that light is coursing around it. If you change the Amiga's colors fast enough, they glow, and if you get the entire screen flashing through a color cycle, it looks like a light show and is dazzling.

CHAPTER
SEVENTEEN

The Source of the Picture

It's a good thing to reduce the bits each pixel needs from 12 to 5, but it raises another difficulty. Five is a somewhat awkward number, at least for computer memory. Memory units come in bytes of 8 bits apiece. If each pixel required 4 bits, we could cram 2 into each byte and lose no space. But with 5, we've got 3 bits left over for every byte. It's as though, instead of reducing bits per pixel from 12 to 5, we only reduced it from 12 to 8.

Now, of course, a computer isn't forced to have an integer number of pixels in every byte. For instance, if the Amiga used six bits per pixel, it could conceivably arrange the bytes in sets of four, where bits 1–6 of the first byte would be one pixel, and bits 7–8 plus bits 1–4 of the second byte would be the next pixel, and so on. But it's clumsy. You could write software to do this with five bits per pixel, and it would be even clumsier.

The Amiga's designers came up with an unusual solution to this problem. They took a three-dimensional approach. Imagine, they thought, a bitmap for a 320 × 200 screen that's 320 bits by 200 bits. That's bits—one bit per pixel. Now suppose each bit is the top of a bit tower, 5 bits deep. We then have essentially 5-bit planes overlaying each other. Since a bit tower would have 5 bits, it could refer to one of the 32 color registers. Therefore, each bit tower could represent one pixel.

That's what they did. They stacked the information vertically. Now the bytes themselves lie horizontally. Hence, to get the register number for pixel 1, you go to the first five bytes and look at bit 1 in each of them. The five bit 2's would represent pixel 2. For pixel 9, you go to the second five bytes and look at their bit 1's, and so on. You access five different bytes for every pixel, but you fill each byte completely.

You can see that you get a cubelike structure. The Amiga's bitmap is divided into a series of bit planes, each of which takes up 8K. Thus, if you're in 320 × 200 resolution with 32 colors, you need five planes, or 40K. If you're in 320 × 400, you need twice as many pixels, or 80K. In high resolution, at 640 × 200, you need 64K, and at 640 × 400, you need 128K. But high resolution uses twice the pixels of low, so why not twice 40K and 80K? It's a good question, and we'll see the answer in a moment.

Resolutions

The Amiga actually has six bit planes rather than five. With six bit planes in constant action, the Amiga could display 64 colors at once. But six are simply too many for the Amiga to access in time to get all the signals to the cathode gun. The gun can't be slowed down. It must cover the screen once every 1/60 second, and so the computer is limited to 32 colors.

At high resolution, you have many more pixels than low, and you must again adjust to the uncompromising electron gun. You do so by cutting the number of bit planes back to four. Four bit planes means only 16 different colors onscreen at once. Why? Because a four-bit binary can't refer to all 32 color registers, but only to 16. This fact in turn leads to the memory figures above. Each bit plane takes up 8K, but now we have only four of them instead of five. Four bit planes occupy 32K rather than 40K. But since 640 × 200 is double the height of 320 × 200, it needs two times the number of pixels. That is, it needs a bit plane that's twice as large, or twice 32K, that is, 64K. And 640 × 400, of course, needs twice that sum again, or 128K.

The Amiga also has two interlaced modes, through which it displays pictures 400 pixels high. In a way, they work like interlaced fingers. In the first 1/60 second, the CRT electron gun covers a 320 × 200 or 640 × 200 screen, leaving empty spaces between each line it strikes. In the second 1/60 second, it covers another 320 × 200 or 640 × 200, but it shifts slightly down to fill in the empty lines. It's an easy task for the Amiga's video chip. The phosphor glow from the first display lingers on, and the mind knits the two images into one.

That's the theory, anyway. In practice, the phosphors from the first spraying have started to fade by the time the second one arrives. Hence, the two images don't quite merge. The result is quiver, slight but clearly noticeable. There's no way to avoid it short of reconstructing the monitor so that it shows images faster than 60 times a second. The Macintosh uses this approach, but of course it displays only in black and white.

With everything said so far, you may be wondering about the third resolution mode, hold and modify, which allows you to display all 4096 colors at once. If the Amiga has 32 color registers and six bit planes, how is it possible?

In fact, hold and modify works on a completely different

basis from everything we have discussed so far. Basically, it is a relative rather than absolute system. It defines each pixel in terms of the pixel just before it. Hence, it holds the previous value long enough to modify it and get the new value. Hold and modify uses all six bit planes, but, again, in an unusual way. Bit planes 5 and 6 determine which part of the previous pixel value gets changed. Bits from planes 1 through 4 are then substituted into the prior values.

As you might guess, hold and modify is more complicated than the Amiga's other modes, and will likely be difficult for programmers to work with. It is poorly suited for animation and other shifting images, and will thus probably be used mainly for static pictures. But if you are an artist, that may well be enough.

Playfields

The Amiga's screen is more than just the product of its colors and its resolution levels. Its graphics chips give it special powers. Since they take over much work from the CPU, they allow for faster display, so the line you draw appears at once. But they also confer a structure on the screen and grace it with brilliant prowess in animation.

The first and most obvious element of that structure is the playfield. A *playfield* is essentially an independent screen, the same width as the screen itself, but of variable height. Two playfields are available on the CRT. They constitute another reason for having that sixth bit plane. A playfield uses three bit planes, and, since three bits can refer to eight registers, it can have eight different colors.

Playfields have interesting properties. First, one playfield can have priority over the other so that it lays over it. At the same time, parts of the dominant playfield can be transparent, so you can look through and see what's happening on the playfield beneath. This fact fits playfields well for games. In *Skyfox*, for instance, one playfield, the cockpit, can have transparent spaces through which you view the second playfield, the hostile world around. Both work together to heighten the effect of soaring over countryside.

Sprites

Sprites originated as a hardware solution to the difficulties of animation. They are small objects that move across the playfields. A sprite can be 16 pixels wide, that is, 1/20 of the screen in low resolution. It can also be as tall as the screen. The Amiga offers you eight of them, and you can get more by reusing some on the same screen. Each pixel of a sprite can have one of four colors. It's also possible to attach two sprites to each other, making one sprite with the capacities of two, hence with a range of 16 different colors.

Sprites have several features in common with playfields. First, you can give them a hierarchy so that one will always appear atop another. Indeed, you can have up to seven layers of priority. In addition, you can make one of their colors transparency so that you can see through one sprite onto another. In fact, in some ways you can think of playfields as simply large sprites and vice versa. They have different hardware backgrounds, but they can work in very similar ways.

Animation

The Amiga's talent for animation really brings it alive. A computer screen can sparkle like a handful of gems, but it's still static. Motion gives it past, present, and future, as well as verve and élan, and it can bewitch us.

The Amiga has two animation systems, one for playfields and one for sprites.

The Blitter—the odd-sounding component of the Agnes chip—controls playfield animation and confers noble capacities upon it. First, it works at high speed, always a blessing for animation. It basically transfers images from one place to another. Such an operation means moving an image about in the bitmap, and *Blitter* in fact derives from *bitmapped block transfer*.

Animation on the playfield works like this. A programmer indicates an image on a background. The image and background are saved in memory. The programmer can then tell the Blitter to move the image around as a block. The alternative, constantly redrawing the image against the background, is painstaking and slow. With playfield animation, you can move around several dozen objects, as well as fill spaces quickly and draw lines at an eye-popping one million pixels per second.

CHAPTER
SEVENTEEN

The second kind of animation is sprite animation. It works faster than playfield animation and generally controls the darting about of sprites on the screen. Intriguingly, if you run out of sprites, you can always use the Blitter to set up other independent, spritelike objects, of which there is no limit. Playfield animation is so good and can replicate sprite animation in so many ways that the latter has lost some of its importance.

Both types have a built-in collision detection capacity. The Amiga can tell when two sprites, a sprite and a playfield, or two playfields have bumped into each other. It's a useful feature. In games, objects strike each other all the time, and if the hardware can sense the impact, the software can move on to better things. The game can be made richer and faster. Collision detection also lets you confine roving objects to a prescribed territory.

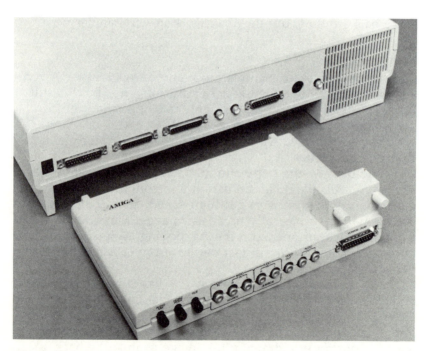

The Genlock Interface

CHAPTER SEVENTEEN

The Genlock Interface

You will undoubtedly hear talk about the genlock interface and wonder what it is. In fact, it's a means of working with external video signals, like those from a VCR, video camera, or even another computer. With a genlock interface, you can read in a video frame, like, say, a picture of Molokai, and use it as a background for graphics on your Amiga. It's a useful way of manipulating images, but it's mainly for professionals, and you are not likely to start playing with it tomorrow.

The Amiga's graphics hardware simply sweeps the field clean. There is nothing else even nearby. But, as with all hardware, it needs software to realize its potential. And programmers aren't shirking their responsibilities here. It's like asking them to dive for rubies.

Graphics Software

G raphics software can turn you into an artist, or at least more of an artist than you are. It can transform the screen into a magic canvas, where lines flow easily, outlines fill at once, and mistakes vanish like they never occurred. It can bring forth a square, rectangle, polygon, circle, or oblong out of the void in one or two seconds. It can magnify the screen so that you paint in scintillas, creating extraordinary detail. In short, a graphics program gives you control over artwork.

That kind of control, that power, is exhilarating, especially if it elevates you from a bumbler to an apparent competent. The individual who has never before drawn for amusement, being discouraged by the wretched product of the effort, may now spend hours at the computer screen, lord of the blank page. Graphics programs are fun and can be fascinating. And the Amiga was born for them.

The graphics programs below will not, of course, make you into the new Vermeer or Delacroix. They can't even bestow talent. But they can help compensate for the void of talent most of us were born with.

Graphicraft
Commodore-Amiga, Inc.
1200 Wilson Drive
West Chester, PA 19380
215-431-9100 ext. 9707
$49.95

Graphicraft was one of the first, simplest, and least expensive graphics programs for the Amiga. At release, it lacked many of the features of a typical Amiga graphics program. Even so, it lets you cruise on air.

Graphics programs come in two slightly different formats. In one, various options are permanently displayed on the screen, as icons, so you can reach them at once. If you want to draw, you click the brush icon and instantly gain that power. This approach is quick and easy to use, but takes up drawing space. *Graphicraft* uses the other format. Instead of permanent onscreen icons, it places everything in pull-down menus. It's slower, but it gives you canvas room.

Graphicraft has the following menus: Project, Edit, Special, Color, Shape, and Brush. As it happens, we can go straight through them, from right to left, and gain a pretty good idea of how this and most other graphics programs work.

The brush is the basic drawing tool. As an artist has several types of brush, so does *Graphicraft*. The Brush menu offers about a dozen brush shapes, including different-sized squares and circles, and dotted brushes, which leave parallel lines behind. If these aren't enough—and they may not be— you can easily create your own brush.

The Shape menu is a potpourri of operating modes. It contains four icons and one verbal command. The Draw option, shown by a wriggling line, is the normal mode and lets you draw freehand. The Straight Line links your starting point to your endpoint by a straight line, no matter where the mouse has wandered in between. It's an automatic straight edge and very handy, as you know if you've ever tried drawing a straight line unassisted. The third mode is the Rectangle. It lets you create and size instant rectangles, another nice power. The fourth mode, Fill, looks like a Baggie half-filled with ink. It allows you to click on any enclosed area and fill it at once with the color of your choice. The fifth and final mode is Text, represented by the command Text. It displays six options. There are two text sizes, and each can appear over or under graphics, or in a whitened area that slashes through them.

The Color menu contains your palette. When you roll it down, it displays the hues in each color register. It also shows three scales, one each for red, green, and blue. To get a new color, you click one of the 32 register colors. Its hue then appears in the color square, and at the same time, the sliders on the scales shift into the positions that generate the color. You can move them back and forth and watch the metamorphosis of the color square. When it's what you want, click OK, and the new tint enters the register. At the same time, anything painted in the old color instantly changes. If you want to preserve your existing colors, make sure you alter a color that hasn't been used.

You can also play with the palette. Suppose you are doing delicate color work and wish one color to shade gradually into another. You'll want the palette to hold the range of hues in between the two. Instead of creating them from scratch, you can get that minispectrum by clicking Range, then two colors on the palette. This act will give you their intermediaries.

The Special menu is aptly named, for it contains the tricks of this software: Magnify, Mirrors, Cycle Draw, and Cycle Color. Each is a pleasure.

Magnify. The Magnify command is a virtual zoom lens. It magnifies small sections of screen so that you can work dot by dot and give your drawings a finesse that friends will attribute to a keen eye and special gifts.

Mirrors. Mirrors lets you mirror the course of your paintbrush so that you can draw two, four, or more symmetrical lines at once. In Mirrors, even gross and thoughtless dabblings have a way of turning into candidates for printout.

Cycle Draw. We've already seen Cycle Draw. It lets you draw in multicolored segments. When you select Cycle Draw, a box appears onscreen with the palette and a timer. You set the timer, which determines how frequently the color will change. You also pick the colors you want. If you click the Range box, then two colors, you'll automatically get all the palette colors in between.

Cycle Colors. We've seen Cycle Colors, too. It makes the onscreen colors change in sequence, from, say, red to blue to silver to green to red, and so on. You can run them through all 32 colors in the palette. This feature also has a timer, and if you set it high, the Amiga will shiver with iridescence.

The Edit menu offers further intriguing powers. First, it has the Undo command. Undo is like a spirit looking over your shoulder, ready to forgive and eliminate any mistake you make. It allows you to take one step backward, to retract completely your very last action. Hence, if you can't get a line exactly right, you can keep Undoing your attempt until it's finally acceptable. Undo also lets you withdraw catastrophic errors. For instance, if you start drawing and forget you are in Fill, the screen will flood with color. Instead of laboriously erasing this mistake, you can simply Undo it.

The Edit menu has other features. It lets you frame certain areas, that is, select them for cutting or copying elsewhere. You can also erase the entire screen, a useful command if you're just playing around. In prerelease, *Graphicraft* had no specific eraser to let you white out in fine detail. But you can always use the paintbrush with white to get the same result.

Graphicraft is a very basic program. *Deluxe Video Construction Set*, from Electronic Arts of Menlo Park, California, is more sophisticated. It uses the faster, onscreen-icon format and has a much greater array of powers than *Graphicraft*. *Aegis Images*, from Aegis Development, is another superior program. It does almost everything *Graphicraft* does, and its extra capacities give a better idea of the Amiga's powers:

Patterns. *Aegis Images* comes with 16 preset patterns, which you can use as fill. For instance, if you wanted to fill a rectangle with a herringbone pattern, you could select the pattern, click the rectangle, and you would have it. This feature lets you give the appearance of delicacy to your work. You can also create your own patterns.

Instant circles. The software lets you create a circle or oblong at once. If you are attempting a human face, for instance, you can start with a basic oval, insert small circles for eyes, add arcs for the eyebrows, and so on.

Grid. The software lets you place a grid over your work to place lines and images more accurately.

Wash. Wash softens the contrast between adjacent colors, creating a watercolor effect.

Gradient Fill and Dithering. These capacities allow you to fill a shape with a range of colors and blend them smoothly together.

Rotate. Rotate turns an image around an imaginary axis running from you through its center.

Enlarge and Shrink. Images can make your image grow or shrink to whatever size you want, a handy feature to have.

Amiga graphics programs not only ease the artistic labor, but speed it up. In moments, you can create effects that might otherwise take hours. And the end result can be a versicolored blazonry.

Using Color

If you've never worked in color before, you may be a bit overwhelmed by the possibilities. Of course, you can splash the Amiga's colors around just for their own sake. It's fun, and some painters have elevated it to a genre. But you can also use them for more interesting effects.

Color can convey distance. The common means of creating this impression include reducing an item's size, placing it behind other objects, and subjecting it to perspective. Color lets you enhance the impression with at least three techniques:

Pallor. Distant colors lack the vibrancy of nearby ones; hence, paler and grayer items seem farther away. If you want a hillside to look miles off, don't paint it electric green.

Receding colors. Even in abstract art, reds, yellows, and browns seem to advance toward you, while greens and blues recede. Hence, landscape painters tend to put brownish hues in the foreground, greens and yellows in the middle distance, and blues and grays far away.

Blue. Blue is not just a receding color, but the typical cast of far-off objects. Sunlight stimulates air molecules to emit this color, so the more distant a sight, the more blue creeps into it. Don't overdo it. It's subtle, and most people are not consciously aware of it.

Color can also convey solidity with shadow. Solid objects obstruct light, so a shadowed typeface, for instance, at once suggests block letters. But what color is a shadow? Until the nineteenth century, most artists used neutral tones like browns and grays, which correspond to our sense of what a shadow should look like and, in fact, suffice. But if you examine a shadow closely enough, you'll see it's a bit more complicated. Sand in shade can actually appear purple next to sand in sunlight. Shadows on pink look greenish. Renoir even painted healthy flesh a bright green, and it was convincing in the context. Again, the effect is subtle, but you can explore it freely on the Amiga since it lets you change colors so easily.

You can eschew shadow and achieve a light, airy feel. The early Impressionists, for instance, filled their canvases with colors of uniform brightness, and it suggested a world full of sunlight, but also one without corporeality. If your work on the Amiga seems to lack body, you may be overusing the brilliant colors.

Programs like *Graphicraft* and *Aegis Images* are the classic graphics software. But they are not the only graphics-oriented programs you will run across. Indeed, there are a great many others.

Animation

The Blitter makes the Amiga a true animation machine. You can create shapes, move them around, change their shapes and colors, and then reprise the entire sequence on the screen. Animation programs are easy enough for anyone to learn, and if you ever watched Saturday morning cartoons as a kid, playing with them may give you a slight sense of levitation.

Aegis Animator
Aegis Development
2210 Wilshire Boulevard, Suite 277
Santa Monica, CA 90403
$139.95 (with *Images*)

Aegis Animator was one of the first animation programs for the Amiga, and it clearly shows what such software can do. It rests on the basic concept of the *tween*. A tween is an automatic, mobile transition from one figure to its successor. For instance, if you move a polygon from the left side of the screen to the right, the tween will play back the shift from start to finish. It's like a tiny movie.

Tweens on the *Aegis Animator* are not limited to simple shifts. They can move objects on complex courses, rotate them around three different axes, expand or shrink them, change their shapes and colors, and move them in front of or behind other objects. A single tween can do all these things, and you can link tweens together to form a longer piece of animation.

The software has further capacities. It permits control over such global features as speed of playback. It also has a storybook mode. Storybook divides the screen into nine equal compartments, where you can cut and paste objects from one animation into another or splice whole animations together.

Aegis Animator has several other ingratiating aspects. It offers onscreen icons as an option, so you can click commands immediately or select them from menus at your pleasure. It accepts detailed pictures from *Aegis Images*, heightening its utility. Its palette contains a continually cycling color, which you can choose with a click of the mouse. And, when the pointer touches a menu item, its color begins to cycle. It's a small thing, but pleasant, and it indicates care. *Aegis Animator* is the kind of program the Amiga was made for.

Letterhead Programs

Letterhead programs let you make letterhead, greeting cards, and other useful designs. The leader in the field is *The Print Shop*, a bestseller from Brøderbund of San Rafael, California, and it was due out for the Amiga soon after launch.

The Print Shop is an easy-going program for enhancing letters and playing with type. In versions for other computers, it helps you make letterhead, banners, signs, and greeting cards. For letterheads or signs, the software offers numerous fonts and such styles as solid, outlined, or three-dimensional. You can thus create several distinct letterheads or signs whose sizes and fonts underscore their messages.

The Print Shop offers two ways to make greeting cards. The first is akin to shopping. You peruse a variety of predesigned cards—such as birthday, season's greetings, valentine, anniversary, or invitation—select one, and fill in the recipient's name. The second approach is more creative. You make your own cards. First, you choose a border, anything from a thick line to a pattern of hearts. Then you pick an illustration. *The Print Shop* comes with scores of them: houses, bells, rabbits, clocks, musical notes, and a Christmas tree. If none pleases you, you can draw your own from scratch. The software allows you to incorporate graphics from other programs into your works and to superimpose letters on the drawing.

The Print Shop frees you from the limitations of the greeting-card rack and lets you send more personal and even more attractive cards. It also saves money and shopping time.

Clip Art

A graphics program, like a spreadsheet or database, is a blank slate. Your ability determines the quality of what you draw. If it is slender, you may want to purchase the work of someone whose isn't. You can buy drawings already on disk. This is called clip art.

Clip art is pleasant stuff. There's nothing complicated about it. It's just a disk full of pictures, usually of everything imaginable—portraits of famous people, animals, skylines, frames, little symbols, and so forth. You can generally move these pictures into your letters and adorn them with illustrations. You can even move them into your own artwork.

Clip art can come in different guises. For instance, one program for the Macintosh lets you print out designs of award-winning paper airplanes. The paper rolls out of your printer, and you fold the craft along the lines indicated. You can also print decorations on the plane. It remains to be seen whether this unusual software will be adapted to the Amiga.

Business Graphics

Business graphics programs generally render graphs and charts and hence are often, but not always, tied to spreadsheets. Good business graphics programs will let you choose among pie charts, bar graphs, line graphs, area graphs, scatter charts, and many more. They are now appearing with 3-D graphs, which Amiga programs may offer as a matter of course.

Amiga business graphics can be very impressive. For instance, Aegis has announced a program called *Impact*, which comes in two parts. The first allows you to create numerous kinds of charts. Bar graphs can be of three types (stacked, group, or overlapped), can line up horizontally or vertically, and can exhibit 3-D. Line graphs can have either single or multiple plots in regular, area, and scatter formats. Pie charts can be normal or exploded, and can appear in 3-D. The program uses the Blitter to move parts of the display around as independent objects, and it comes with text in five fonts, five styles, and point sizes from 4 to 18.

The second half of the software controls slide presentation. Among other things, it lets you determine type of transformation between the slides, including fade in and out, spiral in and out, curtain up or down, random, and trickle. It also allows for wipe delay and pause delay. Since you can use this software with the Polaroid Palette slide capture system, it should enter the market for business presentation slides, which amounts to $11.8 billion per year.

Computer-Aided Design

Computer-aided design, or CAD, software is for the professional drafter. It is characterized by a grid, which covers the screen and orients you to horizontal and vertical alignments, telling you precisely where you are. This grid is merely an aid and disappears when you tell it to.

Once again, Aegis Development has announced one of the first graphics programs in the area. Its *Aegis Draw* offers such features as Rulers; Zoom, for doing detail work on one part of the screen while another part displays the whole diagram; Automatic Scaling, for changing the scale instantly; and a Parts Library, for repeated use of certain segments of drawings.

Aegis Draw is a general-purpose CAD program; more professional ones, like *Aegis Draw Pro*, may contain such special

CHAPTER
EIGHTEEN

features as drafting symbols, commercial floor plan layouts, and printed circuit designs. Much CAD is done on expensive, dedicated workstations, but the Amiga could make significant inroads on these devices.

Indeed, the Amiga will encroach on many fields. In sensory terms, it's like a celestial bird. It wings are brilliant, and they enable it to soar. And it can sing.

Music and Voice

The Amiga can act as a Moog synthesizer. Now, what on earth does that mean? Well, it means that the computer gives you incredible power over music and voice. It lets you compose music at the computer, whether you understand musical notation or not. It also lets you control the characteristics of the sound you generate. The Amiga can not only act as an entire band, but it can let you create tones never heard on traditional instruments.

The synthesizer has been victimized by associations with "electronic music," the often atonal, experimental music of people like Karlheinz Stockhausen, which was not exactly "Moon River." But, as performers like David Bowie, Tangerine Dream, and The Captain and Tennille have shown, the synthesizer is not restricted to the avant-garde. In fact, George Harrison's solo on synthesizer in "Maxwell's Silver Hammer" went almost unnoticed. It is a musical instrument with fantastic flexibility.

The synthesizer stands in relation to traditional instruments as the computer does to traditional machines. Because it's computerized, it can mimic any other instrument. Of course, good instruments have tones of particular complexity, depth, and subtlety, and the world still has a place for a Guarneri violin, not to mention the average clarinet. But the degree to which the synthesizer can approach other instruments is often astonishing to people.

The Amiga, as a universal machine, can act as a synthesizer, the universal machine among musical instruments. But to understand this power fully, we need to take a brief excursion into the world of sound itself. You have to know the properties of this special medium before you can understand what the Amiga does with it.

Sound

Sound is simply the tiny, rapid fluctuations of air pressure in the ear. A well-protected structure called the cochlea sits at the end of the ear canal. It is filled with fluid and has numerous little hairs. These hairs detect the minute changes in pressure and pass the information on to the auditory nerve, and thence to the brain.

The changes in air pressure are referred to as sound waves. These waves must strike the ear very often to be heard; hence, we do not hear changes in air pressure when we drive up and down a hill. We measure their rapidity by the ubiquitous hertz (Hz), which here means one crest of a wave per second. The average ear can hear sounds from around 20 Hz—a very low groan—to 20,000 Hz—the most ethereal squeak.

Where all these frequencies are present at once in random volume, the ear hears *white noise*, a dense crackle like static on a radio. White noise is generally unpleasant and useless. But one variant of it, *pink noise*, is more interesting. Consisting of sounds between 18 and 1000 Hz, it can be filtered and refined in such a way as to suggest the wind or the ocean, and is often an intriguing accompaniment to music.

Where a sound has an identifiably constant pitch, we call it a note. The note is the atom of music, and the main object of our scrutiny.

The Note

Notes make up melody. They can take many different forms, but every note is composed of four elements: duration, pitch, volume, and timbre.

If you are familiar with musical notation, you know that it can represent only the first two of these accurately. Let's go down the list.

Duration. Duration is the simplest part of a note. On a musical staff, it is indicated by symbols representing fractions of time. The whole note, the longest, is a small hollow circle. A half note, half that length, is a hollow circle with a pole rising from it. A quarter note, half that length again, is a filled black circle with a pole. And so it goes, down through eighths, sixteenths, and thirty-seconds. The scheme is purely relative. All depends on the length of the whole note, and the notation alone offers no clue to this benchmark. Hence, composers put Italian phrases like *largo*, slow, or *scherzando*, quick and playful, above the staff. Duration is critical to composition and melody, but need detain us no further.

Pitch. As we saw above, pitch is determined by the numbers of waves striking our ear per second. This aspect of a sound is sometimes called its *frequency*. The higher the frequency, the higher the pitch. Another way to think of pitch is as the length of the waves. Long waves are lower in pitch.

Notes are rarely of precisely one pitch. Indeed, if they were, they would be less interesting, for the ear favors a certain complexity of tone. For instance, when an individual sings a note, there is a slight but rapid variation in the pitch, which lends richness and warmth to the sound. This effect is called *vibrato* and is generally considered desirable.

Volume. Musical notation can only attempt to indicate volume. Hence, the Italian phrases appear once more. *Pianissimo*, for instance, means very soft and quiet. What produces volume? It is actually the second major characteristic of any wave: its height. The higher the sound wave, the louder the sound seems to our ears. The height of a sound wave is sometimes called its *amplitude.*

A single note is not the same thing as a single wave. A note contains many waves. Moreover, their heights can change over the course of the whole note. For instance, a note can oscillate rapidly in volume, fluttering back and forth in a manner similar to a vibrato. We call this effect a *tremolo.*

But there is another, more important way in which the waves of a note fluctuate in height. Take the piano. When you strike a piano key, the note rises rapidly to peak volume, then slowly dies away, perhaps lingering on for several seconds. On the other hand, a flute note begins and ends quite suddenly. In order to describe these distinctive patterns of volume, we employ the concept of the envelope.

An envelope is the life history of a note's amplitude. In the case of the piano, for instance, it somewhat resembles the cross section of a mountain range. We can divide it into stages and discuss them separately. The first is called the *attack*. It is the trajectory the note takes on its rise to top volume, and is usually brief, though it need not be. The part from peak to disappearance is sometimes called the *release*, though it is commonly broken down even further.

Let's look at the envelope of a piano note. When you strike the key, the volume rapidly increases to apex (see Figure 19-1). Its attack is very fast. It then exhibits three stages of release. First, as you hold the key down, its volume declines about two-thirds. This slide is the *decay*. The volume then lingers at that plateau for a while, during the *sustain*. Finally, when you release the key, it declines into silence. We call this last stage, again, the release.

Figure 19-1. Phases of an Envelope

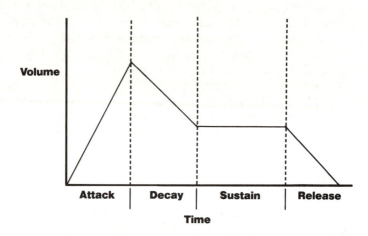

The Amiga and any other synthesizer will let you dictate the envelope of your notes. It's one way you can give them a distinctive, novel tone. If you play around with the envelope generator, you'll see how it affects the sound, and pretty soon you'll be able to sense the envelope of a note just by hearing it. Here are some of the effects you can create.

Pizzicato. If you set the middle stages, decay and sustain, to zero, and make attack and release very quick, you wind up with a sharp, picking sound, like plucked strings. The envelope looks like an upside-down golf tee.

Broad. If you set the outer ends of the envelope, attack and release, to zero, you get a bright, flat sound, like that of brass instruments.

Lingering. Make the attack brief and the decay, sustain, and release relatively long, and you get the envelope of the piano, guitar, and vibes.

Rounded. Use a gradual attack, no decay, a long sustain, and a gradual release, and the note will slowly rise to peak, stay there awhile, and slowly decline, like bowed strings. The envelope looks like a mesa with gentle slopes.

Volume goes far toward determining the exact sound you can get. But there is one other quality, and it is perhaps the most intriguing of them all.

Timbre. Two notes can have the identical duration, pitch, and volume envelope, and they will sound very different if played on a cello and a french horn. That difference is timbre. Musical notation rarely indicates timbre since, for the most part, it's inherent in the instrument and you can't do anything about it. Composers control it by writing different parts for a whole orchestra.

What causes timbre? We've already exhausted the measurements you can make on the two-dimensional sound waves. Their length causes pitch and their height causes volume. What else is there?

Well, there's one thing left and it's the most basic of all: shape.

We tend to think of sound waves as ripples, oscillating regularly up and down in a series of hill, valley, hill, and so on. In fact, this pattern is merely the most basic of sound waves. We call it the *sine wave*. Its timbre is almost bodiless. In its pure form, it is a thin tone like a whistle.

The sine wave is the building block for all other waves. You can easily add extra waves to the basic sine; they are called *harmonics* by engineers and *overtones* by musicians. They let you create several other fundamental waveforms which don't look much like the sine (see Figure 19-2).

The *triangle wave* resembles the sine wave in its symmetry, but is made of straight lines and angles. Instead of rounded hills and valleys, it has triangular ones. The wave rises up in a line until it hits a sharp apex, then instantly turns down at the same angle to the bottom of the wave, and so on. The triangle wave has more body than the sine wave, and its sound resembles a flute or a trumpet.

The *pulse*, or *square*, *wave* is also symmetrical, but completely rectangular. It rises instantly from the low point to the high point, remains there for a while, then drops instantly to the low point, remains there for a while, and so on. It looks like a fretwork and creates a richer sound than the triangle, somewhere between that of a flute and an oboe.

The *sawtooth wave* abandons the symmetry of the three other waves. It rises steadily up to its highest point, then drops instantly down to the bottom and starts rising again. This wave has a full, reedy sound, like a saxophone.

Figure 19-2. Wave Forms

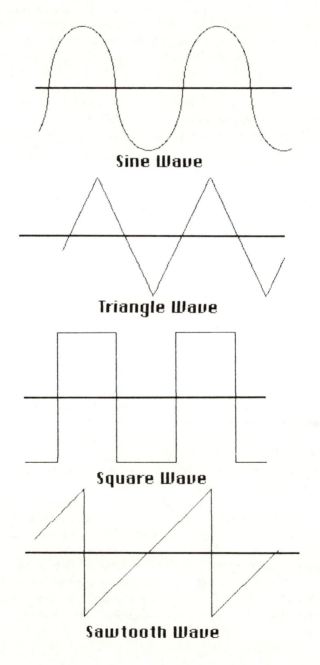

Sine Wave

Triangle Wave

Square Wave

Sawtooth Wave

These are the fundamental waveforms, and are often called simply *fundamentals.* You don't often hear them in their unmodified state. Usually, they are much altered by overtones and look almost like seismograms. But they are the building blocks.

A synthesizer lets you control these elements of sound. And, in fact, its means of control can become quite involved. The territory is fascinating but intricate, a domain where people spend their lives; this book can only introduce you to it. But it is certainly worth the look.

The History of the Synthesizer

The first music synthesizer was invented in 1929 by Edouard E. Coupleux and Joseph A. Givelet, who displayed their "Automatically Operating Musical Instrument of the Electric Oscillation Type" at the Paris Exposition. It somewhat resembled a player piano, with its roll of punched paper tape, but it went much further. The paper tape controlled not only pitch, but also volume, tremolo, and timbre. It represented an attempt to resolve sound into its constituents, then use them to create music. That is, it synthesized music from its parts. That's all a synthesizer does.

The Coupleux-Givelet device was purely mechanical, and did not set the planet ablaze. The next advance in the field would have more impact.

The first electronic synthesizer was invented in 1963 independently by Donald Buchla and Robert Moog, though Moog's name wound up attached to the machine. The Moog synthesizer works by modifying an electrical model of sound. To understand that, we need to examine briefly the relationship between sound and electricity.

We've seen earlier that electricity can give a very good replica of sound. It can be made to fluctuate in strength exactly as sound waves do. If it couldn't, we wouldn't have the telephone, the record player, the tape recorder, and many other familiar devices we associate with life in the twentieth century.

Let's look at a simple public address system on a stage. You speak into a microphone, which converts your voice into electrical waves that parallel the original sound waves. The current travels to an amplifier, which increases the amplitude, and then to a speaker. The speaker has a cone which shudders back and forth, creating tiny fluctuations in air pressure: sound. The more often it reverberates, the higher the pitch, and the more forcefully, the greater the volume. The cone can duplicate even convoluted waveforms because it can adapt its shudder to them precisely. Hence your original utterance is reproduced, in your own voice, with all its nuances.

The system is an analog one. That is, the current is a direct analog of the original sound, and the broadcast sound is a facsimile of the current. There are no bits, no binaries, no ons and offs.

The synthesizer invented by Moog and Buchla is also an analog device. It generates electrical waves and alters them to your specifications before they reach the speaker. In 1975, Robert Moog defined it as a device with a minimum of five parts:

1. A *controller*, such as a keyboard, to let you issue commands to the instrument. The keyboard determines pitch and duration, but controllers can give vibrato, trills, and other effects as well. The controller is analogous to your arm as it moves a violin bow back and forth.
2. An *oscillator*, the primal element in the machine, to create the electrical wave. The oscillator resembles the string in a violin.
3. A *filter* to alter and enrich the pitch of the waves. Many oscillators generate a high, bright sound which you do not always want, and a lowpass filter, for instance, cuts off some of the higher frequency overtones for a more pleasant sound.
4. An *amplifier* to strengthen or mute the volume.
5. An *envelope generator* to control the amplifier.

The last three elements are analogous to the hollow body of the violin, which receives the primary sound of the strings through the bridge and sound holes, and modifies it to give greater depth and resonance.

The difference between a violin and a synthesizer, of course, is that the violin is fixed. The synthesizer more resembles a violin whose hollow body you could expand, contract, and otherwise alter to give you an array of timbres and volumes. Moreover, the synthesizer is hardly limited to the five basic elements above. It can have many more attachments and capacities.

The analog synthesizer, as we've seen, works on waves carried through wires. That's the way telephones and record players work as well. But waves are meaningless to a computer, which understands only ons and offs. The next advance in electronic musical instruments was the digital synthesizer.

Digital Synthesizers

Newton and Leibnitz discovered the essential principle of digital synthesis back in the seventeenth century. While developing calculus, they realized that if enough points on a curve could be numbered, the whole curve could be described. It's rather like a connect-the-dots puzzle. You don't need every single point. You just need enough to draw an accurate line between them.

Thus, we can represent the waveform of any sound by assigning numbers to it periodically. Each number specifies a dot's position. If the intervals between them are short enough, we'll get a wave we can reproduce. And computers work fast enough to handle such intervals.

The first digital synthesizer was invented in 1975 and called the Synclavier. Digital synthesizers revamp the standard analog layout. First, they have a microprocessor at their core. It creates waveforms by generating a series of binary numbers. When the waveforms are fully described, they go to a digital-to-analog converter, which turns the binaries into voltage levels, that is, electrical waves. The waves flow to the speaker and emerge as sound. The digital-analog converter, then, is similar to the oscillator.

But notice where the waveforms are created: before they become electrical. The digital synthesizer completely builds the signal before passing it on to the converter. And it does so with software. A music program, for instance, will let you specify in detail the waveform, the volume envelope, and all the other features of a note. The synthesizer transforms your commands into numbers, converts them to analog, and plays them out. The increase in versatility is dramatic.

The first complete computer musical instrument was the Fairlight, developed in Australia in 1979. The Fairlight was impressive enough to interest musicians like Stevie Wonder and Keith Emerson, and it did many things the Amiga can also do. For instance, it performed both accompaniment and sound sampling. It allowed you to use a light pen to draw waveforms on the video screen. It had over 400 preset sounds, let you record live sounds over recorded ones to create overdubbing, and was resilient enough to take on the road. It cost between $25,000 and $30,000.

The Amiga as Synthesizer

The Amiga rivals the Fairlight in everything but price, and its Portia is one of the most advanced sound chips ever designed. At the basic level, the Amiga has all the powers of any synthesizer. Each of its four voices can have its own volume envelope, so you can set the attack, decay, sustain, and release of your notes. Each also has a volume control with 64 different levels, a very wide range. You can also regulate timbre. In addition, the Amiga imitates instruments like the vibes with a realism that is truly startling. Such mimicry is not just a trick. Retail prices for a set of vibes start at $2,500.

The computer has four independent channels of sound, and their autonomy is significant. Since you can program each channel separately, each is technically a synthesizer, and the Amiga is really a quartet of the devices. You can also combine channels in pairs to achieve bona fide stereo so that hooking up two speakers to the audio ports yields more than just extra volume. And the Amiga does not limit you to four different sounds. Each channel itself can play multilevel tones, so the computer can emit a panoply of sounds at once.

You can also use any of these channels as a music sequencer. A sequencer is an electronic instrument that generates a series of notes over and over again. It's not much use on its own, but it has an important role in creating musical background, especially in rock, which thrives on a sense of throb beneath the surface. Groups like Tangerine Dream and Kraftwerk have made extensive use of sequencers.

Moreover, the Amiga, like the Fairlight, can do sound sampling. It's a marvelous attribute. You attach a microphone to the Amiga and play in a specific sound, say, a finger snapping. The Amiga digitizes the waveform of that sound and stores it. Now it's simply one more instrument to the computer. It treats the finger snap waveform just like the vibes. You can play out melodies with it, alter its volume envelope, send it through filters, and manipulate it generally. And, of course, you aren't limited to finger snaps. You can read in the sound of musical instruments, your own voice, a cat's meow, a washing machine, the Amiga disk drive, anything you want. With several such sounds, you can create a polyphony of the parlor.

The Amiga also has a built-in faculty for voice synthesis, male or female, in a range of eight to nine octaves. Its initial quality was outstanding for personal computers. Nonetheless, few people would confuse it with human speech. It tended to partition diphthongs like *oi* into *oh* and *ee*, and to articulate those unstressed vowels—like the second *i* in *imitate*—that we in English reduce to a schwa. But programmers can work with it on a phonemic level, and it is possible that the machine will soon be addressing us in very lifelike tones indeed.

Software

Little sound software had actually appeared by the time of the Amiga's launch, though there was much in the offing and even more in the planning. At the outset, the following programs seemed to hold promise:

Musicraft, from Cherry Lane, is a basic synthesizer program. It gives you access to the four sound channels of the Amiga, and lets you control volume, timbre, and the other fundamental elements of sound. It lets you play on your Amiga keyboard, and if you want greater ease and comfort, you can also buy a piano-style keyboard.

Harmony, also from Cherry Lane, is an accompaniment program. It offers a choice of songs, initially from the Beatles and Lionel Richie. Each has five parts. You sing or play one part of the tune, and the Amiga generates the four-part accompaniment. If you speed up, the computer speeds up. If you play softly, the computer plays softly. You don't have to hit each note exactly, since the software deduces your goal if you get close enough. The company planned to sell this product for $79.

Texture, another Cherry Lane program, will let you modify a prior digital recording. You can have eight different tracks and manipulate any note on any track. For instance, you could filter out pitches in a range you don't want or shift the key of what you've recorded or alter the tempo. It uses graphics to show you the recorded notes and aid modification. It was to be priced at $199.

PitchWriter, also from Cherry Lane, digitizes pitch, as

through a microphone from an instrument you are playing,
and turns it into monophonic sound.

All of this Cherry Lane software is designed to work together. In addition, the company intended to release a sound
sampling program as well as educational music programs,
such as one to train the ear. It may even offer a voice-library
manager, a database for sounds created by sound sampling.

Cherry Lane will not be the only company selling Amiga
music software. Electronic Courseware Systems plans a line of
educational music software to teach, among other things,
blues, keyboard chords, intervals, jazz, and piano sight reading. Passport Designs of Half Moon Bay, California, will market them as well as issue its own music synthesizer program,
The Music Shop.

And this is just the overture.

The MIDI Interface

Finally, the Amiga is compatible with the MIDI interface, MIDI
for Musical Instrument Digital Interface. What is this feature
and why has it attracted so much attention?

The MIDI is a recently standardized means of communication between synthesizers. It allows you to hook up several of them to your Amiga and control them all from there.
Why do that? Aren't four synthesizers enough for anyone?
Well, not necessarily. Synthesizers are different. Some specialize in certain timbres and give a unique sound. That's why
you commonly see performers with more than one synthesizer
on stage.

If you use MIDI to attach two digital or analog synthesizers to the Amiga, you can play the computer and both
"slave" synthesizers will respond to your commands. You will
be playing three machines at once. You can also, if you like,
store prerecorded music in the adjunct devices so that it
accompanies you. You can thus achieve in live performance
the kind of layered sound you otherwise get only in a recording studio with multiple tracks. In fact, you can attach up to
16 other devices to the Amiga, including not just synthesizers,
but digital drums, which will control the timekeeping just as a
drummer does in a live band.

Moreover, you can create other, even more wide-ranging
effects. J. L. Cooper Electronics of Marina del Rey, California,
sells a MIDI Lighting Controller, which lets you prerecord

lighting and special effects to synchronize with the music. MIDI can even allow a good composer to dispense with the orchestra and record an entire motion picture sound track at home.

The MIDI interface is a hardware device and does not come with the Amiga. You have to buy one for about $60 to $90. But for music professionals, it's an open sesame.

The Amiga's sound capacities are like a boulevard down which we peer without seeing an end. They give us instrument, voice, band, and even a sound studio, and we can only guess what else lies farther on except that it should be magnificent.

PART FIVE
Communications

*"Now, Sal, we're leaving everything behind
us and entering a new and unknown phase
of things. All the years and troubles and
kicks—and now this! so we can safely think
of nothing else and just go on ahead with
our faces stuck out like this, you see, and
understand the world as, really and
genuinely speaking, other Americans
haven't done before us."*

Jack Kerouac
On the Road

Modems and the World

The Amiga is really more than a computer. It is your key to a universe. It can exchange information with other computers, large and small, all over the globe. It can increase your access to knowledge and your power to communicate incredibly.

The Amiga can make available:

- Electronic mail and bulletin boards. You can send messages to individuals personally or lodge them in the computer equivalent of a bulletin board.
- Electronic shopping and banking. From the chair in front of your Amiga, you can instantly order products, pay checks, and transfer money among your bank accounts.
- Electronic education. You can take college courses via computer and earn degrees from accredited colleges and universities.
- Telecommuting. With the right job, you can stay at home and send your work in to the office through the Amiga.
- Encyclopedic databases. You can scan the vast memory of mainframes and conduct research in minutes.
- Information utilities. You can turn to these multifaceted services for everything from wire news to restaurant reviews to random sonnets.

This power is of a very different order from that of the computer by itself. It means that, in addition to a typewriter, a calculator, a file cabinet, a game board, an easel, and a musical instrument, the Amiga can be a super-telephone.

The Amiga as Terminal

The communicative aspect of the Amiga is one of the most surprising of all to a beginner. We are all somewhat accustomed to computers as word manipulators, number jugglers, and videogames, and even their graphics capacity follows naturally from the games they run. But to understand how

CHAPTER
TWENTY

they can work as telephones, we have to pull back a bit and take the larger view.

As we have seen, the CPU of the Amiga sits at the core of an entire system, which also includes input, memory, and output. All parts of this system communicate by electrical signals, as through the cables on your desk. And since electricity travels at the speed of light, it doesn't much matter where these devices are physically in relation to each other. They will work well together as long as they are electrically linked.

Moreover, to enter data and get feedback, you really need only the keyboard, mouse, and screen on your desk. The CPU and memory can be elsewhere. A large company may have a single mainframe in the basement and terminals (keyboard and video without the computer) in every office. When you touch a key on the terminal, the signal travels down to the mainframe, which sends a character back to your screen. It happens virtually as fast as it does on the Amiga. Yet such terminals themselves have no memory or logical capacity, and for this reason are sometimes called dumb terminals.

The geographic range of such a setup is hardly restricted to a building or city. A terminal can tap into a mainframe anywhere. A terminal in Dallas can use a mainframe in New Delhi as long as there is a working electrical circuit between the two. Conveniently, a dense network of such circuitry already covers the globe. It's the telephone system.

If you can hook your Amiga up to the phone lines and connect it to the mainframe of, say, an encyclopedic database, you can turn the Amiga into a terminal for a while and enjoy stupendous capacity.

And that's not all. You can also use the phone system to link up with another individual at a personal computer. You can talk by typing in sentences. You can send reports and have the laugh on overnight delivery services. You can even play online chess.

What do you need to bring this trick off? First, of course, you must get your computer signals into the phone system. Second, you must have some way of controlling the communication.

So, the next question is how to unlock the telephone system. The answer is simple. The key is a modem.

The Modem

It's an axiom of the computer world, repeated over and over in these pages, that digital computers understand only on/off states. They must therefore communicate in them. And they do, issuing rapid streams of on/off pulses to the printer and other devices in the outside world. If you plugged an Amiga directly into a phone jack, it would try to pump its rat-a-tat-tat message into the lines.

The phone lines would reject it. The telephone system carries electrical models of sound, that is, waves. Digital ons and offs are not waves, and the system won't touch them. (AT&T does plan to digitize the wires so they'll carry these signals, one indication of how important computer communication has become. But this transformation will not be completed for several years.)

Therefore, as in so many other places in a computer system, you need a converter. The device that does this job must translate the outgoing signals from digital to audio, or *modulate* them, and translate the incoming ones from audio to digital, or *demodulate* them. It is thus called a modulator-demodulator, or *modem*. The Amiga will accept almost any type and brand of modem.

For all their magical capacity to open the phone system, modems look pretty unprepossessing. They are squat, rectangular objects, shaped like thick notepads. Setting them up is simple. You plug one end of an RS-232 cable into the modem and the other into the modem port of the Amiga. Then you connect the modem to a phone jack, that is, the outlet with the square hole that a small plastic plug clicks into. Newer modems are even smaller and even easier to install.

The phone jack is the only element of this equation that should cause any difficulty at all. If you have an old phone without a modular jack, you can buy a conversion part from most electronics stores for about five dollars. And if you want to use the modem in an office or any place where there is a multiline system, you can have the phone company put in a single-line adapter. However, if for some reason you wish to use a modem in hotels, you should know that many hotels place their jacks behind the walls to discourage phone theft. In such places, you need an old-fashioned type of modem called an acoustic coupler, which is otherwise inferior and moribund.

CHAPTER TWENTY

Buying a Modem

Modems have been falling steadily in price as the demand for them encourages mass production. They are also slowly relinquishing many of their functions to communications software, which handles them more adeptly. Nonetheless, there are still certain features to look out for, and for most people we recommend:

• 2400 or 1200 baud, rather than 300
• Autodial and autoanswer
• Call status monitor

Here is one more little freshet of technical terminology. But bear with it. The concepts again are essentially simple, and they have implications for your pocketbook.

The most important is modem speed. The speed at which a modem can send and receive signals is measured in *baud*. This term, which smacks of the comedies of Plautus and other notorious wags, derives from J. M. E. Baudot, inventor of the Baudot telegraph code. The speed of modem transmission can also be stated as *bits per second* (bps).

In truth, *baud* and *bps* refer to quite different concepts, and people almost always use *baud* incorrectly to mean *bps*. A modem that sends at 1200 bps, for instance, is usually called 1200 baud, though it actually sends at 600 baud with two bits per baud. *Baud* is simply easier to say. Moreover, since usage determines meaning, and since so many people now use *baud* to mean *bps*, the latter term is slowly vanishing. But we will hew to *bps*. When you start looking more deeply into the technology, it can make a difference.

Most modems you'll see handle 300 bps, 1200 bps, or 2400 bps. Since a character in transmission requires ten bits, rather than eight, these modems move about 30, 120, or 240 characters per second, which corresponds to about half a typed line, two lines, or four lines per second. The higher speed option usually includes the lower as well, so a 2400 bps modem is really a 2400/1200/300 modem.

A 1200 bps device is clearly preferable to a 300 bps unit, since it has the 300 bps option. Because 1200 bps is four times faster than 300 bps, total fees for commercial information services are usually lower at 1200 bps, even though per-minute fees may be higher at this speed. In addition, if you are sending or receiving documents, you finish four times as fast and save on phone bills. Moreover, 1200 bps modems have almost become the norm, and the day may arrive when 300 bps is simply antiquated. Since modems on both ends of the line must have the same rate, 300 bps could slowly narrow the range of your communications.

However, 300 bps has advantages. It is clearly the cheaper initial investment, currently beginning at around $80. The least expensive 1200 bps modems start at around $300, and most sell for around $500. Moreover, 1200 bps saves money online only if you are receiving or sending large documents to or from disk. If you are receiving messages directly on the screen, you will find it generates text so quickly that it is hard to read. And if you are keying in messages, you will have to type two lines per second to fully exploit the 1200 baud speed. No one types this fast. Thus, if you want to converse with others or access news or merely explore a system like CompuServe, 300 bps is more economical.

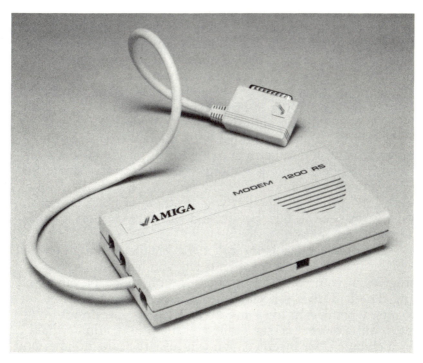

Amiga 1660 Modem/1200 RS

CHAPTER
TWENTY

With a 1200 bps modem, you set the speed to suit your purposes. You can also communicate with both 1200 and 300 bps modems, and even though it is more expensive than 300 bps, if you use a modem frequently, it could pay for itself.

The 2400 bps modem has appeared within the past year and is still somewhat dewy behind the ears. It is twice as fast as the 1200 bps, and it costs more. Moreover, it remains a bit rare, and unless there is a 2400 bps modem on the other end, the extra speed is useless. However, information utilities like The Source and Dow Jones News/Retrieval now offer 2400 bps service, and it could become the next standard fairly soon.

Recently, a super-fast modem has appeared, called Fastlink. Fastlink works at around 10,000 bps, an extraordinary speed for the telephone lines. It circumvents existing limitations in telephone technology by sending signals in a way that resembles parallel transmission. It currently costs about $2,000, and is available from Digital Communications Associates of Alpharetta, Georgia.

Two other features are *autodial* and *autoanswer*. These two are becoming de rigueur in modems, but if you are buying an inexpensive model, you should make sure it has them. Autodial lets you dial a phone number at the computer itself, through its software. You type in the number, then issue a command, and the number is dialed. It also makes possible the automatic redialing of busy numbers, called *autoredial*, and the automatic logging onto the large databases, called *auto-log-on*. Without autodial, you must hook a telephone up to the modem, dial the number manually, them quickly switch over to the computer. There is no longer any reason to tolerate this arrangement. Autoanswer lets the modem pick up the phone and admit messages whether you are there or not. You may not always need it, but if your modem won't support it, your software can't either.

The third feature is the *call status monitor*. Though termed *monitor*, it is usually a speaker. It lets you listen in on the progress of your call. You can hear the phone at the other end ring. The feature is especially useful when calling bulletin boards, which seem to spring up and vanish like desert flowers. If an operator message tells you the phone number has been changed, for instance, you can hear the new number and write it down. Sometimes, also, flesh-and-blood individuals will answer the phone, and you can hear them say, "Hello!" a

couple of times. The call status monitor can be simply a series
of messages on the screen, but the speaker is much more
informative.

Several reputable companies market modems, and their
imprimatur generally guarantees quality. Hayes is the leader in
the field, and its Smartmodem 1200, at around $700, is one of
the most popular and best-regarded of them all. It's expensive,
but if you keep your eyes open, you may be able to find it at a
discount. Other respected makers include Novation, US Robot-
ics, and Universal Data Systems, and their prices for 1200 bps
modems are around $500. Apple sells 1200 and 300 bps
modems for $495 and $225, and these, too, perform well,
though they will not work with certain software made by
Hayes. Modems at 2400 bps are somewhat more costly. The
Hayes Smartmodem 2400 runs about $900, but you may find
other decent brands for $700 or so.

Other Communications Hardware

The modem is the basic communications tool for personal
computers. However, if you use a computer in an office, you
may come across certain other kinds.

One is the telephone-modem combination. The fusion is
natural, and these devices cover the spectrum in terms of
complexity. Some are little more than a telephone and modem
in the same box. Others come with computers of their own,
and can let you dictate and edit completely oral memos, store
voice messages digitally, and perform numerous other tele-
phonic feats. They are expensive, however, and most are now
made only for the IBM PC.

A network is a group of computers wired directly together, without the intervening telephone connection.
Computers in a network can exchange data easily and at great
speed, up to 9600 bps or higher, but their main advantage
probably lies in their capacity to share costly equipment. For
example, you can buy Apple's LaserWriter printer and, with
the proper network, everyone can use it. Since you don't have
to buy a separate printer for everyone, you can save money
and obtain a remarkable product besides.

Picture phones also exist, up in the canopy where the rare
orchids grow. Currently, they cost around $75,000 for the
hardware—cameras, TV screens, and the 65-pound modem-
equivalent. This last runs $56,000, and not only digitizes the

TV signal but condenses it, so it can convey 90 million bps over a 56,000 bps line. If you would like such an item, you should be aware that the expenses don't end with purchase. To communicate, you'll have to link up to AT&T's Accunet network, which will cost $1,000 per hour.

Communications Software

The modem lets us get computer signals into the phone system. It's the gateway that makes communication possible. But once the channels are thrown open, we still need to control the exchange that occurs. And for that, we need software.

Communications programs can be an adventure into arcana. They control the whole communication process. And telephony is a full-blown technology, another one of those worlds that the Amiga leads us into, where we gape and wonder at the twisted rock forms and pastel skies. Don't worry if you occasionally stumble or find some of the terminology opaque or irrelevant. It is.

When the Amiga sends its on/off message into the wires, it pumps out not only characters, but a lot of hidden procedural information. Some of this you must decide upon yourself. For instance, you normally set the variable called character length at 7 or 8. Neither of these settings is superior to the other. But the one you pick must match the setting at the other end.

Why? Well, it's something of a Catch-22 situation. A variable like character length refers to how bits are formatted in transmission. That formatting constitutes a sort of code. The remote computer can't decipher it merely by listening to ons and offs. It just sees a parade of bits. Even if you were to send it information about character length over the wires, it wouldn't comprehend. You might as well explain hieroglyphics in hieroglyphics. The remote computer needs a clue to divine the meaning of the on/off stream. It must have prior knowledge of your formatting. That is, its settings must match your own.

And formatting is a matter with a great many variables. Communications programs can, thus, beset you with a flock of complexities. If that happens, just remember Rule One of telecommunications: You don't have to know what the individual variables mean. You just have to make sure that both sides match.

Let's leap into the pit. When shopping for a good communications program, look for these features in particular:

- Compatibility with your operating system and modem
- Autodial, autoanswer, autoredial, and auto-log-on
- VT 100 or VT 102 terminal emulation
- Easily set parameters
- XON/XOFF and XMODEM protocols
- Amiga-to-Amiga file transfer
- Disk/buffer downloading
- Extras

The first is essential, the next six are important, and those in the last category can approach the status of a sunroof in a car.

Compatibility. Compatibility is the sine qua non. Communications software is still software and must dovetail with your system. It must run on your operating system, and it must support your modem. Most communications programs will work with any modem, but some are choosier. If you purchase your modem and software at the same time, you should minimize the risk of buying an odd couple. It is also worth getting software that supports your printer. Such software allows you to print out information as it comes in over the screen, and it's a quick way to get hardcopies from the mainframe.

Automatic operations. We've seen that a modem should support autodial and autoanswer. Your software should, too, and today most of it does. But look particularly for autoredial and auto-log-on. Autoredial, as we've seen, will automatically redial a busy number and help you get on the often-congested bulletin boards.

Auto-log-on will let you into a giant database with a minimum of fuss. To enter one, you must first log on. That is, you must supply the mainframe with numerous pieces of information—access number, service code, password, and so forth. It's rather like filling out an address and personal identification form. The task is mechanical, a challenge to the patience rather than the intellect; many communications programs thus provide you with auto-log-on. The first time you go online with a particular database, you log on completely. The software stores the data on disk and henceforth enters it automatically.

VT 100 or 102 emulation. As we've seen, for the Amiga to communicate with a mainframe, you have to trick it into thinking that the clever Amiga is really just one of its crude terminals. The Amiga has to emulate its terminal. As you might expect, there are many kinds of terminals of different quality. Almost every program will emulate the Teletype, or TTY, terminal. The TTY is just a screen version of the old print Teletype that used to make the stock exchange sound like a rifle range. It's very primitive, and you can do better. Most decent programs will also emulate the widespread VT 100 or 102. A few also mimic the IBM 3278. If you have special need to emulate one of the others, you may want to look for a program with a terminal emulation language, like *Telescape* on the Macintosh.

Parameters. *Parameters* is one of those words that range in dictionary definition from the highly specific to the grossly vague, as in its synonyms *factor* and *element*. When you go online, however, it means only one thing: the technical variables of communication, like bps, stop bits, parity, and character length, that you and the remote computer must agree upon beforehand.

It's not really hard. Except for *bps*, you don't even have to know what the terms mean. If you have a list of the parameters required by, say, CompuServe, you just feed them in. A decent program will save them and call them up every time you want to access CompuServe. It will also let you change the settings while you're online, rather than forcing you to withdraw and reconnect later. In addition, it should limit the number of parameters you have to specify. Some rather advanced programs present you with a startling number of variables, offering the potential for great control over the communication. But such control is the province of experts and can baffle a beginner. For most people, the parameters should be few and fundamental.

Protocols. Certain kinds of parameters are called *protocols*, another unsettling name. Though in society as a whole, this term most commonly denotes strict codes of etiquette, *protocols* has a variety of other meanings, for example, preliminary diplomatic memoranda, which tend to obscure the whole word. In computer communications, it refers to a set of rules for one aspect or another of transmitting data.

Your software should have at least two protocols: XON/XOFF and XMODEM. XON/XOFF will halt the flow of incoming data for a moment while the Amiga performs some operation, such as moving data from RAM to disk. Without it, you may simply lose information that arrives during the halt. Most of the mainframes require XON/XOFF, so it is vital if you are to take complete advantage of your modem. Almost all communications software now has it.

XMODEM, sometimes called the Christensen protocol, has become popular partly because its inventor, Ward Christensen, released it into the public domain. It is an error-checking routine. Error checking is vital since, without it, static and noise on telephone lines will pepper your documents with mistakes. The XMODEM protocol essentially counts the bits you send and automatically retransmits the message block if the number differs from that in your document. Again, of course, if the software in the remote computer does not support XMODEM, you cannot use it.

Amiga-to-Amiga file transfer. The sixth feature involves the special nature of Amiga files. Currently most communications software sends prose in a *text file*, that is, a simple stream of ASCII numbers with an occasional carriage return tossed in. That's fine for a computer like the IBM PC, which is incapable of more. But the Amiga gives you documents with various fonts, print sizes, styles, and many other enhancements. The text file mode strips the document of all these and compels refurbishing at the other end. If you're sending files between yourself and, say, an IBM PC or a mainframe, you may not be able to avoid text mode. But between two Amigas, it's a pointless hardship. Look for programs that will handle full Amiga prose. They should be able to send graphics, voice, and music, too.

Disk/buffer downloading. The power to store incoming information as fast as it comes into your computer is called *downloading*, and it lets you snare a piece of the mainframe's memory at electronic speeds. Since it works so quickly, it saves you money online. There are two distinct capture methods: downloading to a disk and to a buffer, that is, to an area of RAM. Each has advantages. Downloading to a disk gives you greater convenience and capacity. It gets data to disk immediately, and it lets you record as much as the disk will hold—a great deal in the case of the Amiga. A buffer is

CHAPTER
TWENTY

merely a way station en route to the disk, and usually holds a maximum of 10 to 30K before you must save to disk. However, downloading to a buffer is faster, hence more economical if you want to access a relatively small amount of information. Many programs offer both disk and buffer downloading, and these are preferable to software with disk or buffer only, especially since they all sell for around the same price. Uploading is the reverse of downloading. The software normally takes a file directly from your disk and sends it over the wires.

Extras. The extras range from the handy to the decorative and come in an impressive variety. We cannot list them all, for there are far too many, and programmers are inventing new ones all the time. However, certain of them appear fairly often and are generally pleasing:

- *Directory.* Some programs will keep a list of the numbers you phone and let you click one to place a call instantly. You will appreciate this feature more than you might imagine.
- *Voice/data switch.* A voice/data switch can be a big help if a lengthy topic of conversation looms up while you are linked to someone else's computer. It lets you jump easily from data connection to voice connection over the phone so that you can discuss the matter orally, hence faster and less expensively.
- *Macros.* Macros let you create commands which will execute a bundled series of other commands in one or two strokes, as you can in Logo or Forth. Auto-log-on is a kind of macro.
- *Languages.* A few programs come with their own languages for executing fancy operations. Several Macintosh programs have such languages. They are not usually as hard as they seem, and good ones can expand your power dramatically.
- *Unattended operation.* Some software will download and upload your Amiga when you're not there, thus allowing you to exploit late-night phone rates and otherwise send and receive at your pleasure. Note that your modem must also be able to handle this feature.
- *File editing.* Many programs let you write or edit text without going back to a word processor, a useful but often primitive feature called file editing. There is a trend toward combining communications software with word processors. Since the latter create most of the documents that the former transmit, fusion is a natural. So far, however, most such programs have shirked one side in favor of the other. You may prefer

to put a complete word processor on the disk with your communications program and run both concurrently.

• *Tutorials.* Communications software is harder to understand than most other kinds, and so tutorial programs are especially useful. Good documentation and online help are also very desirable.

Modems, software, and all of their appurtenances are, of course, means to an end. They are like roads. We value them not for their own sake, but because they can take us places, and the less aware we are of the pavement, the better the road has done its job. This chapter has dealt with the smoothness of ride. The next is about destinations.

The Other End of the Rainbow

Once you buy a modem and software, what do you do with it? Chitchat with total strangers? Send birthday cards to drooling babies across the continent? Well, yes, you can do these things. But you can also do innumerable others, and the discussion below only hints at the possibilities.

Electronic Mail

In a broad sense, of course, all computer telecommunication is electronic mail. It transmits characters rather than speech. However, the term generally refers to a narrower kind of system run by certain very large companies. If you subscribe to an electronic mail service, you get a numbered "box" in the mainframe. Correspondents can leave messages for you there, and you can retrieve them at your convenience. You can send and receive written reports almost instantly.

Among the best-known providers of electronic mail are The Source, CompuServe, and MCI Mail. You should investigate the costs of these services carefully. MCI Mail will let you send a 7500-character document—three to five typed pages— for $1.00, while the others are generally more expensive. You should also be aware that, unlike the postal service, some of these companies make you pay to log in and receive your mail. Among the three, MCI Mail is the most convenient and the cheapest, at least during daylight hours. SourceMail is relatively easy to use and full of useful features, but is more costly. EasyPlex on CompuServe offers such aids as different modes for different levels of experience, online instructions, and an address book for user ID's on up to 50 people.

Electronic Bulletin Boards

Electronic bulletin boards resemble electronic mail except that the contents of the messages are public rather than private. The Source and CompuServe have bulletin boards, where you can find want ads, for sale notices, and virtually everything else you would find on the bulletin board of a supermarket.

Private citizens also run bulletin boards, which tend to act as community forums. You can call in and simply peruse people's notations if you want. There's no guarantee the comments will always be interesting or illuminating, but neither is TV, and people are paid to write that. Or you can play a more active role and type in your own comments, queries, or declarations. You can also download a great deal of free, public-domain software, though you should first make sure it will run on the Amiga. While the quality of such programs is uneven, you are unlikely to complain about the bargain. There are at least 450 bulletin boards in North America, and probably many more, as their numbers are increasing rapidly.

In addition to the general-purpose bulletin boards, there are many devoted to special subjects, such as genealogy, astronomy, sex, the space shuttle, medicine, Pascal, satire, law, and numerous others. Some offer games such as *Adventure.* Others concentrate on particular computers, such as the Apple line or the IBM PC. These too are growing in number and diversity, and offer intriguing potential for bringing people with related interests together.

These bulletin boards are very easy to log onto. All of them have a Help function that explains the various commands and guides you safely in to touchdown. However, if you plan to use particular boards fairly often, it is only decent to download the commands and keep them on your desk so that other people don't get constant busy signals as you dawdle through the sign-on.

There is a spirit of excitement and even ferment in the bulletin board milieu, like an underground that trembles with a sense of important secrets. And, again like an underground, finding your way around among them can be an interesting challenge. New ones are always appearing as older ones change or fold. Two of the best ways to locate bulletin boards are by examining those on The Source and CompuServe, and those on the numerous free boards themselves.

You can set up your own bulletin board system if you like. With the Amiga, you need only an autoanswer modem, bulletin board software, and a second disk drive. If you have a particular interest that is unmet by existing systems or if you just like presiding over a forum, a bulletin board could be a source of satisfaction.

CHAPTER
TWENTY-ONE

Electronic Education

If you can earn a college degree by regular mail, you should
be able to earn one by electronic mail. One company, The
Electronic University, has now made such telediplomas possible. The Electronic University is not a university itself, but
rather an intermediary. It is a national system that links your
computer to accredited colleges throughout the nation and
provides courses from live instructors. These colleges offer
associate degrees in business and general studies, baccalaure-
ate degrees in business and the arts, and several MBA degrees.
Course fees include all communication costs. The University
also has a vast Electronic Library, interactive seminars, and a
counseling center. Its number is 1-800-22LEARN (1-800-
44LEARN in California).

Electronic Shopping

If you can have electronic mail, there is no reason why you
can't have electronic mail order. And one service, called
Comp-U-Store, has long specialized in this field. It offers customers a remarkable range of products: VCRs, luggage, stereo
sets, guitars, cameras, watches, and much more.

Comp-U-Store also gives you a number of bonuses. First,
and most important, it discounts almost all items by 10 to 60
percent. Moreover, prices include not only tax, but shipping
and handling, and the company delivers all orders right to
your door. Comp-U-Store states officially that your goods will
arrive in four to six weeks, though they often come sooner.

You can browse through Comp-U-Card listings on The
Source, Dow Jones, or CompuServe, but you can't buy anything until you take out a subscription, which costs $25 per
year. You can get one by contacting the firm directly at 777
Summer Street, Stamford, Connecticut 06901 (800-252-4100).
You can access Comp-U-Card at any time of day, any day of
the year.

CompuServe also has an Electronic Mall, which sells
books, records, airline tickets, computer equipment, magazines, and other consumer items. The Mall requires no
subscription fee and offers few discounts. Like a real mall, it is
composed of independent outlets, such as Sears, Walden-
books, and American Airlines, and though most deliver, rates
depend on the company you are dealing with.

Of course, no matter what the advantages of electronic shopping, you're still ordering by mail. You don't have the opportunity to pick up the item, turn it 360 degrees, hold it up to the light, pay for it, and rush right home with it. The problem is particularly acute where esthetics is important, as in buying crystal or silverware. However, Comp-U-Store specializes in more technological offerings, and since it gives you the catalog numbers of the major brand names it carries, you can often check elsewhere to find the caliber of, say, its Magnavox video camera or Okidata dot-matrix printer. It also has a much wider variety of goods than most stores, so you can often find what you're looking for at once instead of calling all around town.

Home Banking

If you can mail letters, coursework, and order forms with your Amiga, you should be able to mail bills with it, too. Home banking is in its infancy, but it is growing apace because of the considerable savings it offers to banks and customers alike.

Most people have already engaged in a form of computerized banking. Every time you step up to an automatic teller machine (ATM) and punch in commands, you are telling a computer to manipulate your money. That computer is not the ATM itself, which is merely a terminal like your Amiga when it logs on. It is a mainframe in some carefully anonymous building somewhere.

If you use the Amiga as a home banking terminal, you won't be able to get money out of it, since, unfortunately, it does not come equipped with tall columns of cash. But you can personalize your dealings with the remote computer in a way impossible with an ATM. You can tell the bank whom you want to pay, how much, and even when. Thus, you could say, in effect, "Pay the phone company whatever I owe on the third of every month." These transfers will take place automatically unless you change the order.

You can also use home banking for other purposes. It can display your present savings and checking account balances, and all the checks that have so far cleared. It can let you shift assets from savings to checking and vice versa. It can indicate the current interest rates for its investment instruments, and let you purchase them as well as travelers check and money orders. It can let you call up your bank credit-card statement and even make loan applications.

Not every home banking system offers all these services, but the banks are clearly eager to promote them. Home banking can give them a bonanza. At the present, the average check is handled by over ten bank employees. Home banking would sidestep so much of this routine that Robert Lipp, president of Chemical Bank, has said that it could lower the cost of processing the average bill payment from $1.02 to 35 cents, saving Chemical millions per year.

You also profit. Paying off creditors from your easy chair is convenient and postage-free. Instant access to your account figures is reassuring and can sometimes help you negotiate the white water of cash-flow problems. And, as home banking spreads, you may expect the banks to make it much cheaper than traditional check writing.

Telecommuting

Telecommuting sounds like a dream. Instead of threading your way through traffic twice a day, always on the alert for brain-damaged motorists, or enduring the shuttle by bus or train to your place of employment, you simply stay at home and work at the terminal. You escape the pressures of the office, spend more time with your family, wear what you please, work more flexible hours, and save the approximately $1,000 per year the average worker spends on commuting.

Telecommuting benefits the employer as well. It increases productivity. New York Telephone, for instance, found that the output of telecommuters rose by as much as 50 percent, because they no longer wasted time going back and forth from work, and they were free from the distractions of the office. Moreover, since it cuts down on the need for office floor space, it reduces rent and utility expenses.

Computer communication makes telecommuting possible today, and some have estimated that as many as 50 million Americans have jobs that lend themselves to it. However, it is not for everyone. Many people enjoy the social interplay of the office and would feel lonely at a home terminal. Others believe that participation in office politics boosts the chances for promotion. Others find that the constant presence of the family creates unexpected friction. And still others find themselves eating and drinking too much, unable to resist the lure of the refrigerator. For these reasons, telecommuting could become a matter of controversy if employers try to implement it across-the-board on a wide scale.

Yet managers seem to fear telecommuting more than employees do. They have two somewhat inconsistent worries: that home workers will lapse into revelry and that their own job of oversight, of peering over the shoulder to insure that work is well done, will stand revealed as unnecessary. Some employers also worry about the chance that eavesdroppers may tap into their data.

Despite the foregoing, if telecommuting appeals to you, you might seek to persuade your boss to let you try it, perhaps one or two days a week. The best managers tend to sympathize with the idea, and even in companies where high-level executives oppose it, telecommuting arrangements are blooming on the sly. In the right situation, it has advantages for everyone.

Encyclopedic Databases

The encyclopedic databases are realms unto themselves, vast halls of seemingly endless knowledge which you can scan at the speed of light. There is no way to convey the immensity of these resources. They are actually collections of component databases, themselves enormous, and they probably offer more information than you can get anywhere else on earth without rising from your chair.

There are three main encyclopedics: Dialog, BRS, and Orbit. They all began in the early to mid-1970s, when they served institutions such as libraries, universities, and large corporations. Their rates were high, and they required expensive equipment. Carried forward by inertia, they continued to advertise mainly to institutional users until the early 1980s. Thus, most people have never heard of them.

Their rates are still relatively high. Ten minutes on Dialog, for instance, can cost around $15. But in that time you can do hours worth of work. Instead of going through the various indexes, tracking down journal articles, and photocopying them while people fidget in line behind you, you finish in about the time it takes to eat a sandwich.

The encyclopedics have no card catalog, so you have to search them with a special technique. First, you enter a set of

CHAPTER
TWENTY-ONE

keywords, words likely to appear together only in the articles you want. The remote computer scans the entirety of its database for them and returns with the number of articles that contain them. If that number is, say, 45,000, then you must enter more keywords to narrow the field. If the number is 0, you must change some to expand it. Keyword selection is a mysterious art, full of surprises, and often the keywords you think will strictly define the topic open floodgates a mile or so high. But some principles are obvious. If you are researching annual variations in wheat harvest along the Nile in the time of Ramses II, do not just feed in *Egypt*. You need more specific clues. *Wheat*, *Nile*, and *Ramses II* would do far better. But even here, if you omit the English term for wheat, *corn*, you may miss useful information. You should always think out your keyword strategy in advance, since it's expensive to do so online.

When the number of articles seems reasonable, you ask to see the bibliographical citations for them. These will normally cost a little extra, say, around 25 cents apiece. They enable you to reduce the search still further. You will find articles listed that happen to contain all your keywords, but have little bearing on your topic. There are fewer of these than you might expect, but they crop up. Nonetheless, it is worth downloading all the citations for future reference.

If a citation looks especially promising, you can order up an abstract of it. The abstract will generally encapsulate the issue, the methodology (if any), and the conclusions. Each abstract costs an additional sum.

The encyclopedic databases usually do not offer the full text of the articles cited. This feature would consume too much memory, though it would be exceptionally useful. However, all three will let you order the material online. You can also go to your local library and flush out the citations there, a much cheaper approach, but one that takes more time and confines you to the books and periodicals in stock.

The three encyclopedics have a startling range. The list below conveys their scope about as well as the buffalo pen at the zoo conveys a herd.

Biography Master Index lets you peruse the life histories of over two million individuals who have achieved note.

Biosis Previews is a worldwide index that cites from over 8000 journals in the life sciences, as well as symposia and many other kinds of reports.

CLAIMS™ has millions of patent abstracts, some dating to 1950.

Comprehensive Dissertation Index holds the subject, title, and author of almost every dissertation written in the United States since 1861.

Electronic Yellow Page lets you search over two million phone listings in more than 4800 United States phonebooks.

Standard & Poor's News Daily gives you the latest information on over 10,000 publicly held corporations.

Other available databases cover popular magazines, commercial software, microcomputers, chemistry, advertisements, American studies, book reviews, grants, math, physics, environmental research, books in print, the *Harvard Business Review*, medicine, associations of all kinds, and UPI stories. And there are many, many more.

The largest of the three services is Dialog, owned by Lockheed. Dialog has close to 200 separate databases, compared with between 60 and 80 for its rivals BRS and Orbit. Many databases are common to all three, but others appear on only one; to see the full spectrum you should contact all of them. Their toll-free numbers are:

Dialog:	**800-334-2564**
BRS:	**800-833-4707**
	800-553-5566 (in New York)
Orbit:	**800-421-7229**
	800-352-6689 (in California)

Two of the encyclopedics, Dialog and BRS, also provide more limited, economical services in the evening and on weekends. Dialog offers Knowledge Index, which charges a one-time fee of $35, and $24 an hour for connect time; it gives access to 28 databases. BRS offers BRS/After Dark, which costs $35 to join and from $6 to $20 an hour online, with a $12 monthly minimum. It has 42 databases. While the two services duplicate each other to some extent, BRS/After Dark excels in chemistry, education, and social sciences, and also includes the *Academic American Encyclopedia*. Knowledge Index focuses more on engineering, computers, legal research, magazines, and newspapers. These miniencyclopedics may be good places to start if you are interested in seeing what the giant databases are all about.

There are many times when you want to find a needle or two in a haystack. The encyclopedics give you a great big magnet.

Dow Jones News/Retrieval

Dow Jones News/Retrieval, or DJN/R, is one of the three main information utilities. These services specialize in breadth and offer news, sports, games, horoscopes, and a potpourri of other items to engage your attention. The encyclopedics, in contrast, specialize in depth. Information utilities are tools for frequent, but often casual, consultation, whereas encyclopedics are for less common, but more intensive, search. The former are like enormous newspapers; the latter, like reference books.

And insofar as information utilities resemble newspapers, DJN/R is the *Wall Street Journal* of them. The similarity is more than casual, for Dow Jones & Company owns them both and sets their tone. DJN/R is part news and financial database and part basic information utility. It offers current stock quotes, delayed 15 minutes by regulation, as well as historical ones. It predicts earnings per share for thousands of companies, offers information disclosed to the Securities and Exchange Commission, compiles a wealth of statistics on individual corporations, summarizes the TV show "Wall $treet Week," presents weekly economic survey charts, and features highlights from the *Journal*. But it also carries general news from UPI, weather reports for cities worldwide, reviews of 50 current movies, a sports report, and access to Comp-U-Store. In addition, it carries the *Academic American Encyclopedia*.

DJN/R is not the easiest information utility to learn, and it automatically displays lengthy help messages. While the beginner welcomes such assistance, the experienced user often finds it exasperating. Moreover, the service is relatively expensive. The DJN/R information number is:

800-257-5114
609-452-1511 (in New Jersey)

Dow Jones News/Retrieval is clearly a solid asset for anyone involved in stocks and bonds, or even affected by them. It is also enjoyable for the simple thrill of being ringside at a little major money action.

CompuServe

CompuServe Information Service is the second big information utility. Located in Columbus, Ohio, and owned by H & R Block, CompuServe offers a broad array of consumer features. It is rather like an amusement park that you wander through, constantly coming across novelties and lacking much sense of its dimensions except that they are huge.

Like DJN/R, CompuServe has business reports. But it also has discussion forums called special interest groups, or SIGs, and they are excellent. SIGs focus on one field, such as cooking or travel, and encourage information exchange. Those that concentrate on particular computers can be a special boon. Some SIGs can be relatively static, but most of those on CompuServe have real vitality. And new ones are springing up as users create them. In addition, much public domain software is available, and it can be directly downloaded. CompuServe also has the best games of the utilities, and many of them can engage several players. For instance, if you live in Fort Lauderdale, you can play galactic war games with people you've never met in Winnepeg or Phoenix.

In addition, CompuServe offers the popular CB Simulator, which connects you to a roundtable of up to 40 people who carry on transcontinental conversation about everything imaginable. Everyone takes a handle, and the talk proceeds quickly and sometimes inscrutably, with comments like the more cryptic messages in "Personals" columns of newspapers.

We cannot list all the services CompuServe provides, but some of them include:

AAMSI Medical Forum
Academic American Encyclopedia
AP Videotex, World News
Arcade SIG
Ask Mr. Fed SIG
Astrology
Calculate Net Worth
CB Interest Group SIG
Children's Games
Color Computer SIG
Computer Art SIG
Computing Across America
Electronic Gourmet
Entertainment SIG

CHAPTER TWENTY-ONE

Financial Forecast
Firstworld Travel Club
Golf SIG
Handicapped Users' Data Base
Hollywood Hotline
Human Sexuality
Intelligence Test
Loan Amortization
Money Market Services
The National Satirist
Official Airline Guide
Rapaport Diamond Broker
Standard & Poor's
TravelVision
Trivia Test
Value Line Financials
Veterinarians' Forum
Whole Earth Software SIG
Work-at-Home SIG

CompuServe also offers prices on commodities and livestock exchanges, movie reviews, weather, electronic mail, online conferencing, and much more. The service is adding features constantly and notifies you of them in its What's New listing, which appears when you log on.

You can join the information utility at one of two tiers: Consumer Information Service (CIS) and Executive Information Service (EIS). EIS is more expensive. It includes all the features of CIS, yet does not offer a great deal more except the satisfaction of sitting in the mezzanine. Its exclusive extras include a superior electronic mail service called InfoPlex, the useful Investors' Forums, the Institutional Brokers Estimate Survey, a demographics database, and a statistical analysis program. Most of its financial services can also be found on CIS.

CompuServe is generally simple to use, and available any time except from 5:00 a.m. to 8:00 a.m. You may be able to get on during this period as well, but the utility uses it for maintenance and access may be limited. Its information number is:

800-848-8199
614-457-0802 (in Ohio)

CompuServe is the most home-oriented of the information utilities, a bag of surprises for children and adults alike.

The Source^{SM}

Owned by Reader's Digest and Control Data Corporation, The Source stands midway between its two competitors, a utility that has long offered news and playthings to its customers and now seems to be pedaling rapidly toward the business market.

The financial services of The Source are thus better developed than those of CompuServe, though they cannot touch DJN/R's. The Source offers stock reports updated all day long, but not as currently as DJN/R's. It also presents news of metal markets, currency trading, and numerous commodities, such as sugar, cocoa, cotton, hogs, potatoes, lumber, rubber, orange juice, cattle, grain, coffee, and poultry. In addition, it has business commentary, financial advice, and abstracts from leading business publications.

But The Source has a great deal more, and again the list below is just a fragment:

Airline Schedules
Amortization of Loans
Ask Dick Kleiner
Aviation SIG
Backgammon
Be Your Own Lawyer
Biorhythm
Book Buying
Classic & Exotic Cars
Coin Flipping
Current Reviews from Filmeter
Dial-A-Date
Ham Radio SIG
Health Care SIG
Health Tips
Hotel Guide
I Ching
Income Tax Calculation
Introduction to the Language Esperanto
IQ Test
Lifestyles

CHAPTER
TWENTY-ONE

Mr. Software's Catalog
Mobil's National Restaurant Guide
Othello
Out of the Closet
Research for a Fee
Ridexchange
Ski Reports
Slot Machine
Software Author SIG
Space War SIG
Super Adventure
Super Blackjack
Today in History
Tri-Weekly Trombone
TV Reviews
UCSD Pascal SIG
W.I.N.K. Magazine

Like CompuServe, The Source also has CB simulation.

The Source and CompuServe vary in the quality of many of their offerings. The Source's SIGs tend to lack the clublike vivacity of CompuServe's. And its games do not equal those of its rival's. However, it clearly surpasses CompuServe in financial news and electronic mail. The Source's toll-free number is:

800-336-3366
800-572-2070 (in Virginia)

Among the three main information utilities, The Source best straddles the gulf between business and pleasure. It offers a great deal of both and, like the others, offers a great deal period.

Conclusion

I'm glad you made it. You've gone from the history of Commodore down to the microscopic circuitry in the Amiga and back up out to the global information network. You've seen the four sides of computer hardware and the software pyramid that makes it all come alive. You've seen how the Amiga and its accessories work and formed at least some idea of its remarkable powers.

This book, of course, is only an introduction. The literature fans out in great detail from almost every topic we've mentioned. And there are big, fascinating subjects, such as artificial intelligence, that we've hardly been able to touch on.

If you would like to learn more about computers, there are many avenues open to you.

Magazines. Computer magazines are invaluable in keeping you abreast of this fast-changing field. Most of them regularly announce new products and, soon after, review them. Their articles of broader scope can also be interesting. Many people subscribe to them for the advertisements alone, often the most current information on available technology. *Amiga-World* is the first magazine devoted to the Amiga, and more general-purpose magazines, like *COMPUTE!* and *Personal Computing*, also run informative stories. *Byte*, one of the best known, is somewhat technical for beginners, but you may like it anyway.

User Groups. User groups are clubs devoted to particular machines. They began in the early days of personal computers, when you had to solder parts together yourself. At that time, they provided a social pool of experience, where hobbyists could swap ideas, warn each other about ripoffs, and even form companies. They still serve such functions. Members at user groups can often answer questions you may have as well as pass along free, public-domain software and opinions of products they've bought. Amiga user groups will likely form throughout North America, and your dealer may know of the groups in your area.

Bulletin boards. Bulletin boards are available from the information utilities, Dialog, BRS, and numerous individuals and clubs. Some specialize in particular machines, and you may well find Amiga bulletin boards springing up. Here, too, you can often download free software or pick up valuable tips.

Books. There are books galore on everything from individual programs to telecommunications to the impact of the personal computer on society. Books can give you a depth of understanding about a topic that is hard to attain anywhere else.

COMPUTE! Publications has a number of books aimed specifically at the Amiga, including *COMPUTE!'s AmigaDOS Reference Guide* by Arlan R. Levitan and Sheldon Leemon, *COMPUTE!'s Kids and the Amiga* by Edward Carlson, and *COMPUTE!'s Amiga Programmer's Guide.*

The Amiga will take you a long way. It is far more powerful than the early "electronic brains," and advances in software and hardware are making it more useful every day. Indeed, computers like the Amiga may be the nearest thing we have to the "open road" of nineteenth-century America, the lane which disappears over the horizon into a realm of unexplored potential. You have already started out on that road, and your desktop will never be the same.

Index

253

COMPUTE! Books

Ask your retailer for these **COMPUTE! Books** or order directly from **COMPUTE!**.

Call toll free (in US) **1-800-346-6767** (in NY 212-887-8525) or write COMPUTE! Books, P.O. Box 5038, F.D.R. Station, New York, NY 10150.

Quantity	Title	Price*	Total
_____	COMPUTE!'s Beginner's Guide to the Amiga (025-4)	$16.95	_____
_____	COMPUTE!'s AmigaDOS Reference Guide (047-5)	$14.95	_____
_____	Elementary Amiga BASIC (041-6)	$14.95	_____
_____	COMPUTE!'s Amiga Programmer's Guide (028-9)	$16.95	_____
_____	COMPUTE!'s Kids and the Amiga (048-3)	$14.95	_____
_____	Inside Amiga Graphics (040-8)	$16.95	_____
_____	Advanced Amiga BASIC (045-9)	$16.95	_____
_____	COMPUTE!'s Amiga Applications (053-X)	$16.95	_____

*Add $2.00 per book for shipping and handling.
Outside US add $5.00 air mail or $2.00 surface mail.

NC residents add 4.5% sales tax _____
NY residents add 8.25% sales tax _____
Shipping & handling: $2.00/book _____
Total payment _____

All orders must be prepaid (check, charge, or money order).
All payments must be in US funds.
NC residents add 4.5% sales tax.
☐ Payment enclosed.
Charge   ☐ Visa   ☐ MasterCard   ☐ American Express

Acct. No._____ Exp. Date_____

Name_____

Address_____

City_____ State _____ Zip_____

*Allow 4–5 weeks for delivery.
Prices and availability subject to change.
Current catalog available upon request.

46202513

If you've enjoyed the articles in this book, you'll find the same style and quality in every monthly issue of **COMPUTE!** Magazine. Use this form to order your subscription to **COMPUTE!**.

For Fastest Service
Call Our **Toll-Free** US Order Line
1-800-247-5470
In IA call 1-800-532-1272

COMPUTE!
P.O. Box 10954
Des Moines, IA 50340

My computer is:
☐ Commodore 64 or 128 ☐ TI-99/4A ☐ IBM PC or PCjr ☐ VIC-20
☐ Apple ☐ Atari ☐ Amiga ☐ Other_____
☐ Don't yet have one...

☐ $24 One Year US Subscription
☐ $45 Two Year US Subscription
☐ $65 Three Year US Subscription

Subscription rates outside the US:

☐ $30 Canada and Foreign Surface Mail
☐ $65 Foreign Air Delivery

Name _____

Address _____

City _____ State _____ Zip _____

Country _____

Payment must be in US funds drawn on a US bank, international money order, or charge card.
☐ Payment Enclosed ☐ Visa
☐ MasterCard ☐ American Express

Acct. No. _____ Expires _____/_____
                                              (Required)

Your subscription will begin with the next available issue. Please allow 4–6 weeks for delivery of first issue. Subscription prices subject to change at any time.

46219333

GET EXCITING
NEW PROGRAMS EACH MONTH
—BY SUBSCRIBING NOW TO
COMPUTE!

Say YES now to *COMPUTE!*—and get up to 200 all-new programs each year.

Issue after issue, *COMPUTE!* delivers at least 20 exciting new game programs...education programs...personal and budgeting programs...sorting and filing programs...programs for the kids ...and programs for the kid in all of us.

And there's so much more to *COMPUTE!*

Interested in writing your own programs? Want to know how to create your own games? How can you convert your Commodore 64 into an 80 column machine? What does it take to customize existing programs to your individual needs? Look no further than the insightful, skillfully written articles in *COMPUTE!* If there's any possible way

to get more from your home computer— any way to make it faster, more powerful or more fun—you can be sure that you'll hear about it right here in *COMPUTE!*

What about other home computer users? What questions do they have? What solutions have they devised? What innovations can they share with you? Turn to our "Feedback" section and tap into one of the largest home computer user groups you'll find anywhere.

The bottom line is this: no other publication gives you more for your home computer than *COMPUTE!* So subscribe today—and start getting the absolute most out of your computer. Return the form below or call 1-800-247-5470 now!